HEADWAY

STUDENT'S BOOK **UPPER-INTERMEDIATE**

John & Liz Soars

Oxford University Press

	Grammar	Vocabulary 1	Vocabulary 2	Revision	Skill	Topic
1	*The tense system* Present, past and future Simple and continuous Perfect and non-perfect Active and passive	Parts of the body Nouns used as verbs Compound nouns Suffixes and prefixes (1)	Keeping vocabulary records	Dates and numbers Fractions and decimals	Exploiting prior knowledge Skimming	English as a world language
2	*Present Perfect Simple and Continuous* Relating past actions and activities to the present	Associating words with a period of one's life	Guessing the meaning of unknown words via linguistic and contextual clues Suffixes and prefixes (2)	Pronunciation of the alphabet Spelling long words English names Abbreviations	Literary appreciation	**The Seven Ages of Man** by William Shakespeare
3	*Gerunds* After certain verbs After prepositions As subject *Infinitives* After certain verbs and adjectives	Categorizing words to do with work	Adjectives describing personal characteristics	Short answers **So do I/neither do I**	Intensive reading Completing a questionnaire	The right job for you
4	*Question forms* Subject/object questions Short questions **Who to?** Indirect questions Tag questions Questions + preposition	Guessing meaning Dramatic and neutral styles	A poem on the irregularities of English spelling Guessing the spelling of words	**Have** – auxiliary verb – full verb – to express obligation	Appreciating popular fiction Predicting content from a book cover	Reincarnation
5	*Narrative tenses* Past Simple and Continuous Past Perfect Simple and Continuous	Means of transport and their associations	Homonyms and homophones Jokes with a play on words	Common expressions Exclamations	Reading for information Summarizing	The nightmare side of international travel
6	*Expressing quantity* Mass and count nouns Compounds with **some** and **any** **Few** versus **a few** **Much** and **many**	The language of statistics Clauses of comparison	Health Illnesses, symptoms and diagnoses Courses of treatment	Modal verbs – a review of forms and concepts	Predicting Appreciating a writer's style	The health hazards of modern-day life
7	*Future time* **Will** and **going to** Present Continuous and Simple Future Continuous Future Perfect **May, might, could**	Nouns and verbs – with the same form and pronunciation – with shifting stress **'increase in'crease**	Gap filling Exploring synonyms	Short answers after verbs of opinion **I think so** **I don't think so**	Predicting Recognizing topic sentences	Monster cities of the year 2000

● SPEAKING		● LISTENING		● WRITING	
Activity	**Topic**	**Skill**	**Topic**	**Focus**	**Activity**
Discussion	How do you learn languages?	Identifying different accents of English Listening for specific information Transferring information	Description of six capital cities Esperanto, the artificial language	Proof-reading to find mistakes	Writing an autobiography
Roleplay	Who should get the part?	Listening for specific information Transferring information	The audition	Word order	Writing a biography
A maze	You've been made redundant. What are you going to do?	Summarizing	An unusual first job	The style of formal letters	Writing a letter of application
A class survey	Fears and phobias	Note taking	A ghost story	Text comparison	Writing an appraisal of a book or film
Discussion	Plus, minus and interest points of international travel	Predicting Completing a map	Adventures of a lorry driver	Conjunctions and prepositions of time	Writing a narrative
Group work	Planning a menu	Listening for specific information Transferring information	Holistic medicine	Formal and informal letters	Rearranging jumbled texts Writing a formal and an informal letter
Discussion Roleplay	Yesterday's and today's problems An optimist and a pessimist	Listening for specific information Note taking	An interview with Jonathon Porritt, Director of Friends of the Earth	Joining contrasting ideas Discourse markers	Presenting both sides of an argument

	Grammar	Vocabulary 1	Vocabulary 2	Revision	Skill	Topic
8	*Description* Relative clauses Present and past participles Modifying adverbs	Compound adjectives Expressing negative qualities Physical descriptions	Describing objects – shape, material, colour	Different meanings of **get** **Get** + preposition Multi-word verbs (1) – used literally	Literary appreciation – a short story	**The Lotus Eater** by Somerset Maugham
9	*Modal verbs of deduction* Expressing degrees of certainty about the present and past **Must, might, may, could, can't**	Multi-word verbs (2) – literal – particle as intensifier – non-literal	Idiomatic expressions Identifying the key word to idiomatic expressions	Words commonly confused **Rob** versus **steal** **Actually** versus **at the moment**	Jigsaw Comparing and exchanging information	The relationship between father and daughter
10	*Expressing present and past habit* Present Simple and Continuous **Will** **Would** **Used to** + infinitive (compared with **used to** + noun/gerund)	Money	Words with similar meaning – synonyms and collocation	Time expressions **The day before yesterday**	Matching topic sentences to paragraphs	Meanness
11	*Hypothesis* **Should have done** **Wish** Third conditional	Driving	Formal versus neutral style	Sentence stress Emphatic **do/does/did**	Inferring	Things I wish I'd known at 18
12	*Articles* **A, the** and the zero article	Multi-word verbs (3) Nouns formed from multi-word verbs	Guessing the meaning of a word from the example in the dictionary entry Poem – **The Things That Matter**	Singular or plural nouns? Countable or uncountable nouns?	Predicting Summarizing	Life isn't a rehearsal

	SPEAKING		LISTENING		WRITING
Activity	**Topic**	**Skill**	**Topic**	**Focus**	**Activity**
Lecturettes	Describing a person, place or occasion	Note taking	Hitch-hiking in the snow	Text comparison Fact and opinion in descriptions	Writing two descriptions of a town
Communication game	Solve the murder!	Intensive listening Summarizing	An arranged marriage	Verb patterns in reported speech	Writing a report of an interview
Roleplay	'Writer seeks companion for a year on a tropical island'	Predicting Note taking	An interview with Johnny Morris about pets in our lives	Rearranging jumbled texts to develop awareness of text cohesion	Writing a dialogue, a letter or an essay
Discussion	Pros and cons Paradoxes	Form filling	Failing a driving test	Sentence combination	Manipulating complex clauses to produce coherent writing
Discussion	Periods in world history Time travel	Listening for information	An interview with Mrs Thatcher about Victorian values	Linking devices	Writing an essay

UNIT 1

The tense system

Languages and language learning

● Discussion point

Answer the questions using the list below.

1 Which language in the world is spoken by most people?
2 Which language has the largest vocabulary?
3 Which is the oldest written language?
4 Which sub-continent has the largest number of languages?
5 Which language has no irregular verbs?
6 Which language has the most letters in its alphabet?
7 In which language is the largest encyclopaedia printed?

Is it . . . Spanish/Cambodian/English/Egyptian/Esperanto/Mandarin Chinese/Indian?

The answers are on the next page.

1987年(昭和62年)

朝日新聞

高松宮さま ご逝去

THE WALL STREET JOURNAL.
EUROPE

© 1987 Dow Jones & Compa

European Report

WEDNESDAY, JANUARY 7, 1987

LE MONDE AFFAIRES : les chevaliers de Bernard Tapie

DERNIÈRE ÉDITION

Le Monde

— SAMEDI 14 FÉVRIER 1987

Demain, les robots à la ferme (Page 11)

Portfolio
MONTANT DU JOUR : + 37
30 000 F à gagner

LE FIGARO
premier quotidien

ÉLET és TUDOMÁNY

EL PAIS

Anno 112 · N. 5 · L. 700 (Arretrato L. 1.)

5. S

MADRID, MARTES

DIENTE DE LA MAÑANA   Precio 60 pesetas / Año XII. Número 3.560

För
fastighetslån

PK KREDIT

SVENSKA DAGBLADET

Telefon
till SvD
08/13 50 00

Nr 4 ★   VECKA 2   TEL: 08-13 50 00   MÅNDAGEN DEN 5 JANUARI 1987   Vardagar 4:- Söndagar 4.50

Gorbac

Mercoledì 7 gennaio 1987 · L. 700

Anno 112 · N. 5 · L. 700 (Arretrato L. 1.400)

CORRIERE DELLA SERA

Reading

Pre-reading task

Work in pairs.
Do you think the following statements are true or false? Write T or F in the boxes.

1 [F] English was already an important world language four hundred years ago.
2 [T] It is mainly because of the United States that English has become a world language.
3 [F] One person out of seven in the world speaks perfect English.
4 [T] There are few inflections in modern English.
5 [F] In English, many verbs can be used as nouns.
6 [T] English has borrowed words from many other languages.
7 [F] In the future, all other languages will probably die out.

Skim reading

Read the article on *English as a world language*. Find out the answers to the true/false statements. There is one statement for each paragraph. Discuss your answers in pairs. Then read the article in more depth.

English as a world language

Countries in which English is spoken as mother tongue.

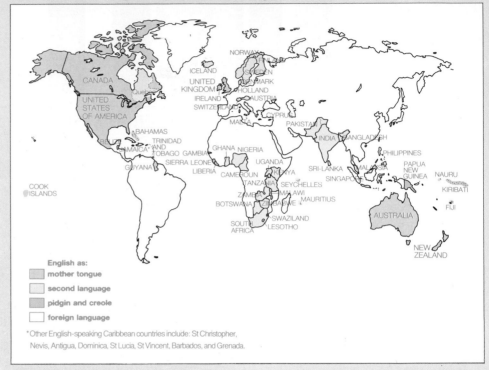

English as:
▨ mother tongue
▢ second language
▨ pidgin and creole
▢ foreign language

*Other English-speaking Caribbean countries include: St Christopher, Nevis, Antigua, Dominica, St Lucia, St Vincent, Barbados, and Grenada.

Today, when English is one of the major languages in the world, it requires an effort of the imagination to realize that this is a relatively recent thing – that in Shakespeare's time, for example, only a few million people spoke English, and the language was not thought to be very important by the other nations of Europe, and was unknown to the rest of the world.

English *has become* a world language because of its establishment as a mother tongue outside England, in all the continents of the world. This exporting of English *began* in the seventeenth century, with the first settlements in North America. Above all, it is the great growth of population in the United States, assisted by massive immigration in the nineteenth and twentieth centuries, that has given the English language its present standing in the world.

People who *speak* English fall into one of three groups: those who have learned it as their native language; those who have learned it as a second language in a society that is mainly bilingual; and those who *are forced* to use it for a practical purpose – administrative, professional or educational. One person in seven of the world's entire population belongs to one of these three groups. Incredibly enough, 75% of the world's mail and 60% of the world's telephone calls are in English.

BASIC CHARACTERISTICS
SIMPLICITY OF FORM. Old English, like modern German, French, Russian and Greek, had many inflections to show singular and plural, tense, person, etc., but over the centuries words *have been simplified*. Verbs now have very few inflections, and adjectives *do not change* according to the noun.

FLEXIBILITY. As a result of the loss of inflections, English has become, over the past five centuries, a very flexible language. Without inflections, the same word can operate as many different parts of speech. Many nouns and verbs have the same form, for example **swim, drink, walk, kiss, look**, and **smile**. We can talk about **water** to drink and **to water** the flowers; **time** to go and **to time** a race; **a paper** to read and **to paper** a bedroom. Adjectives can be used as verbs. We **warm** our hands in front of a fire; if clothes are **dirtied**, they need to be **cleaned** and **dried**. Prepositions too are flexible. A sixty-year old man is **nearing** retirement; we can talk about a **round of golf, cards, or drinks**.

OPENNESS OF VOCABULARY. This involves the free admissions of words from other languages and the easy creation of compounds and derivatives. Most world languages *have contributed* some words to English at some time, and the process *is now being reversed*. Purists of the French, Russian, and Japanese languages *are resisting* the arrival of English in their vocabulary.

THE FUTURE OF ENGLISH. Geographically, English is the most widespread language on Earth, second only to Mandarin Chinese in the number of people who speak it. It is the language of business, technology, sport, and aviation. This will no doubt continue, although the proposition that all other languages *will die out* is absurd.

Comprehension check/Language work

Here are the answers to some questions. Work out the questions.

1 A few million.
2 Because it is the mother tongue of many countries outside England.
3 In the seventeenth century.
4 75%
5 60%
6 Yes, it had a lot of inflections.
7 Simplicity of form, flexibility, and openness of vocabulary.
8 Mandarin Chinese.

What do you think?

1 Does the text come from
– a brochure for an English language school?
– a preface to a book on modern language teaching?
– a dictionary?
– an encyclopaedia?
2 The text says that it is because of the United States that English is a world language. Why?
3 Which of the three groups of English speakers do you belong to? What is your reason for learning?
4 What words are there in your language that have been borrowed from other languages?

Listening

T.1   You will hear six native speakers of English from different countries describing their capital city. Put the number of the speaker in the right box. Try to recognize the different accents, and listen for clues to help you.

American	4	Welsh	
Australian	1	Irish	6 2
Scottish	5	English	3

▶ **Language focus**

Read the *Language review* on page 7. Do the *Controlled practice* exercises 1–4 on page 8 .

Vocabulary 1

The article on *English as a world language* mentioned three characteristics of vocabulary in English: *flexibility of form*, *compounds* and *derivatives*.

Flexibility of form

1 Label the diagram below. Work in pairs.
Can you add any more parts of the body?

1 *palm*
2 ___
3 ___
4 ___
5 ___
6 ___
7 ___
8 ___
9 ___
10 ___
11 ___
12 ___
13 ___
14 ___
15 ___
16 ___
17 ___

2 Complete the following sentences using a verb (in an appropriate tense) which denotes a part of the body.

Example
You have no money. *Face* the facts. You can't go on spending money as though you were a millionaire.

a. Could you Give me that book on the table next to you? Thank you.
b. In the final minutes of the football match, Robson shoot the ball into the back of the net.
c. She Reverse the car carefully out of the garage, and drove off.
d. After his father's death, Tom had to take the responsibility for his family's debts.
e. She _____ the material gently. It felt as smooth as silk. From this she could make the most beautiful gown.
f. The bank robber was Point with a knife and a gun.
g. I ran out of petrol on the motorway, so I had to go a lift to the nearest petrol station.

4

Compounds

1 Look at the dictionary entry of compounds formed with the word **head**. Answer the questions.

> **20** (compounds) ~-ache n [C,U] (a) continuous pain in the ~: *suffer from ~ache(s); have a bad ~ache.* (b) (sl) troublesome problem: *more ~aches for the Department of the Environment.* ~-band n band worn round the ~. ~-dress n covering for the ~, esp woman's ornamental kind. ~-gear n hat, cap, ~dress. ~-hunter n savage who cuts off and keeps as trophies the ~s of his enemies. ~-lamp n powerful lamp fixed to the front of a motor vehicle, etc. ⇨ the illus at motor. ~-land /-lænd/ n promontory, cape. ~-light n large lamp on the front of a locomotive, motor-car, etc. ⇨ the illus at motor. ~-line n newspaper heading; line at the top of a page containing title, etc; (pl) summary of broadcast news: *'Here are the news ~lines.'* ~-man /-mæn/ n (pl -men) chief man of a village, tribe, etc. '~-master/'~mistress nn principal master (mistress) of a school. ~-on adj, adv (of collisions) with the front parts (of vehicles) meeting: *a ~-on collision; meet/strike ~-on.* ~-phones n pl receivers fitting over the ~ (for radio, etc); ear-phones. ~-piece n (a) helmet. (b) (colloq) intelligence; brains. '~-quarters n (sing or pl) place from which (e g police, army) operations are controlled. ~-rest n sth that supports the ~. ~-room n = clearance(2). ~-set n ~phones. ~-ship /-ʃɪp/ n position of a ~master or ~mistress: *apply for a ~ship.* ~-stall n part of a bridle or halter that fits round the ~. ~-stone n stone set up at the ~ of a grave. ~-way n [U] progress. *make some/no ~way,* ⇨ 19 above. ~-wind n one that blows directly into one's face, or against the course of a ship, etc. ~-word n word used as a heading, e g the first word, in heavy type, of a dictionary entry. ~-ed adj (in compounds) *'three-~ed,* having three ~s; *'long-~ed,* having a long skull. ~-less adj having no ~.

a. Why do tennis players sometimes wear a **headband**?
b. Where is the **headquarters** of the United Nations?
c. What is written on **headstones**?
d. If you're making **headway** with a problem, how are you getting on?
e. What are the lights on the front of a car called?
f. What is the first thing you hear on the radio or television news?
g. What do you do if you want to listen to music without disturbing anyone?

2 Work in pairs.

Find the compounds under **hair**, **eye**, and **finger**. Write similar sentences to the ones above, sometimes using the word (as in questions a.–d.) and sometimes not (as in questions e.–g.). Ask the other students your questions to test them!

Derivatives

1 Look at the words made with *suffixes* and *prefixes*.

verb	to cre'ate
nouns	crea'tivity
	cre'ation
person	cre'ator
adjective	cre'ative
opposite	uncre'ative

2 Do the same for the following words.
The *prefixes* and *suffixes* will not always be the same.

photograph   produce   economy

Speaking

How do you learn languages?

1 Discuss the following questions with your fellow students.

– What are the differences between the ways a baby learns its first language and the ways an adult learns a second language?
– What advantages does the baby have?
– What advantages does the adult have?

2 Work alone.
What is most important for you in learning a language? Put the list in order of importance, 1 being the most important.

- ☑ learning grammar
- ☑ learning vocabulary
- ☑ speaking and being corrected
- ☐ speaking and not being corrected all the time
- ☐ listening
- ☑ reading
- ☑ writing
- ☑ pronunciation practice

3 Work in groups.
Compare your lists.
Justify your order, but remember that different people learn in different ways.
Try to agree as a class on an order of importance.

4 Can you think of some suggestions for effective language learning?

Example
Practise as much as possible.
Read books and newspapers.

Listening

Pre-listening task

You will hear a radio programme about Esperanto. Work in pairs. Make two lists.

What I know about Esperanto
It's an artificial language.

What I would like to know
Who invented it?

Listening for information

T.2

1 Listen to the introduction to the programme. Does it mention any of the subjects you discussed? Does it answer any of your questions?

2 Listen to the interview with Professor Nesbit, and fill in the charts.

Advantages of Esperanto as a world language

Disadvantages of English as a world language

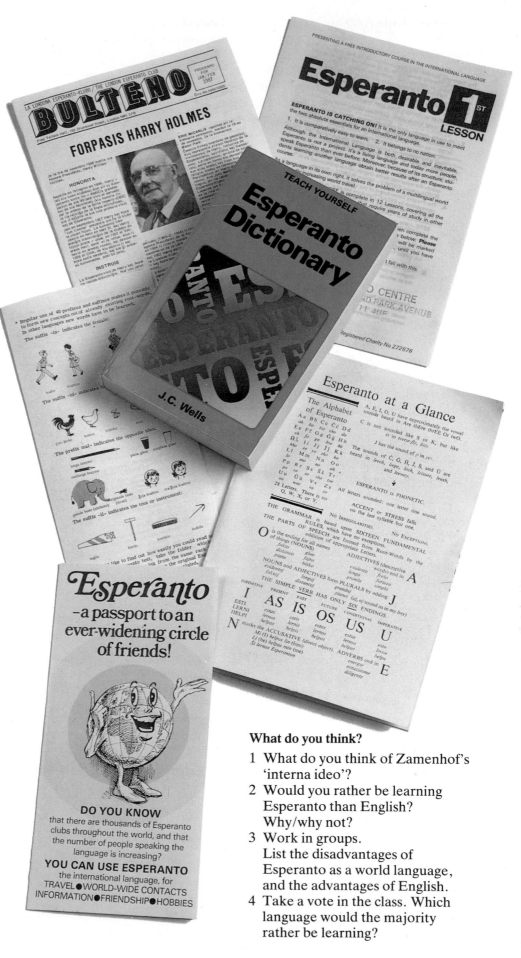

What do you think?

1 What do you think of Zamenhof's 'interna ideo'?

2 Would you rather be learning Esperanto than English? Why/why not?

3 Work in groups.
List the disadvantages of Esperanto as a world language, and the advantages of English.

4 Take a vote in the class. Which language would the majority rather be learning?

● Vocabulary 2

Keeping vocabulary records

It is very important that you decide how you are going to organize your vocabulary learning. You need to keep a record of the words you come across, and review the records regularly. Buy a special notebook.

There are many ways of keeping records, but the best is the one that you think is right for yourself. Here are some suggestions.

The information you need is:
– the word
– its part of speech (noun, verb, etc.)
– its meaning
– its pronunciation
– how to use it in a sentence.

You might want:
– to make a note of the context
– to translate it into your language
– to write a sample sentence of your own or from the dictionary
– to include a word of similar meaning in English.

Different ways of organizing the page.

Another approach is to keep small file cards in an index box.

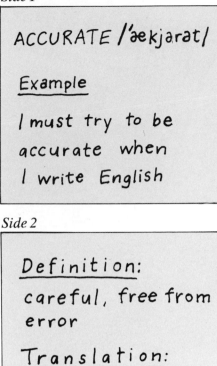

Side 1

ACCURATE /ˈækjərət/

Example

I must try to be accurate when I write English

Side 2

Definition:
careful, free from error

Translation:
preciso, exacto

(in Spanish)

1.

Context A recipe		
Word	Example	Translation
to season	season the dish with salt and pepper before serving	assaisonner (in French)

2.

Word	Pronunciation	Example	Similar word
possession (n.)	/pəˈzeʃn/	I lost all my possessions in the fire	belongings

○ Writing

When you are speaking, mistakes often do not matter if people can understand what you mean. Unfortunately, this is not the case when you are writing. Correct the mistakes in these sentences, and use the signs and abbreviations below to identify the mistakes.

/   This word is not necessary

∧   Add (a) word(s)

P   Punctuation

Sp   Spelling

Gr   Grammar

T   Tense

Ww   Wrong word

Wo   Word order

Example

Gr   *She lives in Rome.*

Wo   *I like very much skiing.*

_____ a. My friend she came to see me last night.

_____ b. I am going to the village where live my parents.

_____ c. He told to me a story, wich was very funny.

_____ d. When I arrived to home, I had the dinner.

_____ e. She speak english, french and russian.

_____ f. The dog broke it's leg.

_____ g. He gave to me a pen for my bithday.

_____ h. She's doctor.

_____ i. She's a doctor for five years.

_____ j. I explained the teacher why was I late.

_____ k. The American people is very generous.

_____ l. I made my homework very carefuly.

Correct this composition in the same way. There are twenty mistakes.

My name is Luis González, and I come from Mexico. I born in 1951 in one small village outside Mexico City. When I was six years I went to the nursery school, and I enjoyed it very much. When I was eleven I've moved to Brazil, because my father is diplomat, so my all life I live in differents countries. After school, I was for four years in a business college, and I got a degree in business administration. I working for a company that products small calculator. It's a good work, and I'm very interesting for computors. I want to learn english because my father and I will start our own business in America soon.

Write a similar composition about yourself.

Include information about:
– your background
– your education
– your work experience
– countries you have been to
– what you hope to do in the future.

Practise checking your own and your colleagues' written work for mistakes before giving it to your teacher.

Language review
The tense system

1 Continuous and Perfect aspect
There are two aspects in the tense system of English, *continuous* and *perfect*. Tenses have two elements of meaning, the *time of the verb action* and *aspect*. Aspect is *the way the speaker sees the verb action*.

Continuous aspect
a. *Ann sings well.*
b. *Ann is singing well.*
In both sentences the tense is *present*, but the *aspect* is different. In a. Ann's ability as a singer is *permanent*; b. refers to a performance on a *particular occasion*.
Continuous tenses are less frequent than simple tenses.

Perfect aspect
a. *Peter lived in Rome for five years.*
b. *Peter has lived in Rome for five years.*
(a.) refers to a time in the past, *now finished*; (b.) refers to both past and present, and expresses an action which *began in the past* and *still continues*.
The *Present Perfect* is a very common tense, and is particularly frequent in spoken English.

2 Active and Passive
English has *active* and *passive voices*.
a. *Maria speaks several languages.*
b. *English is spoken all over the world.*
In (a.) the agent, Maria, is the *subject*.
In (b.) the agent is not given.
Passive sentences are less frequent in spoken English, but they are very common in scientific and official writing.

▶ **Grammar reference:** page 109 and 110

CONTROLLED PRACTICE
The tense system

1 Complete the tense charts opposite.
 Use the verb **work** for the active and **mend** for the passive in the third person singular.

 Notice that not all continuous tenses are included. They are rare because they are so long.

 Complete the following sentences.
 Continuous tenses are formed with the auxiliary verb _____ + the _____ participle.
 Perfect tenses are formed with the auxiliary verb _____ + the _____ participle.
 Passive tenses are formed with the auxiliary verb _____ + the _____ participle.

2 Look again at the article on *English as a world language*. There are ten verbs in italics. What tense are they?

3 You are going to interview someone about her/his past, present and future. First work in pairs. Prepare the questions.

ACTIVE	Simple	Continuous
Present	*he works*	~~work~~ ~~the~~ *working*
Past	*He worked*	*worked*
Future	*He will ~~work~~* *~~He work~~*	
Present Perfect		
Past Perfect		
Future Perfect		

PASSIVE	Simple	Continuous
Present	*it is mended*	
Past		
Future		
Present Perfect		
Past Perfect		
Future Perfect		

background	*Where were you born?*
education	*What schools did . . . ?* *. . . university?*
travel experience	*What countries have you . . . ?* *When . . . ?* *What . . . ?*
family	*. . . married?* *Have you got . . . ?*
sports and hobbies	*Do you play . . . ?*
work experience	*. . . job?* *How long . . . ?*
reason for learning English	*Why . . . ?*
hopes and intentions for the future	*What do you want . . . ?* *When are you going to . . . ?*

 Ask your teacher the questions to check you have formed them correctly.

4 Change partners. Ask and answer questions about each other.

BIRTH:

I was born in Australia.

SPORTS:

I play cards.

HOPES:

I hope to make it through the day

8

REVISION
Numbers and dates

Dates

1 The way dates are written and spoken is different.

Written
17/9/1951
17 September 1951
17 Sept. 1951

Spoken
the seventeenth of September, nineteen fifty-one
September the seventeenth, nineteen fifty-one

2 Work in pairs. Practise saying the following dates.
16 April/21 July/3 February/29 January/4 November
1986/1916/1960/1804/1991/1620
28/1/58   6/6/80   25/4/76
the 20th century/the 18th century/the 12th century

Numbers

1 **0** is pronounced in different ways. The number is called nought /nɔːt/ in British English and zero /zɪərəʊ/ in American English.
When numbers are said one by one, we say /əʊ/ like the letter 'o'.

Example
Telephone numbers
3098 /θriː əʊ naɪn eɪt/
Account numbers
36024 /θriː sɪks əʊ tuː fɔː/

Sports are different!
Football 3–0 /nɪl/
Tennis 15–0 /lʌv/

---

2 **Dictation**

T.3 You will hear four news items. On the tape there are sixteen numbers. Write them down on a separate piece of paper. Write the numbers, not the letters.

Example   *13*

3 Work in pairs. Practise saying the following numbers.

Numbers
13/14/15/16/17/18/19
30/40/50/60/70/80/90
14/40/16/60/18/80

13 years old/19 people/16 cars

105/238/950/1,200/2,780/
5,060/11,900/120,000/450,000/
843,926/5,600,420

Money
£6.70/90p/15p/£15/£1.50/£17.99/
$20/10FF/50DM

Telephone numbers
01 491 2598/0943 78855/
010 44 368 31120

Fractions
$\frac{1}{2}/\frac{3}{4}/\frac{1}{4}/\frac{1}{3}/\frac{2}{3}/\frac{7}{8}/\frac{3}{5}/4\frac{3}{4}/18\frac{1}{2}/24\frac{7}{16}$

Decimals
4.32/7.886/27.9%/33.406/
11.02/3.141592

---

4 Answer these questions.
– What's the date today?
– When's your birthday?
– What's your date of birth?
– When's Christmas Eve?
– When's New Year's Day?
– What's the population of your country?
– What's your address?
– What's the rate of unemployment in your country?
– What's the exchange rate between sterling and your currency?
– What's your telephone number?

Present Perfect Simple and Continuous

The seven ages of man

● Discussion point

People in developed countries can expect to live for about seventy years.

Suggest age groups for the following people and ages.

0 – ☐ a baby (babyhood)

☐ – 13 a child (childhood)

13 – ☐ a teenager (the teenage years)

☐ – ☐ an adult (adulthood)

☐ – ☐ a middle-aged person (middle age)

☐ – ☐ an old person (old age)

What are some of the joys and problems of each age?

Are you happy with your present age?

How do you feel about growing older?

'I'm at that difficult age — too old to work and too young to be a world leader'

Vocabulary 1

Work in pairs.
With which age or ages do you associate the following? Use your dictionary and discuss together.

- nappies
- a pension
- wrinkles
- moo cows and gee gees
- a mortgage

- comics
- false teeth
- swings and roundabouts
- a satchel

- swotting
- going grey

- going bald
- playing truant

- expecting a baby
- an inability to sleep
- an inability to get up

being
- wise
- innocent
- mature
- responsible
- ambitious
- naughty
- absent-minded

Reading

T.4   This is an extract from a Shakespeare play *As You Like It*. It is a famous speech, known as *The seven ages of man*, by a character called Jaques (pronounced /'dʒeɪkwiːz/).

What are the seven ages that Jaques describes? The glossary on the next page will help you.

'AS YOU LIKE IT' (by W. Shakespeare) Act II, Scene 7.

Jaques
                    All the world's a stage,
    And all the men and women merely players:
    They have their exits and their entrances;
    And one man in his time plays many parts,
5   His acts being seven ages. At first the infant,
    Mewling and puking in the nurse's arms.
    And then the whining school-boy, with his satchel,
    And shining morning face, creeping like snail
    Unwillingly to school. And then the lover,
10 Sighing like furnace, with a woful ballad
    Made to his mistress' eyebrow. Then a soldier,
    Full of strange oaths, and bearded like the pard,
    Jealous in honour, sudden and quick in quarrel,
    Seeking the bubble reputation
15 Even in the cannon's mouth. And then the justice,
    In fair round belly with good capon lin'd,
    With eyes severe, and beard of formal cut,
    Full of wise saws and modern instances;
    And so he plays his part. The sixth age shifts
20 Into the lean and slipper'd pantaloon
    With spectacles on nose and pouch on side,
    His youthful hose well sav'd a world too wide
    For his shrunk shank; and his big manly voice,
    Turning again toward childish treble, pipes
25 And whistles in his sound. Last scene of all,
    That ends his strange eventful history,
    Is second childishness and mere oblivion
    Sans teeth, sans eyes, sans taste, sans everything.

Glossary (by line number)

6 *mewling and puking*
crying and being sick (archaic)

7 *whining*
making a complaining, miserable noise

8 *creeping like snail*
moving slowly like a snail

10 *furnace*
enclosed fireplace for heating metals

woful
sad (poetic; modern spelling woeful.)

12 *oaths*
swear words, rude words

bearded like the pard
with a beard like a priest

15 *justice*
judge

16 *belly*
stomach (colloquial)

capon
male chicken fattened for eating

18 *saws*
sayings or proverbs (archaic)

instances
examples

20 *lean*
thin

slipper'd
with slippers on

pantaloon
trousers (archaic)

22 *hose*
kind of trousers

22/23 The trousers which were saved from when he was young are now much too big for his body, which has shrunk.

27 *oblivion*
forgetfulness

28 *sans*
without (French word)

Comprehension check

1 What is the modern word for **players**? (line 2)

2 What are **exits** and **entrances, parts** and **acts** in the theatre?
What are they in a person's life?

3 Does the baby seem attractive?
What doesn't the school-boy want to do?
What is the lover doing?
Do all of these words describe the soldier?
violent   quick-tempered   clever
What does the judge like doing?
How old is the man in the sixth age?
What can't the man in the seventh age do?

4 There is a negative criticism of each of the seven people.
Who . . .
– keeps on complaining?
– wants fame so much that he'll probably kill himself?
– looks rather ridiculous?
– sounds and smells awful?
– probably wouldn't notice either the sound or the smell?
– will probably mature with age?
– sounds a real bore?

5 The lover writes a ballad 'to his mistress' eyebrow'. What point is Shakespeare making about the lover?

6 Explain the phrase **bubble reputation**.

What do you think?

1 *As You Like It* was written nearly four hundred years ago. How much are Shakespeare's descriptions of people still true today?
Do you know anyone that resembles one of the characters?

2 Shakespeare describes the ages of man very cynically. How could each person and age be described in a more flattering way?

► Language focus

Read the *Language review* on page 16. Do the *Controlled practice* exercises 1–3.

● Vocabulary 2

Guessing the meaning of unknown words

When you meet a new word, the best advice is initially to ignore it. Sometimes, however, it might be an important word, and rather than look it up in a dictionary, you might be able to guess it.
It is not always necessary to be 100% right, 50% is often enough.

1 **Suffixes** and **prefixes**

In *Unit 1* (page 4) we saw how *prefixes* and *suffixes* are used to form different parts of speech.
*fashion**able*** = adjective
*happi**ness*** = noun
*electric**ian*** = person
They can also add a new meaning.

Example
bi = two
***bi**lingual*
***bi**plane*
If you understand the meaning of the suffix or prefix, you can often guess the meaning of a new word.

2 What meaning do the following *suffixes* and *prefixes* add?
a. **non**-fiction
b. **dis**honest
c. **mis**understand
d. **over**sleep
e. **under**cook
f. **re**decorate
g. an **ex**-president
h. a manag**eress**
i. help**less**
j. use**ful**
k. **anti**-social
l. **auto**graph
m. **pro**-American
n. **de**frost
o. **micro**scope
p. **post**-graduate
q. **pre**dict

3 Context

Examining the context will provide the best help. Look closely at the context to see:

a. the part of speech. Is it a noun/adjective/verb/person?
b. any other references to the unknown word. Is it described or defined?

Example

Smallpox used to be a highly dangerous disease, but nowadays, thanks to modern medicine, very few people die of it.

Smallpox is a *noun*.
It is a *disease*.
It *used to kill* a lot of people, but not now.

4 Work in pairs.

Read the newspaper article. Try to guess the meaning of the words in italics.

Can you guess 50%?/90%?/100%?

DANGER BOY — Allen swings into action, after climbing up a lamp post.

The boy who fell down stairs, drank antiseptic, chopped off a finger and then plunged into an empty swimming pool . . .

Allen is a little disaster

ACCIDENT PRONE Allen Davies is only five, but already his parents are *convinced* he's a walking disaster.

The youngster has *cracked* his head falling into an empty swimming pool, has *chopped* the end of his finger *off* with a *penknife* and has made himself ill by drinking half a bottle of *Dettol*.

Each time another disaster *strikes* Allen, he is taken to the Children's Hospital in Sydenham, where he has been such a regular visitor he believes the *nursing sister* is a member of his family.

Now Allen's *grateful* father, street trader Alan Davies, has *raised* £6500 for the hospital to buy a neonatal monitor to *measure* babies' breathing and temperature.

Stitches

His wife Margaret said, 'It all started when little Allen was a year old. He fell over and cut himself and had to have *stitches* in his *forehead*. Since then he hasn't stopped. He's been taken to hospital at least ten times.

'The latest accident happened when he climbed on to a *shelf* and managed to open his father's penknife.

'He chopped the end of his finger off and had to have it *sewn back* on.'

Doctors at the hospital also had to stitch Allen's head when he *plunged headlong* into a pool.

Mr Davies, *supported* by the Lewisham and Berwick Street Traders' Association, raised the cash with the help of *celebrities* including actor Richard Harris, *songwriter* Andrew Lloyd-Webber and Spike Milligan, who *donated possessions* to be auctioned at a charity disco and buffet.

Mr Davies, of Avondale Road, Bromley, said, 'Little Allen is a regular patron of the hospital. He's always having accidents. He's been going there since he was just one.'

Holidays

'Everyone in the hospital has known him for years, and he firmly believes he's got a real sister in the hospital because he knows the sister who looks after him so well.'

A sister at the hospital said, 'Whenever we see Allen coming in again, we all shout "What have you been doing this time?"'

Allen's older brothers have also had their share of accidents and had to be taken to the Children's Hospital.

Robert, 15, *tore* some *ligaments* on a skiing holiday and *slipped* off his *crutches*, breaking his ankle a few days later and Lee, 13, injured his neck doing a motorbike *stunt*.

(Standard 3 March 1980)

13

► **Language focus**

1 Underline in a solid line _____ the examples of the *Present Perfect Simple*, and in a broken line _ _ _ _ _ the examples of the *Present Perfect Continuous*. One example is interchangeable. Which one?

2 Work in pairs.
Ask and answer questions about the accidents you have had.

Example
Student A *Have you ever broken a leg?/been in a car crash?/had to have stitches?*
Student B *No, .../Yes, ...*
Student A *When/how/where did ...?*

3 Work in pairs.
Complete the following questions, using either the *Present Perfect Simple* or *Continuous*. If both are possible, use the *Continuous*.

a. How long *Do you* _____ (know) the teacher?

b. How long *have you being* _____ (learn) English?

c. How many other languages *Do you speaking* _____ (learn)? *worky* *you*

d. How long *are you* _____ (work) as a _____?

e. How long _____ (live) in _____?

f. How long _____ (have) your watch/car/_____?

g. _____ you _____ (see) any good films recently?

Now ask and answer the questions.

4 In the article about Allen, first it says:
Allen ... has chopped the end of his finger off
Allen's father ... has raised £6,500
but later:
He chopped the end of his finger off ...
Mr Davis ... raised the cash ...

Why are both tenses possible?

14

● Listening

| **T.5** | A TV company is about to start filming a new serial of Charles Dickens' novel *David Copperfield*. They are trying to find an actor to take the part of Mr Micawber (pronounced /mɪˈkɔːbə/).

Mr Micawber is a comic character. His plans always go wrong, he is always in debt, but he is always optimistic. He is a gentleman, about fifty, who talks too much because he likes the sound of his own voice.

The producer and director have just auditioned three actors for the part.

Listen to their discussion and fill in the chart opposite.

	Good points	Bad points
Bill Frindall		
Harry Lime		
Victor O'Brian		

► **Language focus**

Look at the tapescript on page 126. Find the examples of the *Present Perfect*.

Do the *Controlled practice* exercises 4 and 5.

Speaking

Discussion

Work in groups of four. Appoint a spokesperson.

Talk together to decide who should get the part, and why. When you have come to a decision, the spokesperson should report to the rest of the class.

Roleplay

Work in groups of three.

Student A and B   You are the producer and director. You are going to talk to Student C, who is one of the actors you have just turned down for the part of Mr Micawber. Break the news to him, tell him why, but try not to hurt his feelings.

Student C   You are one of the actors turned down for the part of Mr Micawber. You're very disappointed, and want to know why.

Writing

Word order

Word order in English is relatively fixed. *Subject + verb + object* is the most common order.

Frequency adverbs (**always, sometimes**) usually come before the main verb.

We always go skiing in winter.
I have never seen so many people.
But they come after the verb *to be*.
He is always late.

When there is more than one adverbial phrase at the end of a sentence, the usual order is *manner, place, time*.

He was lying quietly in bed.
(Manner, place)
You worked hard today.
(Manner, time)
We played in the garden for hours.
(Place, time)

Adverbs of time can go at the beginning or end of a sentence, but for reasons of style, we try not to put too many adverbials at the end of a sentence.

Last year I travelled by train right across America.
is more common than
I travelled by train right across America last year.

1 Correct the mistakes of word order in the following sentences.
   a. Always I get at Christmas the same presents.
   b. A pair of socks sends me my aunt Freda.
   c. I last year got from my relatives ten pairs of socks.
   d. I like very much reading.
   e. I don't know why doesn't somebody buy me a book.
   f. I used often to read in bed a book before going to sleep.

2 Put the following into a normal order.

a. In 1951/in Leicester/was born/my sister.
b. At Newcastle University/English literature/she studied/from 1967 to 1970.
c. As a lecturer/she has worked/since 1974/at Oxford Polytechnic.
d. In 1980/happened/to her/something rather interesting.
e. Jobs and houses/for a year/she swapped/from a New York university/with a lecturer.

Biographies

Write the biography of someone (still alive) who you admire. It might be a friend, a relative, or someone who you have never met.

Include the following information:
– background, education and family
– character, and the reasons you admire her/him
– achievements in life, professional and personal.

● Language review

Present Perfect Simple and Continuous

When the *Present Perfect* is used, the **time when** the action happened is not important.

I've lost my diary. Have you seen it anywhere?
It doesn't matter *when* I lost it. The important thing is that I haven't got it *now*.
I've learnt my irregular verbs.
It doesn't matter when, the important thing is that I *know* them *now*.

If the **time** of the action *is* important, we use the *Past Simple* or *Continuous*.

I lost my diary yesterday while I was tidying up.
The *Present Perfect* enables us to look at a past action and express its relationship to the Present. A sentence in the present tense can often summarize the *idea* of the Present Perfect.

a. *I've lived here for five years.* (I still live here.)
I've been learning English since 1984. (I'm still learning.)
b. *Your taxi has arrived.* (It's waiting outside.)
I've been working very hard. (That's why I'm tired.)
c. *I've read all of Shakespeare's plays.* (I know all about them.)

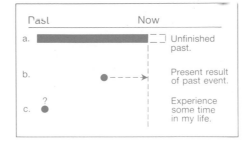

► Grammar reference: page 111.

CONTROLLED PRACTICE
Present Perfect Simple and Continuous versus Past Simple

1 Work in pairs.

Read the biography of William Shakespeare.

SHAKESPEARE, William, 1564–1616, English dramatist and poet, considered the greatest of all playwrights; b. Stratford-upon-Avon. He was the son of a glove maker and leather craftsman, and attended the local grammar school. In 1582 he married Anne Hathaway, and his first child, a daughter, was born within six months. Two years later they had twins. Little else of his life is known before 1592, when he appeared in London as an actor and playwright with a growing reputation. In 1594 he joined a group of actors known as the Lord Chamberlain's Men, which became the King's Men under the patronage of James I. In 1599 he bought the Globe Theatre. He retired to Stratford in 1613. He wrote at least thirty-seven plays: history plays, comedies and tragedies. Their appeal lies in his human vision, which recognises the complexity of moral questions, and in the richness of his language.

Ask and answer questions about Shakespeare.
– When . . . ?
– Where . . . ?
– What . . . ?
– Did he . . . ?
– Who . . . ?
– How many . . . ?
– What sort of . . . ?

THE GLOBE

2 Read the biography of Jeffrey Archer.

ARCHER, Jeffrey was born in 1940, and was educated at Wellington School and Oxford University. In 1969 he became a Member of Parliament when he won a by-election. At 29, he was the youngest member of the House of Commons. He resigned from Parliament in 1974 because he had debts of over £427,000, following the collapse of a Canadian company in which he had invested.

In the same year he wrote his first novel, 'Not a Penny More, Not a Penny Less', which was based on his business experiences. He has been writing ever since, and all six of his novels have been best sellers. They have been translated into over fifteen languages. His most successful novel, 'Kane and Abel', has sold more than four million copies worldwide, and has been made into a television series.

After the success of his books, he decided to return to politics. From September 1985 to October 1986 he was Deputy Chairman of the Conservative Party. He married his wife in 1966, and they live with their two children in Cambridge and London.

Ask and answer questions about Jeffrey Archer.

When . . . ?	How many . . . ?
Where . . . ?	How long . . . ?
What . . . ?	Have any . . . films?
Why . . . ?	

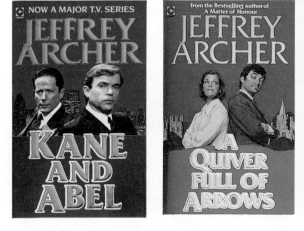

Captain Justin Barlow (left)
— ex RAF, now British Airways'
most experienced pilot

Chris Dexter — has climbed mountains in four continents.

Sister Andrea
— has worked for the poor all over the world.

Tina Turner — world-famous singer

3 Work in pairs.
  Student A You are one of the people opposite. Decide which one. Prepare to talk to a journalist about your life.
  – Which countries have you been to?
  – What were you doing there?
  – What are you doing now?
  Student B You are a journalist. You are going to interview Student A, who is one of the people opposite.
  Talk to her/him to decide which one.
  Prepare your questions to find out about her/his past and present.

  When you are ready, conduct the interview.

4 Compare the use of tenses in the following pairs of sentences. Say which tense is used and why.
a. She lived in New York for two years.
   She has lived in New York for two years.
b. My husband always bought me flowers on my birthday.
   My husband has always bought me flowers on my birthday.
c. Have you ever met anyone famous?
   Did you meet anyone interesting at the party?
d. I've written a novel.
   I've been writing a novel.
e. How long have you been smoking?
   How many cigarettes have you had today?
f. What have you done to your eye? It's red.
   What have you been doing since I last saw you?

5 In the following pairs of sentences one of the tenses is wrong. Say which one, and why.
a. He has been to most countries in the world.
   He has been to Venezuela last year.
b. My first job was in a factory. I did it for three months.
   My first job was in a factory. I've done it for three months.

c. President Kennedy has been assassinated in Dallas.
   President Kennedy was assassinated in Dallas.
d. He's broken his leg.
   He's been breaking his leg.
e. Who's been eating my sandwich? It was here a minute ago.
   Who's eaten my sandwich? It was here a minute ago.
f. I've been writing all morning.
   I've been writing four letters.

REVISION

The Alphabet

1 Of course you know the alphabet, but are you sure you can pronounce all the letters?
  Put the letters in the right column, according to the pronunciation of the vowel.

1 /eɪ/	2 /iː/	3 /e/	4 /aɪ/	5 /əʊ/	6 /uː/	7 /ɑː/
a	b c d	f	i			q

2 **Dictation**
  T.6 You will hear ten English names (people and places) dictated. Write them down on a separate piece of paper.

3 When we are spelling out loud, notice how we break up a long word to allow the other person time to write it down.
  Example
  Henderson   Hen (pause) *der* (pause) *son*
  Gillian   Gill (pause) *ian*
  Remember that vowel sounds link with any consonant sound that comes before, and this happens a lot when you are spelling.
  Example
  Holmes /eɪtʃ əʊ el em iː es/

4 Work in pairs.
  Spell your name and address to your partner.
  Try to say it with speed and rhythm.
  If your partner makes a mistake, you might have to help like this!
  Not p, b for ball!
  Not e, a for apple!

5 **English names**
  Are the following English names girls' names (g), boys' names (b) or surnames (s)?
  Sometimes the same name will fit two categories.

Jane	Atkins
Tracy	James
Frances	Green
Jean	Ellis
Pat	Wilmot
Joe	Hughes
Graham	Joyce
Terry	Robson
Joan	Alan

  Practise spelling them out loud.

6 **Abbreviations**
  Practise these abbreviations.
  What do they stand for? Your dictionary will tell you in the *Appendix*.

PM	BBC	RSVP	UNO
BA	PhD	PTO	PS
MP	EEC	VAT	eg
BSc	UFO	mph	ie

Instructions for the quiz

Simply indicate whether you think the statements are True or False. There are no right or wrong answers, just answers which are true for you and those which are not. Circle only one alternative for each statement.

People

Circle *true* or *false* to the following:

	True	False
I always think of other people's opinions before making decisions	A	C
I like working with statistics	C	A
I always help a colleague who has family problems	A	C
I frequently forget where I leave things	B	C
I cannot often persuade others to see my point of view	C	B
Personal insults don't worry me	C	A
In a new group of people I often feel anxious	C	B
I enjoy telling other people about my achievements	C	A
I am bored by mundane tasks	B	C
I always like to win when I take part in an activity	C	A
I am easily persuaded by the majority opinion	C	B
If I can choose, I do things my way first	C	A
Success in my job is very important to me	B	C
I like tasks which require a lot of physical and mental energy	B	C
I often question myself about how I really feel	A	C
If someone upsets me, I tell them that they have	C	B

Scoring

Total A answers	
Total B answers	
Total A and B answers	

Procedures and Systems

Circle *true* or *false* to the following:

	True	False
I like to keep things in order	A	C
I am quick at making conclusions about most things	C	A
Traditional solutions are the best	A	C
Other people's problems don't interest me	B	C
I rarely question or doubt what other people say	C	B
I don't always finish tasks on time	C	A
I feel comfortable in nearly all social situations	C	B
I like to predict results before beginning to do anything	A	C
I like working under pressure	B	C
I enjoy being challenged by new tasks	C	A
People are usually convinced by my arguments	C	B
Checking detail is not one of my strong points	C	A
Clear and distinct thought is important to me	B	C
I find it hard to express myself in groups	B	C
I always try to finish what I start	A	C
The beauty of nature often astounds me	C	B

Scoring

Total A answers	
Total B answers	
Total A and B answers	

Interpretation

Ignore all C responses. They simply indicate a lack of interest in a particular area, and should not be included in your scoring.

You should now have four scores, each between 0 and 16. A score of 0–4 shows very little interest in a particular area. 5–12 is about average. A score of 13 and over shows a strong interest, and the highest of your four scores indicates which area of work is most likely to suit the requirements of your individual personality.

People

A	B
Caring	Influence
Medical	Control
Welfare	Commercial
Education	Managerial

Procedures and Systems

A	B
Words	Data
Administrative	Financial
Clerical	Data Processing
Legal	
Information	

Communications and the Arts

A	B
Media	Visual Arts & Design
Literary	Art
Languages	Design

Science and Engineering

A	B
Research	Practical
Physical	Physical
Biological	Biological
Mechanical	Mechanical
Electrical	Electrical
Construction	Construction
Process	Process

Communications and the Arts

Circle *true* or *false* to the following:

	True	False
I would like to present TV programmes	A	C
I sometimes find it difficult to say what I mean	C	A
I think I could write good short stories	A	C
I could do drawings for new designs	B	C
My knowledge of the arts is rather limited	C	B
I prefer doing practical things to reading or creative writing	C	A
I rarely notice the design of clothes	C	B
I enjoy talking to others about their opinions	A	C
I am full of creative ideas	B	C
I find most fiction rather uninteresting	C	A
I am not very inventive	C	B
I am a very down-to-earth person	C	A
I would like to exhibit my photographs or paintings for others to see	B	C
I could design something which was visually attractive	B	C
Translating foreign languages would appeal to me	A	C
Unconventional people make me feel uncomfortable	C	B

Scoring

Total A answers	
Total B answers	
Total A and B answers	

Science and Engineering

Circle *true* or *false* to the following:

	True	False
I am good at finding the weaknesses in arguments	A	C
I nearly always make spontaneous decisions	C	A
Thinking up new ideas is easy for me	A	C
I'm not good at persuading others	B	C
I enjoy organizing things in advance	C	B
Thinking in the abstract helps to solve problems	C	A
Mending things is not one of my strong points	C	B
Talking about possibilities that might never happen is enjoyable	A	C
Other people's comments about me don't hurt me	B	C
I try to solve problems by intuition and personal feelings	C	A
I don't always finish what I begin	C	B
I don't try to hide my emotions	C	A
I find it easy to find solutions to practical problems	B	C
Traditional methods are usually the best ones	B	C
My independence is very important to me	A	C
I enjoy reading classical literature	C	B

Scoring

Total A answers	
Total B answers	
Total A and B answers	

People

Within the world of People, if you have more A than B answers, you are more interested in caring for people than in influencing them. You should therefore be looking for a career in the medical, welfare or education fields: for example, doctor, dentist, psychiatrist, health visitor, radiographer, social worker, speech-therapist, teacher or lecturer. But if you have scored more B than A answers, you are more likely to feel at home in a job involving control, commerce or management: for example, the armed forces, police, prison officer, security guard, sales representative, marketing manager, property developer, advertising executive or market researcher.

Procedures and Systems

If your original score places you in the world of Procedures and Systems, more A than B answers points to a career in administrative, legal or clerical work: for example, Civil Servant, office manager, personnel manager, company secretary, solicitor, professional secretary, librarian, archivist, book researcher or records officer. If you have more B than A answers, the chances are your interest in Procedures and Systems will be better catered for in finance and data processing. Suitable careers include: accountancy, banking, valuing, economics, computer programming and systems analysis.

Communications and the Arts

In the world of Communications and the Arts, a higher A than B score should point you towards the media, literature or languages. Occupations include: journalist, radio or television researcher, advertising copy writer, translator or public relations officer.

A higher B than A score, on the other hand, indicates that you are more suited to design and the visual arts. Careers include: graphic designer, cartographer, architect, interior designer, window dresser, theatrical designer, fashion designer or photographer.

Science and Engineering

The main division in this area is between research and practice. More A's suggest research, more B's suggest practice. Since most careers in this world have opportunities for both research and applied work, it is not possible to make specific suggestions to individuals on the basis of their A and B responses. Careers include: biologist, physicist, chemist, mechanical and civil engineer.

John Nicholson is a lecturer in psychology at London University.

What do you think?

1 What professions did the quiz suggest would be best for you? Do you agree?

2 The quiz sometimes asks a similar question more than once.

Example
I cannot often persuade others to see my point of view.
People are usually convinced by my arguments.
I'm not good at persuading others.

Find other examples where the same or similar questions are asked more than once.

3 Many of the statements are asking you one of these questions:

Can you express yourself and your feelings?
Are you confident in your dealings with other people?
Are you ambitious?
Are you an original thinker?
Do you enjoy being a leader or being led?

Do you think these qualities are necessary in all jobs?

4 In the quiz, all C answers must be ignored. Therefore, according to the people who wrote the quiz, scientists and engineers . . .
– don't make spontaneous decisions
– don't enjoy organizing things
– don't think in the abstract
– follow traditional methods
– don't enjoy reading classical literature.
Do you agree?

5 Look at the answers for the other areas of work. Do you agree that A and B answers mean *This quality is important for this area of work* and C answers mean *This quality isn't important*?

► **Language focus**

Read the *Language review* on page 26.
Do the *Controlled practice* exercises 1–4.

● Vocabulary 2

Describing personal characteristics

Look at the statements under *People* and *Procedures and Systems* on page 22. Match one of the following adjectives with one of the statements.

Example
considerate
I always think of other people's opinions before making decisions.

helpful   conventional
insecure   self-centred
proud   cautious
competitive   careless
frank   thorough
organized

Look at some of the other statements.
Think of an adjective to describe that sort of person.

● Speaking

A maze

Work in groups of four.
You have a problem, and you must decide collectively what you are going to do.

Talk together until you all agree on the decision to make. Your teacher will then give you a card with more information, and another decision to make.
Carry on talking and making decisions until you get out of the maze!

24

1

You were working in the textile industry, but you have been made redundant because of new technology. Your company has given you £3,000 redundancy money. You have a family to support, and can't survive very long without an income.

What are you going to do?

a Start applying for jobs. You've seen several jobs that you are qualified to do. **GO TO 3.**

b Go on holiday. You feel depressed. **GO TO 6.**

c Do a retraining scheme to become a sales representative. It's a risk because you'll have to live off your redundancy money. **GO TO 10.**

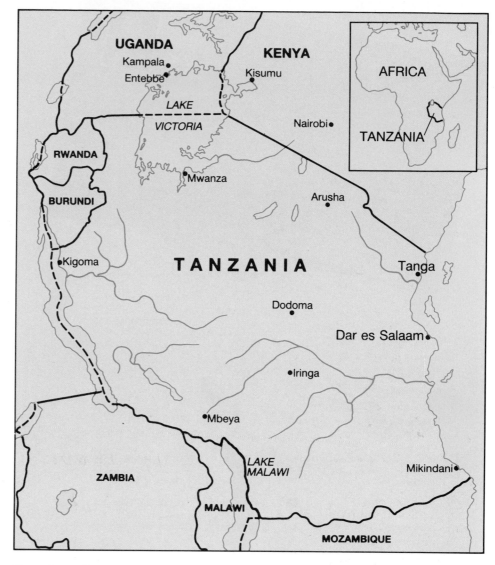

Post-maze activity

When you have finished, discuss these questions.

1 How did you make your decisions?
  Was everybody involved?
  Did one person dominate?
  Were your decisions democratic?
2 In retrospect, did you make any wrong decisions?
  What should you have done?
3 Games such as these are used in management training to practise qualities of leadership. What are the qualities of a good leader?

Listening

T.7 You will hear a woman called Liz talking about her first job, teaching in Tanzania.

Pre-set questions

Listen for the answers to the following questions.

1 What did Liz hope to do at first in Tanzania?
2 Did she manage to do this? Why/why not?
3 What sort of school did she teach at?
4 What happened when a snake appeared?
5 What was Liz's attitude to problems of discipline?
6 Why did she teach the children about the geography of Sweden?

Summary

Work in pairs.
Here is a summary of the conversation, but it contains factual mistakes. Find the mistakes and correct them.

Shortly after her marriage, Liz and her husband went out to Tanzania, where he had a job as a teacher. Liz hoped that she too would be able to teach after a while. However, on the first day, she was asked to teach at the local school because of her valuable university experience. She found the job difficult because she had not taught before, and the children were unused to discipline. When she looks back, Liz thinks that she didn't teach particularly well because she didn't know enough about the subjects she was teaching.

► Language focus

Do the *Controlled practice* exercises 5 and 6.

James Henderson

Kings rd, 18

Birmingham

Trans Europe Tours

Bridge street

Cambridge

Dear P. Bradley

I was reading a magazine the other day - I think it was the February edition of sunshine holidays, and I saw your advertisement for travel couriers, and I thought I'd really like a job like that.

You see, I've got a degree in modern languages from bristol university, and I speak lots of languages - french german spanish and just a little bit of greek too. I've been to all sorts of places in europe.

Last year me and my friend Paul went camping in France and Italy, and we saw the museums and all the places like that. I think I'd be really good at showing people round these places, well I'd really like the chance to try anyway. I'm not doing anything at the moment, so I could come and see you anytime.

Just give me a ring - 381229.

I'm looking forward to meeting you.

Yours

Writing

Style of formal letters

Here is a letter of application for a job. There are no grammatical mistakes, but there are mistakes of other kinds:

– the punctuation is wrong
– the style is too informal
– some of the information is irrelevant
– conventions are broken e.g. of address, salutation, position of sender's name.

In pairs, study it carefully and discuss the mistakes. Then rewrite the letter correctly.

There are similar mistakes on the envelope. Correct them.

Write a letter of application for a job. Include where you saw the advertisement, and say briefly why you are interested in the job and what your qualifications are. Conclude by asking for further details and/or an application form.

Language review

Gerunds

Gerunds are verbs used as nouns, and are formed by adding **-ing** to the verb stem.

They are used:

1 after prepositions.
*I always think of other people's opinions **before making** decisions.*
*I am quick **at reaching** conclusions about most things.*

2 after certain verbs.
*I **like working** with statistics.*
*I **enjoy telling** other people about my achievements.*

3 as the subject of a sentence.
***Checking** detail is not one of my strong points.*
***Translating** foreign languages would appeal to me.*

Infinitives

Infinitives are used:

1 after certain verbs.
*I always **try to finish** what I start.*
*I cannot often **persuade** others **to see** my point of view.*

2 after certain adjectives.
*I find it **hard to express** myself in groups.*

◀ Look again at the quiz on jobs. Find the examples of gerunds and infinitives.

▶ **Grammar reference:** page 111.

CONTROLLED PRACTICE

Gerunds and infinitives

1 Complete the following sentences using a gerund.
Example
I'm good at mending things.

a. I have difficulty in _____

b. I'm very interested in _____

c. I'm thinking of _ _____

d. He saved up £1000 for a holiday by _____

e. I sometimes worry about not _____

f. Thank you for _____

g. I'm looking forward to _____

h. She left the room without _____

i. I stayed in bed all day instead of _

2 Use your imagination to complete the following sentences.
Example
Working in a coal mine is dangerous, but well paid.

a. Finding a good job these days _____

b. Living in a big city _____

c. Taking regular exercise _____

d. Travelling by air _____

e. Being self-employed _____

f. Learning a foreign language _____

3 Complete the following sentences using infinitives.
Example
It is easy to find cheap places to eat.

a. How do you do. Pleased to _____

b. When you're old, it can be difficult to _____

c. I was surprised to _____

d. If you haven't got much money, it's impossible to _____

e. It can be expensive to _____

f. When you travel abroad, it's important to _____

4 [**T.8**] Listen to an interview with a man who went to live and work in a windmill.
Then make sentences about the man using the following prompts.
Example
stop *He stopped working as an accountant.*

a. didn't enjoy
b. couldn't afford
c. interested in
d. decided
e. managed
f. finished
g. were thinking of
h. decided not to
i. doesn't regret
j. prefer
k. the boys . . . used to

Look at the tapescript on page 127 and find more examples of gerunds and infinitives.

5 There are many expressions with **go** + gerund which are concerned with activities, sports, and physical recreation.
go dancing/go skiing/go running

Complete these sentences with **go** + a suitable gerund.

a. I _____ yesterday, but I didn't buy anything.
b. I _____ by the river tomorrow, but I'm sure I won't catch anything.
c. Whenever there's enough snow, we _____ every weekend.
d. If I had enough money, I'd buy a yacht and _____ in the Mediterranean.
e. We had a lovely holiday. We _____ every day. The water was lovely.

6 Fill the gaps with one of the verbs which follow the passage, in either the gerund or infinitive form.

Jane's a nurse, but she's trying (1)_____ a new job. Although she enjoys (2)_____ people, nursing is not very well paid, and she cannot afford (3)_____ all her bills. She finds it impossible to live on such a low salary without (4)_____ her account at the bank. Her flat needs (5)_____, and she would like (6)_____ a car. She managed (7)_____ enough last year for a short holiday by (8)_____ some extra money in her spare time, and this year, she's hoping (9)_____ some friends in France. She has stopped (10)_____ to the theatre, which used to be one of her greatest pleasures. She's thinking of (11)_____ in America, where she could earn a higher salary in a private hospital, but would prefer (12)_____ in this country if possible. She likes (13)_____ to see her parents whenever she wants to. A friend of hers went to America after (14)_____ university, but began (15)_____ her friends so badly that she had to come back.

earn	work	find
look after	visit	redecorate
miss	save	be able to
leave	buy	overdraw
pay	stay	go

REVISION
Short answers

1 Give short answers to these questions.

Example
Can you speak English? *Yes I can.*

a. Have you ever been to America?
_____

b. Do you smoke? No I don't
_____

c. Did you watch television last night? Yes I did
_____

d. Have you got any brothers and sisters? Yes I have
_____

e. Is it raining? Yes it's
_____

f. Does your teacher wear glasses?
No He doesn't

g. Were you in school yesterday?
Yes I was,

h. Are you going out tonight? _____
Yes I can

2 Work in pairs.
Write five sentences that are factually wrong.

Example
The sun rises in the west.
Maria went to France for her holidays.
Pierre doesn't do any homework.

Read them out loud for the other students to correct.

Example
No, it doesn't. It rises in the east.
No, she didn't. She went to Spain.
Yes, he does. He does it every night.

3 Give short answers to these questions.
Example
Who wrote *Macbeth*?
Shakespeare did.

a. Who was the first to arrive in class today?
b. Who is absent?
c. Who can speak the most languages?
d. Who comes to school by car?
e. Who has had a holiday recently?
f. Who's got children?
g. How many of you smoke?
h. How many of you read a newspaper every day?

Write similar questions about the people in your class, and ask them to the other students.

So do I/neither do I

Stand up and talk to the other members of the class.
You are at a party and you have to make a lot of small talk. Find two things that you have in common and two things that you don't.
Use short answers where appropriate.
Do you play tennis?
Yes, I do.
So do I.
When you have talked to enough people, make sentences like the following.

Things in common:
John likes tennis, and so do I.
He's been to America, and so have I.
He doesn't smoke, and neither do I.
He didn't go out last night, and neither did I.

Things different:
He's married, but I'm not.
He can speak German, but I can't.

Is there anybody there?

● Discussion point

1 In Britain, the objects and actions in the pictures have superstitions attached to them.

What is the superstition?

Is there the same superstition in your country?

touch wood

cross your fingers

lucky horseshoes

Friday 13th

not in the house

Spilt Salt

Wish on a wishbone

Can any of the superstitions be explained logically?

What other superstitions are there in your country?

29

2 Look at the dictionary entry for **superstition**.

> **super·sti·tion** (ˌsuːpəˈstɪʃn) (n.) **1** irrational belief or practice, either cultural, personal or religious, usually founded on ignorance or fear, and characterized by obsessive reverence for omens, lucky charms, etc. **2** any irrational belief, esp. with regard to the unknown.

Do you agree that superstitions
– are irrational?
– are founded on ignorance or fear?

What is the difference between a belief and a superstition?

3 Are the following examples of cultural or personal superstitions?
a. A boy has to have a certain lucky pen to write an exam.
b. A girl who's getting married refuses to see her future husband on the day of the marriage, until they meet at the church. She also believes that she has to wear *'something old, something new, something borrowed, something blue'*.
c. A seven year-old girl's tooth falls out, so she puts the tooth under her pillow.
d. A gambler always puts money on grey horses.
e. A businessman consults an astrologer before making an important decision.
f. A footballer always puts his clothes on in a certain order before a match.
g. On Christmas Eve, a child puts a mince pie and a glass of brandy out for Father Christmas.

h. A person thinks *'If I get to the end of the road before that bus, I'll have a good day.'*

● Reading and question formation

1 You are going to read an extract from a book.
What do we usually want to know before we read? Write questions for these answers.
Example
Who wrote it?
Samuel Johnson/Henry James/ Virginia Woolf.

a. _____
In the seventeenth century/In 1890/In the seventies.

b. _____
A short story/A novel/A biography/Science fiction/A horror story.

c. _____
It's fiction.

d. _____
It's about a couple who fall in love/It's about power and corruption.

e. _____
Yes, it has. It came out some years ago and starred Meryl Streep.

f. _____
A girl called Jenny and her mother/Jane Eyre and Mr Rochester.

g. _____
Well, in the beginning Jenny's working as a teacher, then she marries and has children, and the story's about the children growing up.

h. _____
It ends very sadly/We're left wondering/They all live happily ever after.

i. _____
I thought it was great/I couldn't put it down/It was good in parts.

j. _____
Yes, I would. It's well worth reading.

2 Work in groups.
Here is the front and back cover of the book from which you are going to read an extract.
– Which of the questions a.–j. can you definitely answer?
– Which can you guess?
– What additional questions would you like to know the answers to?

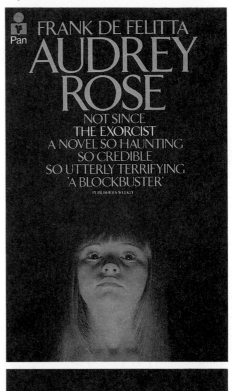

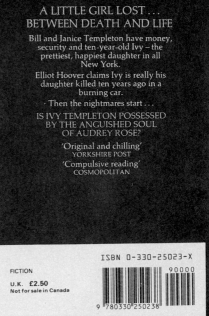

- Who is Ivy?
- Who are Ivy's parents?
- What happened to Elliot Hoover's daughter?
- When?
- What was her name?
- What does Elliot Hoover believe?
- Who do you think has nightmares?
- What about . . . ?

Extract 1 comes about a third of the way through the story. Bill and Janice Templeton have been talking to Elliot Hoover. He wants to be with Ivy Templeton as she grows up because he believes his dead daughter's soul has entered Ivy. Bill and Janice are understandably suspicious, and do not want to believe that their daughter is the reincarnation of Audrey Rose. But Ivy did have nightmares when she was younger . . .

Ivy has been sleeping in a neighbour's spare bedroom. The neighbour calls Bill and Janice to come quickly. Ivy is having another nightmare . . .

Read Extract 1

Comprehension check

1 When Bill goes into the room, is Ivy still or moving about?
2 What do you think her nightmare is about?
3 What happened seven years ago?

Before you read extract 2 what information do you want to learn?

Now read on.

Comprehension check

4 Does Ivy know her parents are there?
5 Why is she knocking into the furniture?
6 What does it seem as though she is trying to do?
7 Why does she draw her hand back from the glass?
8 Who do you think Dr Kaplan is?

Before you read extract 3 what information do you want to learn?

Now read on.

'Everything was fine,' she panted. 'She had dinner . . . went to bed on time . . . then I heard these noises . . . I was in the kitchen . . . I went up . . . and . . . you'll see . . . it's . . . it's frightening . . . I mean . . . she's sleepwalking or something . . . and crying . . . I tried to wake her up . . . but I couldn't . . .'

5   The door to the spare bedroom was half open. Bill waited before entering, listening to the terrified little sounds coming from the room: the running of bare feet on the carpeted floor; the light impact of a body crashing into objects; the soft weeping of childish fear,
10   desperately repeating the same strung-together words, '*Mommy daddy mommydaddymommydaddymommyhothothothothotmommydaddy. . .*' they had heard on certain other nights more than seven years before.

Extract 1

Totally oblivious of their presence, Ivy's eyes shone wildly; her feverish face was swept with a thousand night-time terrors as she raced
15   about the room this way and that, knocking into furniture, chairs, sewing machine, climbing over the large pieces in order to gain some unknown, desperately sought objective. As before, the tiny babylike cries, '*Mommydaddymommydaddyhothothotmommydaddy . . .*' echoed round the room. Each time she'd get by an obstacle and seem to
20   approach the door or window — her hands reaching towards the glass — she would draw back suddenly in pain and plunge into the helter-skelter circle of confusion, weeping, crying, '*Mommydaddymommy daddyhothothotmommydaddymommydaddy . . .*'

Janice's hand grasped Bill's tightly as they stood rooted, just inside
25   the room, helplessly watching the macabre spectacle, knowing, from past experience, how ineffective they both were during these crises.

'Call Dr Kaplan, Janice,' he whispered sharply.

'Wait!'

The voice was Elliot Hoover's, speaking from the doorway directly
30   behind them.

Extract 2

Janice turned and saw him looking intently at Ivy. Hoover's eyes were fixed on the tormented child, critically observing every movement and gesture she made, listening to the exhausted voice repeating, '*Mommydaddymommydaddyhothothotmommydaddymommydaddy . . .*'
35   Janice felt Bill's hand stiffen as he, too, turned and planted a stern, warning look on the intruder.

But Hoover ignored them both, his eyes and mind wholly devoted to their daughter, trying to define the meaning of the terrible hallucination in which she was caught. And then a look of inexpressible sadness
40   swept across his face; his eyes grew large as he uttered, '*My God,*' in a barely audible breath.

He quickly stepped past them into the room and worked his way closer to Ivy, who was staggering near the window, her hands seeking the glass, reaching for it, each time pulling back in pain and fear, as if
45   it were molten lava.

'*Audrey!*' The word burst out of Hoover like a shot: sharp, imperative, holding promise, offering hope. '*Audrey Rose! It's Daddy.*' And he took another step towards the agonized child crying at the window, waving her thin arms at the glass despairingly, begging in a
50   high-pitched voice, '*Mommydaddymommydaddyhothothotmommydaddy mommydaddy . . .*'

'*Audrey Rose! I'm here, Audrey! Here!*'

Bill's hand sought release from Janice's grip, and she knew he was about to move, about to seize Hoover and throw him out of the room.
55   She saw the murderous intent in Bill's eyes, and held onto him even more tightly.

Extract 3

31

Comprehension check

9 How does Hoover feel as he looks at Ivy?
10 Why does he call Ivy 'Audrey'?
11 Why should Bill want to murder Hoover?
12 How do you think Janice feels?

Before you read extract 4 what information do you want to learn?

Now read on.

Comprehension check

13 How does Ivy react to Hoover calling her Audrey?
14 How does Janice feel as she watches her daughter's nightmare ending? Why?

What do you think?

1 These extracts come at a significant moment in the book. Why, do you think?
2 How do you think the story continues?
  What does Bill do?
  How does Janice feel?
  What does Hoover want?
  What happens to Ivy?
  What happens in the end?
3 Which religions believe in reincarnation?
  What do other religions say happens after death?

▶ Language focus

Read the *Language review* on page 36.
Do the *Controlled practice* exercises 1–4.

● Vocabulary 1

1 Work in pairs.
  Try to work out the meaning of the following words from *Audrey Rose*.

(4) sleepwalking (26) ineffective
(8) bare   (39) inexpressible
(13) shone wildly   (62) breathless
(14) raced   (78) worn
(24) tightly   (86) wearying
(25) helplessly

'*Audrey! This way, darling! Audrey Rose! It's Daddy!*' Suddenly, Ivy swung about from the window and turned her fear-ravaged face to Hoover, gazing up at him, begging for mercy, the chant changing to
60 '*Daddydaddydaddydaddydaddydaddydaddydaddy . . .*'
'*Yes, Audrey, It's Daddy! It's Daddy! This way, darling!*' he desperately urged in a breathless voice. '*This way, Audrey Rose! This way! Come!*' And taking a step backwards, he stretched out his hands to the startled child, offering direction, inviting trust. '*This way,*
65 *darling. This way!*'
Slowly, the anguish and panic seemed to drain from their daughter's face; the rapid, feverish intensity of the words seemed to relax, to space out and become more defined, '*Daddy, Daddy, Daddy, Daddy . . .*'
'*Yes, darling, this way*', Hoover coaxed, bending down and stretching
70 out his two arms fully to her. '*Come, Audrey, come!*'
'*Daddy . . . Daddy?*' Her eyes remained fixed on a point just beyond Hoover.
'*This way, Audrey Rose! COME!*' His voice rose to a command. '*COME, AUDREY!*'
75 A prickle of fear ran down Janice's spine as she saw the face of her own child begin to soften with recognition, begin to lose the look of terror. Teardrops hanging on her eyelids — the great blue eyes which now shone so large and brilliant out of her white and worn face — she slowly stretched out her hands to Hoover, in a tentative, testing manner.
80 '*Daddy?*'
'*Yes, Audrey Rose! It's Daddy!*' Hoover encouraged, in a voice charged with emotion. '*Come, darling . . .*'
'*Daddy?*' And with a smile that seemed to answer him, she ran forward into his arms, clutching him in a deep embrace. And thus they
85 remained, holding onto each other, like a pair of lovers finally meeting after a long and wearying journey.

Extract 4

2 The extracts from *Audrey Rose* are extremely dramatic, and this is reflected in the vocabulary.

Example
*Bill hears a body **crashing** into objects.*
This is similar in meaning to **hitting** objects, but **crashing** is more extreme and descriptive.

Match a word from the extracts in column **A** with a more neutral word in column **B**.

A	B
(7) terrified	dive
(13) oblivious of	horrible
(14) feverish	holding
(21) plunge	looking at
(24) grasped	looking for
(25) macabre	fast
(32) tormented	held
(32) observing	bright
(43) seeking	frightened
(54) to seize	got louder
(67) rapid	troubled
(73) rose	unaware of
(78) brilliant	to take hold of
(84) clutching	hot

Listening

Pre-listening task

You will hear two friends, Stephanie and Rob, talking about Stephanie's experiences with strange powers whilst living in an old house in London. She thought it was the spirit of someone who had lived in the house a long time before.
Fortunately it was a happy spirit!

Make up a ghost story, as a class. These are the opening lines.
Take it in turns to continue this story.
Last night I was lying in bed. It was quite late when suddenly I was woken by a strange noise. I . . .

Listening and note taking

[**T.9**] Listen to the tape and take notes under the following headings.

Stephanie's first encounters with the spirit

_____

_____

_____

_____

The night she first saw the spirit

_____

_____

_____

_____

The night the pictures fell off the wall

_____

_____

_____

_____

The night her husband communicated with the spirit

_____

_____

_____

Compare your notes with another student's.
Listen to the tape again to check your notes.

What do you think?

1 Do you believe Stephanie's story? If you don't, how can it be explained?
2 How did Stephanie feel about the ghost?
  Would you have felt the same?
3 We hear about many stories that science finds hard to explain. For example, people who can bend objects without touching them, people who can read the thoughts of others, people who have premonitions about future events, and unidentified flying objects. What stories do you know? Is there a rational explanation for them?

▶ **Language focus**
Do the *Controlled practice* exercises 5–9.

Vocabulary 2

Spelling

As you know, English spelling is not phonetic. The same sound, especially vowel sounds, can be spelt in many different ways.

1 Work in pairs.
Read the following poem together. Pay particular attention to the pronunciation of the words in italics. You can work out the pronunciation in two ways.
– The poem rhymes aa bb cc
– You know that, in line 2, **break** does *not* rhyme with **weak**.

T.10 Now listen to the recording of the poem and check your pronunciation.

When the English tongue we speak

Why is *break* not rhymed with *weak*?

Won't you tell me why it's true

We say *sew*, but also *few*?

And the maker of a verse

Cannot rhyme his *horse* with *worse*?

Beard is not the same as *heard*,

Cord is different from *word*,

Cow is cow, but *low* is low,

Shoe is never rhymed with *foe*.

Think of *hose* and *dose* and *lose*,

And think of *goose* and yet of *choose*,

Think of *comb* and *tomb* and *bomb*,

Doll and *roll* and *home* and *some*.

And since *pay* is rhymed with *say*,

Why not *paid* with *said* I pray?

Think of *blood* and *food* and *good*;

Mould is not pronounced like *could*.

Why is it *done*, but *gone* and *lone* —

Is there any reason known?

To sum it up, it seems to me

That sounds and letters don't agree.

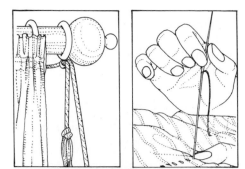

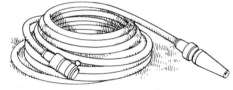

2 Put the words in italics on the right line according to the vowel sound. Use your dictionary if necessary.

a. /eɪ/ _____

b. /iː/ _____

c. /əʊ/ _____

d. /uː/ _____

e. /ɔː/ _____

f. /ɜː/ _____

g. /ɪə/ _____

h. /aʊ/ _____

i. /ɒ/ _____

j. /ʌ/ _____

k. /e/ _____

l. /ʊ/ _____

3 Add some more words with the same vowel sound, and if possible, with different spelling of the vowel sound.
Example
a. *eight*   b. *week*   c. *goal*

4 **Listening and dictionary work**
T.11 Finding a word in the dictionary when you have only heard the word, not seen it, requires you to guess the spelling.
You will hear a tape twice. It is a radio programme about phobias. First listen for general comprehension.
Then listen again. There will be pauses on the tape (and the teacher or you should also stop the tape recorder) after words that you probably don't know.
Work in pairs.
Find the word in your dictionary and make sure you understand it.
Then carry on listening.

Speaking

Fears and phobias

How afraid are you of the following? Score *1* to *10* for each one, *1* being total calm and *10* being absolute panic.

☐ Being stuck in a lift
☐ Standing on top of a tall building

☐ Being all alone in the middle of the countryside
☐ Flying in planes
☐ The dark
☐ Crowds
☐ Snakes
☐ Spiders
☐ Mice
☐ Violence
☐ Thunderstorms
☐ Public speaking

Conduct a class survey to find out what the most common fears and phobias are amongst your classmates.
Can they be explained?
Are they born out of a bad experience or ignorance?
Would Dr Jones' (who spoke on the tape on page 34) approach of graded exposure help?

● Writing

An appraisal of a book or film

1 Work in groups of three.
Here are two appraisals of a book. Read them carefully. Compare their organization, and the way they present points.

I once read a book called 'The Collector'. It's about a man who kidnaps a girl, and she eventually dies. It's quite a horrible story, but I liked it. Ferdinand Clegg is very inhibited with women, he doesn't know how to talk to them, so he kidnaps a girl he's seen in the town. He keeps her in a cottage and takes her photograph. In the end she dies but he didn't kill her. It was written by John Fowles. I liked it very much.

'The Collector' is a novel written by John Fowles. It was first published in 1963, and it is a sort of horror story. It is one of the most sinister
5 *books I have ever read. It holds your attention from the start and becomes more shocking as it progresses. 'The Collector' is a good title. The 'hero', Ferdinand*
10 *Clegg, collects butterflies, but he adds to his collection the girl of his dreams, Miranda, who is an art student. We learn enough about his background, an orphan brought*
15 *up by his aunt and uncle, to have some understanding of his behaviour. He is a very lonely character and painfully shy, especially with women. We see him*
20 *following Miranda from a distance, fascinated by her every move. There is a turning point when he wins some money, and his plans become a reality. He buys a*
25 *remote country cottage, captures Miranda and keeps her there just to look at and admire. All he wants of her is to take her photograph. She is his latest and most precious*
30 *'butterfly'. One of the most interesting aspects of the story is the portrayal of Miranda, as she tries to handle the bizarre situation she finds herself in. Her behaviour*
35 *goes to extremes – from trying to understand Ferdinand and be his friend to violence and trying to escape. In the end she falls ill and dies, while he does nothing to help.*
40 *The reader feels all Miranda's hopes and fears until the final dreadful outcome. This is a book which, once you have started, is impossible to put down.*

2 Divide the second version into paragraphs.
What is the purpose of each paragraph?

3 What tense is used to tell the story and describe the characters?
Why, do you think?

4 Underline any words or expressions which you think are useful to describe a book or film.
Example
a novel written by

5 Why are the words 'hero' (line 9) and 'butterfly' (line 30) in quotation marks?

6 Write an appraisal of a book or
  film that you have liked.
  Organize your paragraphs like
  this.
  Paragraph 1 Factual information
    about the book or film.
  Paragraph 2 An introduction to
    the setting and the characters.
    A description of the plot.
    (This might need two paragraphs.)
  Paragraph 3 Your reactions, and
    the reasons why you liked it.
  Paragraph 4 A conclusion.
The following expressions might help:
. . . tells the story of . . .
. . . based on real life/the author's
  experience
. . . was directed by . . .
. . . was produced by . . .
It stars *X* in the title role.
X's performance as *Y* was
  wonderful/convincing . . .
As the story unfolds, we see . . .
The story takes place in the 1950's.
The story is set in Texas at the
  beginning of the century.
The relationship that *X* has with his
  mother . . .
In the end . . .
We don't learn until the end that . . .
I was impressed by . . .

● Language review

Question forms

1 **How** can combine with adjectives
  and adverbs to form questions.
  How big is your house?
  How fast will this car go?

  What and **which** can combine with
  nouns.
  What size do you take?
  What films have you seen recently?
  Which soup would you like,
  vegetable or chicken?

  Which is generally used when
  there is a limited choice, but this
  rule is not always applied in
  spoken English.
  Which channel is the film on?
  What channel is the film on?

  With people, English prefers
  which, even when the choice is not
  limited.
  Which authors do you like?

36

2 Many verbs and adjectives are used with a preposition.

look at   get married to
afraid of   give something to
dance with

The preposition comes at the end of the question.

*What are you looking **at**?*
*What are you afraid **of**?*
*Who did you dance **with**?*
*Who did you give it **to**?*
*Who is he getting married **to**?*

3 When **who**, **what** or **which** is the subject of the question, there is no inversion and no **do/does/did**. The word order is the same as the statement.

Peter   broke the window.
Who   broke the window?
Many   animals hibernate in winter.
Which   animals hibernate in winter?

► Grammar reference: page 113.

CONTROLLED PRACTICE

Questions

1 Work in pairs.
Write an appropriate question.

Example
What time did you go to bed last night?
At midnight.

a. _____
Twice a week.

b. _____
Blue.

c. _____
Forty miles.

d. _____
Peter's.

e. _____
30 waist, 32 leg.

f. _____
Air France.

g. _____
Five times.

h. _____
To Alice.

i. _____
Twenty pounds a week.

j. *Which*_____
BBC 2.

k. _____
It was cold and rainy.

l. *How long*_____
It takes me 20 minutes.

m. *What*_____
I've had it permed.

n. _____
The *Daily Mail*.

o. _____
Novels and short stories.

2 Write an appropriate question, using **like** either as a verb or as a preposition.

Example
Do you like fish?   (verb)
What's she like?   (preposition)

a. _____
He's a very nice chap. You'd get on well with him.

b. _____
She's got dark hair and wears glasses.

c. _____
Playing tennis and reading.

d. _____
I'd love to, but I haven't got time tonight. Another time, perhaps.

e. _____
I thought it was superb. The acting was marvellous – Robert Redford is my favourite actor.

3 This is a most unfortunate situation!

Bob loves Sheila, but Sheila doesn't love Bob; she loves Henry. Unfortunately, Henry doesn't love her; he loves Pamela, but . . . !
Ask and answer questions.

Example
Who does Bob love?   *He loves Sheila.*
Who loves Bob?   *Pamela does.*

4 Write a short question with a preposition to follow these statements.

Example
He gave away all his money.
Who to?

a. We're going on holiday next week.

_____

b. I'd like to have a word with you, please.

_____

c. I've just received a big parcel in the post!

_____

d. She danced all night long.

_____

e. I need £1,000 as quickly as possible.

_____

f. Peter's writing a book.

_____

g. She's getting married next week.

_____

h. Could you wipe up that mess on the floor, please?

_____

Indirect questions

5 Turn the following *direct* questions into *indirect* questions, using:

I wonder
I'd like to know | why/when/
I'd love to know | who/if/
We didn't find out | whether . . .

Example
Who was the ghost?
I wonder who the ghost was.

a. What was the ghost's name?
b. Is it still there?
c. Did it ever come back?
d. Why did Stephanie think she was being watched?

e. Did she see a ghost when she was young?
f. How long had the ghost been haunting the house?
g. Why was it so cold when the ghost came?
h. Was Stephanie telling the truth?

6 Work in pairs.
Ask and answer questions for the following situations.
a. One of you has just seen a ghost/ a UFO.
b. One of you has fixed a blind date for the other.
c. One of you has just seen a wonderful film.

7 Do the same for the following situations, but ask your questions indirectly, using:
Could you tell me . . . ?
Do you know . . . ?
I was wondering . . .
a. One of you is looking for a good English language school. The other has just spent six months at a school in England.
b. One of you is selling a second-hand car. The other is interested, but wants more information.

8 There are two main kinds of tag questions.

```
(i)  You're Spanish, aren't you?
     (falling intonation on the tag.)

(ii) The train goes at ten, doesn't it?
     (rising intonation on the tag.)

(i)  means 'I'm sure I'm right – confirm
     this for me'.

(ii) is more like a real question. It means
     'I think I'm right, but correct me
     if I'm wrong'.
```

T.12 Listen to the tape of a man and woman talking about holiday arrangements. There are eight tag questions.

Write if they are type (i) or type (ii).
a. have we?   e. doesn't it?
b. isn't it?   f. haven't you?
c. have you?   g. didn't you?
d. didn't you?   h. can't we?

Practise the tag questions on the tape.

38

9 Work alone.
Write some tag questions to ask to another member of the class. You must decide if you're quite sure of the answer (type i) or not sure (type ii). Be very careful with your intonation.

REVISION

Have

Have is used in different ways.
1. As an *auxiliary verb* in Perfect tenses.
   I've never seen anything like it!
2. As a *full verb* to refer to an action.
   I'm having lunch at the moment, so I can't come out.
3. To *refer to a state*, such as a possession or an illness. In spoken English, **got** is often used, but the concept is still present.
   He has a new car/He's got a new car.
   I have a terrible headache/I've got a terrible headache.
4. As a *modal verb* to express obligation.
   I have to go now. Goodbye!

▶ **Grammar reference:** page 114.

1 Make the following sentences negative.
   Example
   He's got a yacht.
   He hasn't got a yacht.
a. She's been to America.
b. I have a bath every night.
c. She's got long hair.
d. They have to work very hard.

2. Make the following sentences into a question.
   Example
   He's got three brothers.
   How many brothers has he got?
a. He's written three books.
   How many . . . ?
b. I have lunch at 1.00.
   When . . . ?
c. He's got a Rolls Royce.
   What sort . . . ?
d. I have to get up at 6.00.
   What time . . . ?

3 Put the following sentences into the past.
   Example
   I'm having a bath.
   I was having a bath when the phone rang.

a. I have a holiday every year.

   _____
   in Mexico last year.

b. I've got a car.

   _____
   my first car when I was 19.

c. I have to work hard.

   _____
   when I was at school.

4 Put the following sentences into the present.
   Imagine the actions are happening *now*, so use the *Present Continuous* where possible. If not possible, use *have got*.
   Example
   I had lunch with Peter.
   I'm having lunch with Peter.
   He had a bad cold.
   He's got a bad cold.
a. We had a good time at the party.
b. She didn't have much experience of working with children.
c. We had a lovely room with a view over the ocean.
d. The restaurant didn't have any red wine, so we had to have white.
e. He had a row with his neighbour.

UNIT 5

Travel and transport

● Vocabulary 1

1 Work in pairs.
Divide the following means of transport into three groups: transport by air, water, or on land.

a submarine	a tram
a moped	a helicopter
an airship	a jet
a canoe	a double-decker
a rowing boat	bus
a barge	a yacht
a van	a glider
a rocket	an estate car
a liner	a hot-air
a jeep	balloon

2 Choose one of the groups.
Which of the means of transport is
– the fastest?
– for commercial purposes?
– for pleasure?
– the most dangerous?
– old-fashioned?
– romantic?
– for military purposes?

What associations do you have for each one?

Example
Barges make me think of towns like Paris and Amsterdam, where they go up and down the river all day. In Britain, some people live on them.

3 What are the names of these airlines?
Which countries are they from?
Which airline has the best reputation for safety? for comfort?

Do you like flying, or are you afraid of it? Say why.
What was your most/least enjoyable flight?
Where were you going?

Travellers' Tales

Every year a magazine called *Executive Travel* organizes a competition to find the *Airline of the Year*. Travellers from all over the world
5 are invited to vote for the most efficient, the most punctual, the safest and the friendliest airline. The winner in 1985 was *British Airways*. The competition asked travellers what for
10 them was most important from an airline, and the results were as follows:

Punctual departures and arrivals	35%
Attentive cabin staff	35%
Comfort	18%
Safety	9%
Good food and wine	3%

The competition also invited travellers to tell their most horrific stories of the nightmare side to international travel.
15 Replies included six hijacks, fifty-three cases of engine failure or trouble with the landing gear, eleven lightning strikes, twenty-three bomb scares, thirteen cases of food poisoning,
20 eleven near misses and two collisions with airport trucks.

Bad flying experiences begin on the ground, naturally. One American airline managed to double-book an
25 entire 747, but this is nothing compared to what happened on an internal flight on a certain African airline. The flight had been overbooked three times. The local military sorted the problem out
30 by insisting that all passengers with boarding cards should run round the plane twice, the fastest getting the seats. An overbooked flight that was going from Heathrow to America gave

35 one traveller a bit of a shock. Dressed only in trousers, shirt and socks, he had been allowed by the stewardess to leave
40 the aircraft to see if he could get a colleague aboard. He returned a few minutes later to find the 747 closed up and about to start moving — with his shoes, wallet, passport and luggage
45 inside. Banging frantically on the door got him back inside. A similar event was seen by a businessman on a flight from Bangladesh. Passengers were waiting for take-off when there was
50 sudden hysterical hammering on the door. At first the cabin crew paid no attention. The hammering continued. When the door was finally opened, the pilot got in.

55 One frequent flier lost a certain amount of confidence when the cabin staff asked him to sit in the lavatory

40

during take-off, so that they could
occupy the seats nearest the
60 emergency exit. Another lost faith in

the pilot's navigational skills when
passengers were given lifeboat drill
on a flight between London and
Manchester.

65 For nervous fliers, a journey to be
avoided was one between Gatwick
and Montpellier, where the in-flight
entertainment consisted of watching
pieces of the engine falling off.
70 Another passenger was asked to hold
the aircraft door closed at take-off
and landing.

Baggage is a rich source of horror
stories. There was the unlucky traveller
75 who left Chicago in minus-23 weather.
He was going to an important meeting
in Dallas, where the temperature was
80-plus. Unfortunately his suitcase had
gone to LA, where it spent the next two
80 days. The customers he was trying to
impress were more than a little
surprised to see him going round in a
thick suit, heavy overcoat and fur hat.

(Adapted from an article in *Executive Travel*
Magazine, October 1985)

Reading

Pre-reading task

1 What for you is most important
from an airline?
Put the following in order of
importance:
☐ safety
☐ comfort
☐ punctual departures and
arrivals
☐ good food and wine
☐ attentive cabin staff

2 Flying is probably one of the safest
ways to travel, but there can be
problems. Discuss what can go
wrong on the ground and in the
air.

Reading for information

Now read the article opposite.
A group of air travellers was invited
to comment on their flying
experiences.
Was their order of importance the
same as yours?
Did they mention any of the
problems that you discussed?

Comprehension check

1 Look at the list of disasters in
paragraph 2.
Which happened on the ground?
Which happened in the air?
Which could have been both on
the ground and in the air?

2 After paragraph 2, how many
disasters are described?

3 Why did some passengers have to
run round a plane?

4 Why did a passenger and a pilot
have to knock on the plane door to
get in?

5 Why was it surprising to have a
lifeboat drill on a flight from
London to Manchester?

6 What does in-flight entertainment
usually consist of? (lines 67–8)
Was this experience entertaining?

7 Why was the Dallas businessman
inappropriately dressed?

What do you think?

1 The competition was answered by
very experienced travellers.
Why do you think they put safety
so far down on their list of
importance?

2 Why do airlines overbook?

3 Why do you think the cabin staff
on one flight wanted to sit near the
emergency exit?

4 Which of the stories were funny
but dangerous?
Which were funny but not
dangerous?

Pairwork

Student A You have just had one of
the terrible experiences described
in the article. Tell Student B about
it. Use your imagination to add
more detail.

Student B Listen to Student A and
ask questions to get more
information.

Begin like this:
Student A I've just had a terrible
journey!
Student B Why? What happened?
Student A Well, I was going . . .

Summary

Marking a text is one way of
summarizing.
Look at the example.

Every year a magazine called
Executive Travel organizes a
competition to find the *Airline of the
Year*. Travellers from all over the world
are invited to vote for the most

The competition also invited travellers
to tell their most horrific stories of the
nightmare side to international travel.
Replies included six hijacks, fifty-three

Do the same for the rest of the text.
Underline or mark the main ideas
only.
When you have finished, compare
yours with another student's.

▶ **Language focus**

Read the *Language review* on page
45.
Do the *Controlled practice* exercises
1–5.

● Vocabulary 2

Homonyms and homophones

1 Homonyms are words with the same spelling but different meaning.

Example
*I got £50 out of the **bank**.*
*We sat on the river **bank** and had a picnic.*

Notice the two ways in which a dictionary gives different meanings of a word.

– There are two or more definitions in the same entry when the difference is small and the meanings are related.

plain¹ /pleɪn/ *adj* (-er, -est) **1** easy to see, hear or understand: ~ *English*; *in* ~ *speech*; ~ *language*, (of telegrams, etc) not in code. *The meaning is quite* ~. ~ **'sailing,** (fig) course of action that is simple and free from difficulties: *After we engaged a guide, everything was* ~ *sailing.* **2** simple; ordinary; without luxury or ornament: *a* ~ *blue dress*, of blue material without a design on it, or without trimmings, etc; *in* ~ *clothes*, (esp of policemen) in ordinary clothes, not in uniform; ~ *food/cooking*; *a* ~ *cook*, one who can prepare ~ meals. **3** (of persons, their thoughts, actions, etc) straightforward; frank: *in* ~ *words*, frankly; ~ *dealing*, honesty, sincerity. **to be '~ with you,** to speak openly. **,~-'spoken** *adj* frank in speech. **4** (of a person's appearance) not pretty or handsome.

– There are two or more entries when the difference between the meanings is large.

plane¹ /pleɪn/ *n* '~(-tree), one of several kinds of tree with spreading branches, broad leaves and thin bark, which comes off in flakes.

plane² /pleɪn/ *n* tool for trimming the surface of wood by taking shavings from it. ⇨ the illus at tool. □ *vt, vi* [VP2A,15B,2D,22] use a ~; make smooth with a ~: ~ *sth smooth.* ~ *away/down*, remove irregularities with a ~.

plane³ /pleɪn/ *n* **1** flat or level surface; surface such that the straight line joining any points on it is touching it at all points;

plane⁴ /pleɪn/ *n* (colloq abbr for) aeroplane.

Plain and **plane** are homophones. Homophones are words with the same pronunciation, but different spelling and meaning.

Example
*A yacht is a boat with a big **sail**.*
/seɪl/
*I bought this jumper in a **sale**.*
/seɪl/

2 **Homonyms**
In the following sentences there is a word with at least two meanings. You probably know one meaning but not the other. Find the word, look it up in your dictionary and find the correct entry and definition.

a. My brother's a soldier. He's on leave at the moment.
b. She gave me some sound advice. I'll certainly follow it.
c. My uncle left me a thousand pounds in his will.
d. 'Who won the match?' 'It was a draw.'
e. Damn! I've got a parking fine.
f. I'm going away on business to a trade fair soon.
g. One swallow doesn't make a summer.
h. I had to buy a special saw to cut through the pipe.

3 **Homophones**
Look at these words in your dictionary and copy the phonemic script.
Then think of another word with the same pronunciation but a different spelling.

Example
flower /flaʊə(r)/ *flour*

male	war	hire
caught	piece	through
wear	hole	way
stair	rain	saw
die	bored	pair

4 A lot of jokes are made with homonyms and homophones, because there is a play on words. Can you understand the following children's jokes?

Customer Waiter! What sort of soup is this?
Waiter It's bean soup, sir.
Customer I don't care what it was. I want to know what it is now.

Customer Waiter! What's wrong with these eggs?
Waiter Don't ask me, sir. I only laid the table.

Mechanic Your battery's flat.
Driver Oh dear. What shape should it be?

Teacher You missed school yesterday, Johnny, didn't you?
Johnny No, not at all.

Why is Sunday the strongest day?
Because all the others are weak days.

What's the difference between a ball and a prince?
One is thrown in the air, and the other is heir to the throne.

What colour would you paint the sun and the wind?
The sun rose and the wind blue.

Why was the doctor angry?
Because he had no patients.

Why did the teacher have to wear sunglasses?
Because his students were so bright.

Why will you never starve in the desert?
Because of the sand which is there.

What did the salad say to the tomato?
Lettuce get married.

5 **T.13** Listen to the joke on tape about four people on a train. What actually happened in the tunnel?

Speaking

Discussion

1 Work in pairs.
It is now possible to travel to most parts of the world easily, quickly and cheaply. There are both good and bad points to this. Talk together and add to this list.

```
Good points

We can see how people in
other cultures live.

Travelling is exciting.
```

```
Bad points

Countries are losing their
individuality.

Travelling can be dangerous.
```

```
Interest points

Our forms of transport
will change when there is
no more oil.
```

2 What is the most beautiful place you have ever been to?
Why did you like it?
What were you doing there?

Listening

T.14 You will hear a man called Brian talking about his experiences of driving a lorry for the first time. Listen to the first part of the tape and answer the questions.

1 When did the story take place?
2 What had Brian just done?
3 What job was he offered?
4 What sort of vehicle did he expect to drive?
5 What in fact did he have to drive?

The following words are contained in the rest of the story. Look at them, and before you listen imagine what happened to Brian during the rest of the day.

crash   diesel
to brake   pavement
scared   petrol station
flames   roof

Now listen to the rest of the story. There are five incidents. Put a number on the map to show where they happened and briefly describe each one.

Comprehension check/Language work

Here are the answers to some questions.
Work out the questions.

1 While he was a student at university.
2 Five thirty in the morning.
3 No, he drove off.
4 Because Brian had nearly crashed into the garage roof.
5 Ten o'clock in the morning.
6 The manager of the shop.

▶ **Language focus**

Look at the tapescript on page 128. Find the examples of the *Past Perfect tense.*
Do the *Controlled practice* exercises 6–8.

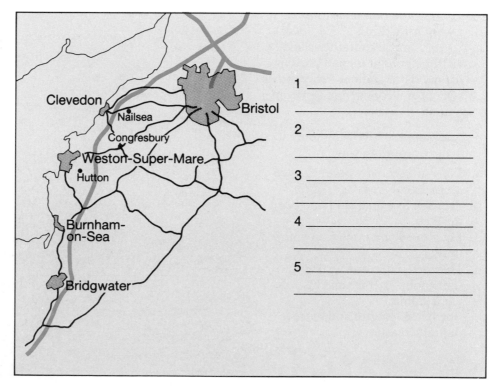

● Writing
Time expressions

1 Conjunctions of time
when   while   whenever
as soon as   by the time   as
Conjunctions join two sentences.

Examples
When Peter arrived, we had lunch.
As I was leaving, the phone rang.

Conjunctions and prepositions of time
until   after   before   since
These words can be used as conjunctions to join two sentences, or as prepositions followed by a noun.

Example

I stayed at the party until | *it ended.*
| *the end.*

After his mother died, | *he moved*
After the death of his mother, | *to Australia.*

2 Put one of the above conjunctions or prepositions into each gap.
a. I met an old school friend _____ I was on the train this morning.
b. I've made a lot of friends _____ I came here.
c. We sheltered under a rock _____ the rain had stopped.
d. I went for a drink _____ work.
e. _____ my grandfather came to visit, he bought a small present for my sister and me – sometimes sweets or a comic, and sometimes a book.

3 Complete the following sentences in an appropriate way.
a. I haven't seen my parents since _____ .
b. As soon as I realized I had been burgled, _____ .
c. I can't pay you now. Can you wait until _____ .
d. He started decorating the bathroom. By the time his wife came home, _____ .
e. She became more and more depressed after _____ .

1 under a lot of pressure
company's profits down

2 working sixteen hours a day
not getting home until . . .
wife and children

4 advised him to give up
work for a while

5 get some fresh air
forget about . . .

7 As Henry was leaving, . . .

8 followed his doctor's advice. bought . . .
As soon as . . . , he started . . .
spent his days . . .

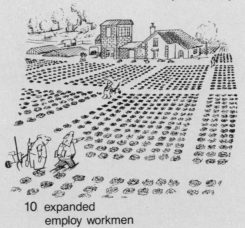

10 expanded
employ workmen

3 listened attentively

6 suggested that he started . . .
the exercise would do him good

9 . . . enjoyed . . . very much
bought . . . built

11 business had grown so much that . . .

4 Writing a narrative

Work in groups of three.
Look at the picture and the words, and write the story about the workaholic.
The beginning has been done for you. The story begins at picture 3.

'Now listen, Henry You've got to learn to take it easy,' said Doctor Clarke. Henry Dunlop, managing director of a large textile company, was lying on his doctor's couch, telling him . . .

● Language review

Narrative tenses

1 **Past Simple and Past Continuous**
The events of a narrative are in the *Past Simple*:
*The journey **began** at 8.00. We **jumped** in the car and **drove** for three hours until we **arrived** at the hotel.*

Descriptions and interrupted activities are in the *Past Continuous*:
*The sun **was shining**, and we **were singing** because we **were going** on holiday.*
*We **were driving** along the motorway when the accident happened.*

2 **Past Perfect Simple and Continuous**
The *Past Perfect* is used to express an action that happened *before* another event in the past:
*The plane **had** already **left** when we arrived at the airport.*
*I **had been trying** to find a job for three months when finally I decided to emigrate.*

Before	Past	Now
●	●		
had already left	arrived	
had been trying	decided	

◀ Look again at the text on page 40. Find examples of *Past Simple*, *Past Continuous* and *Past Perfect*. Some are passive.

▶ Grammar reference: page 114.

CONTROLLED PRACTICE

Past Simple and Continuous

1 Work in pairs.
Compare the use of tenses in the following pairs of sentences. Say *which* tense is used and *why*.
a. When I arrived at the airport, my flight was announced.
When I arrived at the airport, my flight was being announced.
b. During the flight, I read a book.
During the flight, I was reading a book.
c. We had various refreshments on the plane.
We were having lunch when we hit an air pocket.
d. When we landed, I was met by a colleague.
When we landed, it was snowing.

2 What are the following people in history famous for?
What did they do?
When were they alive?

Queen Victoria
Confucius
Alfred Nobel
Churchill
Napoleon
Noah
Marilyn Monroe
Henry VIII
Leonardo da Vinci
Christopher Columbus

3 What were you doing when the following events took place?
What were you doing when you heard the news?
President Kennedy's assassination (November 22, 1963)
First man on the moon (July 21, 1961)
End of the Vietnam war (January 1, 1973)
John Lennon's assassination (December 8, 1980)
Attempted assassination of the Pope (May 13, 1981)
The Live Aid concert (July 13, 1985)

4 **Pronunciation of -ed**

There are three possible pronunciations, /t/, /d/ or /ɪd/. Arrange the following verbs into three groups.
There are six verbs in each group.

needed	laughed
shouted	developed
searched	managed
robbed	mixed
scared	added
banged	staggered
wounded	reached
climbed	persuaded
panicked	hunted

Find the verbs that end in **-ed** in the article on page 40.
Which group do they belong to?

5 **Dictation**

T.15   You will hear a short news item. First listen to it all the way through. You will then hear it again at dictation speed. Copy it down on a separate piece of paper. Pay attention to weak forms such as **was** /wəz/, **were** /wə/, **had** /d/, and **been** /bɪn/.

6 **Past Perfect Simple and Continuous**

Answer the following questions about the lorry driver using a verb in the *Past Perfect Simple* or *Continuous*.

a. How long had Brian been driving when the first accident happened?
b. What had he done?
c. Why did his lorry catch fire?
d. Why was he tired when he got to Bridgwater?

e. Why did the manager come out of his shop?

7 Work in pairs.
Compare the use of tenses in the following pairs of sentences. Say which tense is used and why.
a. When we got to the theatre, the play started.
When we got to the theatre, the play had started.
b. When she saw the photograph, she burst out laughing.
When she had seen all the photographs, she went home.
c. She was tired. She had been writing all morning.
She was tired. She had written three chapters of her book that morning.
d. When I got home, I discovered that someone had stolen my radio.
He was sent to prison. He had been stealing from his employer for years.

8 **Interrogation**

One of you is being questioned by the police. He/she is suspected of having committed a crime last night. The rest of the class are detectives.

Suspect Say what you did last night.
Detectives You want as much detail as possible. Can you find a contradiction in what he/she says?

Example
Suspect *At six o'clock I caught the bus home.*
Detectives *What number bus was it? How long did the journey take? How long had you been waiting? How much was the fare? What were you wearing?*

After a while, choose a different suspect.

REVISION

Common expressions

1 Work in pairs.
Match an expression in column **A** with a reply in column **B**.

A
a. Mind your own business.
b. I've changed my mind.

c. Excuse me!
d. Mind the step.
e. Sorry!
f. Pardon?
g. I don't care what he does.
h. It serves him right.
i. Here you are.
j. Come on!
k. What's up?
l. It's up to you.
m. Do you want this one or that one?

B
☐ Thank you.
☐ Where to?
☐ I don't feel very well.
☐ Ouch! Too late.
☐ I don't mind. You choose.
☐ Never mind. It doesn't matter.
☐ I'll say it again for you.
☐ Oh, no. I hate decisions.
☐ Why? What did he do?
☐ All right. All right. I didn't mean to be nosy.
☐ Yes, can I help you?
☐ What, again?
☐ That's not very nice. I thought you two were friends.

Write short dialogues with two matched expressions either at the beginning, in the middle or at the end of the dialogue. Read them out to the rest of the class. They must guess where the dialogue is taking place, and who the people are.

2 When would you use the following expressions?

Good luck!	Bad luck!
Congratulations!	Watch out!
Good Lord!	Ta.
Have a nice time!	Cheers!

Cheerio!
I'm sorry to hear that.

3   T.16   You will hear ten short dialogues which contain the following exclamations. What do the exclamations mean?

Do you say the same in your language?

UNIT 6

Expressing quantity

How do you feel today?

● Discussion point

1 What dishes is your country famous for?
What kind of food is eaten a lot?
What is a balanced diet?
How does diet affect your health?
Have you changed your diet recently?
2 Answer the questions and add up your scores to see if you have a balanced diet.

TOTAL

If your fat total was less than your fibre total, well done.

If your fat total was about the same as your fibre total (within one or two points), try to cut down on fat.

If your fat total was greater than your fibre total, you need to make changes in your diet.

(Adapted from the *Economist August 31, 1985*)

THE BALANCED DIET

FAT

Which do you usually eat?	
Butter	3
Margarine	2
Nothing	0

Which do you usually use for cooking?	
Meat fat, butter, margarine	3
Vegetable oil	2
Corn, sunflower, olive oil	1

How many times a week do you eat chips?	
Five or more	3
Two to four	2
Once	1
Occasionally/never	0

How often do you eat cream or ice-cream?	
Every day	3
Several times a week	2
About once a week	1
Less than once a week/never	0

Which type of milk do you drink?	
Full fat	3
Semi-skimmed	1
Skimmed/none	0

What type of cheese do you eat most of?	
High-fat (Cheddar, Stilton)	4
Medium-fat (Camembert, Edam, Brie)	3
Low-fat (cottage)	2
Variety	3

FIBRE

What kind of bread do you eat?	
Wholemeal	3
White	1
Mixture	2

How many slices of bread do you eat a day?	
Six or more	4
Three to five	3
One or two	1
None	0

How many times a week do you eat cereal?	
Six or more	4
Three to five	3
Once or twice	2
Occasionally/never	0

How many times a week do you eat high or medium-fat cheese?	
Five or more	3
Three to five	2
Once or twice a week	1
Occasionally/never	0

How many times a week do you eat chocolate?	
Six or more	3
Three to five	2
Once or twice	1
Occasionally/never	0

How often do you eat meat?	
Twice a day	4
Once a day	2
Most days	1
Never	0

How many times a week do you eat sausages/meat pies/burgers?	
Six or more	3
Three to five	2
Once or twice	1
Occasionally/never	0

If you have a choice of how to cook meat, how do you cook it?	
Fry	3
Grill with added oil	2
Grill without adding oil	1

How many times a week do you eat cake, biscuits, or desserts?	
Six or more	3
Three to five	2
Once or twice	1
Occasionally/never	0

How many times a week do you eat rice or pasta?	
Six or more	4
Three to five	3
Once or twice	2
Occasionally/never	0

How many times a week do you eat boiled, mashed or jacket potatoes?	
Six or more	5
Three to five	3
Once or twice	2
Occasionally/never	0

3 A survey

Every student must choose one of the questions that interests her/him.
Try to choose different questions.
Stand up, and ask all the other students your question.
Make a note of their answers.
Prepare a report. The following structures will help you.

Most Some Quite a few A few Few	people eat cream every day.

About half All	of us eat cream once a week.

Only one of us never eats cream.

Everybody Nearly everybody Hardly anybody Nobody	eats cream every day.

4 Work in pairs.

Make a list of five different items of food.
Read out your list.
The other students must say:
– if they are good for us or not
– why
– how much we should or shouldn't eat

Example
Fruit

Fruit is very good for us. It contains vitamins. We should eat a lot.

Biscuits

Biscuits aren't very good for us. They're made with sugar. We shouldn't eat too many.

● Reading

Pre-reading task

You will read an **article** written to a newspaper about the health hazards of modern-day life.
The following words and phrases are contained in the article.
Check them in your dictionary.

to dice with death	a vein
fraught with danger	to pant
lead (n) /led/	to throb
gums	to inhale
liver	a stroke
an early grave	rash

What do you think are some of the health hazards that the article mentions?

Scan reading

The writer describes a typical day in the life of a businessman, and the dangers that he faces at different times of the day.
Read the article quickly and answer the following questions.

1 Was the article written by a doctor?
2 Imagine the businessman gets up at 7.00, it takes him an hour to get to work and he starts at 9.00.
   Where is he, and what is he doing, at the following times?

   7.05/7.30/7.45/8.30/8.55/9.00
   9.10/1.15/4.00/6.00/6.30

Comprehension check

1 According to the writer, what dangers are attached to the following?

2 Why isn't nylon a good material for the skin?
3 How many kilos overweight is the businessman?
4 Who are your nearest and dearest? (lines 26–7)
5 Why should you use the stairs and not the lift?
6 What does his colleague need to be careful of?
7 What effect does the traffic jam have on him?
8 What dangers has his wife faced all day?

DICING WITH DEATH
And living with statistics

BY RUTH JEMMETT

EVERY DAY is fraught with danger. You wake in the morning, rush to the window and take a deep breath. Don't! Hasn't anyone told you about the air being polluted with lead from petrol? Next
5 you go to the bathroom. After touching the lavatory handle, your innocent-looking hands are covered in bacteria, which even a good wash won't entirely remove. You sigh, and get dressed. Good heavens! Didn't you realize that
10 all that nylon won't let your skin breathe?

With a rash beginning to appear on your skin, you make your way to the kitchen for breakfast. Eating *must* be good for you − mustn't it? Of course it is, provided you don't have tea or
15 coffee, which are bad for your heart, or a good old-fashioned English fry-up, which will fill your stomach with cholesterol-building fat.

Depressed − not to mention hungry − you go to clean your teeth. Put down that nylon
20 toothbrush at once! It will ruin your gums. Do you have the courage to weigh yourself? Horrors! You're at least half a stone overweight, which is sure to help send you to an early grave.

Hesitating, you make your way to the car,
25 knowing that (according to statistics) there's a good chance that either you or one of your nearest and dearest will be involved in an accident sometime during your life. After a heart-thumping journey, you reach work.
30 Filled with relief you get into the lift. Get out at once and race up those stairs, unless you want a heart attack tomorrow.

Panting, you reach the office, where you collapse into a chair. The cleaner has just left,
35 leaving an aerosol's delightful aroma floating in the air. You inhale deeply, enjoying the sweet fragrance. Danger! Breathing in the substance will ruin your lungs (not to mention our atmosphere, if we are to believe the experts.)
40 With trembling hands you light a cigarette to calm your nerves. A *what*? How *dare* you? In comes your colleague, Ms Brown, all ready for a busy day, blonde hair and make-up in place. Do you think she's heard about the cancer scare
45 concerning hair dyes and eye-liners?

At last lunch-time comes. You join your mates in the local for a sandwich. White bread, eh? A low-fibre diet is no good at all. You have 'just one more drink', which helps you on your
50 way to liver failure, and you return to the office. You spend the afternoon fighting a battle with high blood pressure and chronic indigestion (or is it your heart at last?) and give a sigh of relief as 5.30 arrives.
55 What a jam on the by-pass tonight. It gets your fingers tapping on the steering wheel, doesn't it? You look in the driving mirror and see a large vein throbbing up and down on your forehead. It throbs even faster as you suddenly remember that
60 article you were reading about strokes.

A nervous wreck, you reach home. You crawl up the path and fall into your wife's protective arms. She won't last much longer, of course. She's inhaled a large amount of washing
65 powder, quite a few asbestos particles from her hair drier and a great number of chemicals from aerosol sprays.

But do not fear, civilization is here. Are we *really* that much happier in our modern
70 technological world with all its new-found knowledge than our ancestors who knew nothing of these things? Is it any surprise that there were no analysts or psychiatrists in any century before ours? I'm sure they didn't need any.

(Sunday Times 22 June 1980)

What do you think?

1 What point is the writer making in the last paragraph? Do you agree?

2 Do you think the writer is . . .
a. much too worried about the dangers of modern life?
b. right to be worried about them?
c. being funny about them to make a point?

3 Read the text again and mark it like this:

✓✓ I agree that this is a real danger.

✓ This could be dangerous, but it's not worth worrying about.

✗ I don't agree that this is a danger.

? I don't understand the point that the writer is trying to make.

Compare your reactions with a partner's.

4 The article deals with quite a serious subject, but it is written in a humorous way. A lot of it sounds like *spoken* English, as though two people were talking to each other. Find examples of this.

▶ Language focus

Read the *Language review* on page 54.
Do the *Controlled practice* exercises 1–4.

49

Vocabulary 1

The language of statistics

Two quotations:
'There are three kinds of lies: lies, damn lies, and statistics.' (Mark Twain)
'He uses statistics as a drunken man uses lamp-posts – for support rather than illumination.' (Andrew Lang)

1 Describing trends

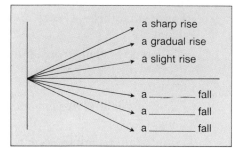

a sharp rise
a gradual rise
a slight rise
a _____ fall
a _____ fall
a _____ fall

Notice the verbs that can be used.

| numbers have | risen gone up | sharply |
| | fallen dropped gone down | slightly |

2 Look at the graphs.

Life expectancy in developed countries has risen from 65 in 1950 to 74 in 1985.
Make similar sentences about Third World countries, America, Japan, and England and Wales.

Life expectancy

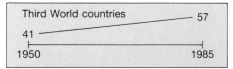

Developed countries
74
65
1950   1985

Third World countries
57
41
1950   1985

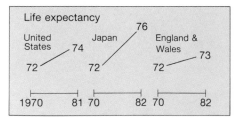

Life expectancy
United States   Japan   England & Wales
72   74   76   72   72   73
1970   81   70   82   70   82

3 Work in pairs.
Look at the graphs and fill in the gaps.

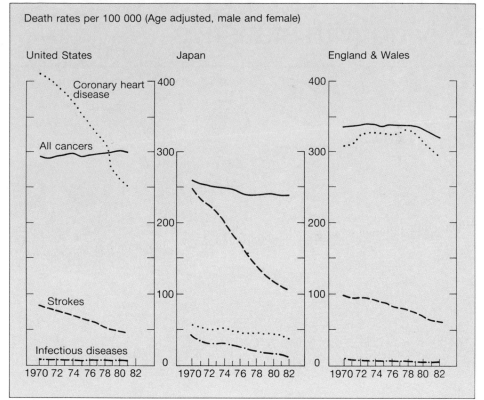

Death rates per 100 000 (Age adjusted, male and female)

United States   Japan   England & Wales

Coronary heart disease   400   400
All cancers   300   300
    200   200
    100   100
Strokes
Infectious diseases   0   0
1970 72 74 76 78 80 82   1970 72 74 76 78 80 82   1970 72 74 76 78 80 82

World Health Organization, The Economist, August 31, 1985

a. In _____, deaths from heart disease have dropped sharply.
b. In Japan, there has been _____ in the number of deaths from cancer, whilst deaths from strokes have _____.
c. In England and Wales, there was _____ in deaths from heart disease in 1978, but since then _____.
d. In _____ and _____, deaths from _____ have hardly changed at all.
e. In England and Wales, deaths from _____ are about the same as from _____.
f. In the United States, many more people die of cancer than of _____.
g. _____ has the lowest rate of heart disease.
h. America has a higher rate of cancer than _____.
i. In Japan, more than twice as many people die of cancer than of _____.
j. In America, about _____ as many people die of cancer as of a stroke.

4 **T.17** Listen to the tape and add to the graph the changing rates of unemployment for West Germany, the United States, and Great Britain.

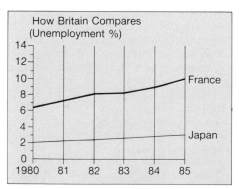

How Britain Compares
(Unemployment %)

14
12
10   France
8
6
4
2   Japan
0
1980 81 82 83 84 85

5 Make similar sentences to those in exercise 3 based on the statistics above and below.

Visitors to Britain and British people going abroad
Where they came from in 1985

	(000's)	Change compared to 1984
North America	4 500	+33%
Western Europe	8 700	+5%
Elsewhere	1 600	−2%

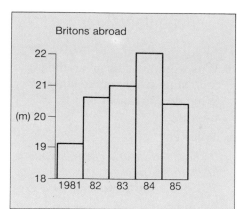

Britons abroad

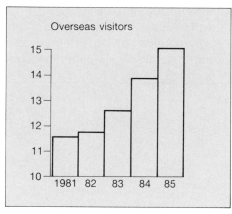

Overseas visitors

Listening

Pre-listening task

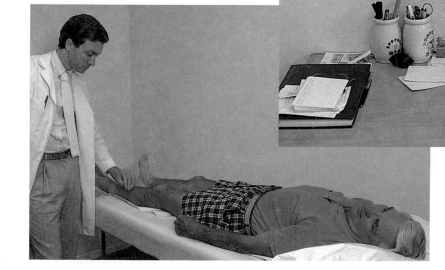

What's the man doing?
Do you think it hurts?
Do you think he's being treated for pains in his foot, his hand, or headaches?
Have you ever had acupuncture treatment?
What do you know about it?

T.18 Listen to the radio programme about holistic medicine.

Comprehension check

1 Complete the chart with some of the differences between Western and holistic medicine.

Western medicine	Holistic medicine

2 What are the three success stories discussed on the programme? What were the patients suffering from?
3 What is the system that Glenna Gillingham is trying to set up?
4 Why, in her opinion, is holistic medicine becoming more popular?

What do you think?

1 Do you agree with Miss Gillingham that we are becoming more health conscious?
Have your own attitudes to health care changed at all?

2 What else would you like to know about acupuncture?

51

3 What do you know about the
following alternative approaches
to medicine?
herbalism   homeopathy
osteopathy   faith healing

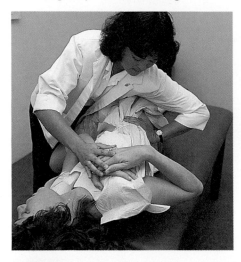

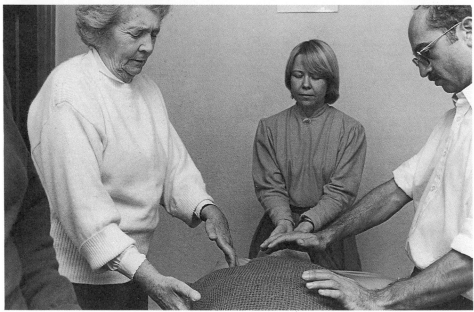

▶ **Language focus**
Do the Controlled practice exercises
5–7.

Vocabulary 2

Health

1 Why would you be given the
following to help make you better?
What do you do with it?

Example
a plaster
*It keeps the wound clean, so that it
heals more quickly.*
You put a plaster on a cut or a graze.

- a course of   – a bandage
  antibiotics   – a sling
- a plaster cast   – antiseptic cream
- a pain killer   – cough medicine
- antihistamine   – sleeping tablets
- a crutch

'*This hypochondria – can you give me something
for it?*'

2 Match the following symptoms
with the correct diagnosis.

Symptoms
1 I've been sick quite a lot.
I can't keep anything down.
I feel terrible.
2 I feel weak and dizzy.
I've got aches and pains all
over my body.
I can't stop shivering.
3 I can't swallow, and my glands
are swollen.
4 I started having a cold a few
days ago, and now I've got a
rash with small red spots all
over my body.

Diagnosis
☐ Influenza ☐ Food poisoning
☐ Tonsillitis ☐ Measles

3 Work alone.
You are ill. Write down your
symptoms.
When you are ready, read out
your symptoms to the rest of the
class. They are doctors, and must
make a diagnosis and suggest
treatment.

● Speaking

Planning a menu

Divide into four groups.
You are going to entertain at your house one of the following groups of people.

Group A
Your uncle and aunt are coming for lunch with their two children, aged six and nine.

Group B
Two old friends, the same age as you, are coming for supper. One of them is vegetarian.

Group C
A potential business client and her/his husband/wife. You need to impress them.

Group D
Two colleagues from work are coming for supper. They are very health-conscious.

1 Plan a menu for them, including first course, main course, and dessert.

2 Now write out your shopping list. If you are in Britain, do this in Imperial measures.
1 pound = 0.45 kilos
1 pint   = 0.56 litres

The following expressions will help you.
one and a half pounds of . . .
a quarter of a pound of . . .
half a pint of . . .
a packet of . . .
a carton of . . .
a tin of . . .
a jar of . . .
a tube of . . .

● Writing

Formal and informal letters

1 Here are two jumbled letters. One is written to a hotel, and the other to a friend.

Work in pairs.
Decide which sentences go with which letter, and put them in the right order.

Letter to a hotel _____

Letter to a friend _____

a. I would like a single room with a shower.

b. I'm writing to ask you a favour.

c. I don't mind where you put me. I'll sleep anywhere!

d. I have a further request.

e. I would like to make a reservation for the nights of 22nd, 23rd, and 24th January.

f. I hope the above is convenient.

g. Write soon and let me know.

h. I'm coming down to London at the end of the month to go to a conference.

i. Could I have a bite to eat when I arrive?

j. I hope you are all well, and that you've recovered from the busy Christmas period.

k. I would be extremely grateful.

l. Could I possibly have a room at the back, as I find the front rooms rather noisy?

m. Could you put me up for a few days?

n. Just a sandwich will do.

o. I look forward to your reply.

p. It's the 22nd – 24th January.

q. As I will be arriving quite late, could you possibly put a cold buffet in my room on the 22nd?

r. I hope that's all right.

s. There's something else I'd like to ask you.

2 Both letters were written by Chris Bright. His address is 47, Angel Road, Blaby, Leicestershire. The hotel is Hotel Regent, 107 Carston Square, London W.1. His friend is called Jan Price. Her address is 33 Alma Crescent, London N.10.
On a separate piece of paper, decide how you would begin and end the two letters.

Think of – the address(es)
– the salutation
– the ending

3 Write replies to both letters. Include the following information.

From the hotel
Confirm the reservation
Price of the room
Arrangements for food in the room

From Jan
Some recent news
Agreeing to the request
Or Refusing the request, saying why

● Language review

Expressing quantity

1 It is important to understand the difference between *mass nouns* and *count nouns*. Mass nouns cannot usually be made plural.

Mass	Count
cheese	pen
water	bottle
snow	tree

2 Expressions of quantity

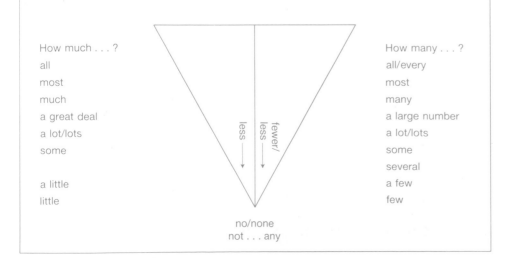

How much . . . ?	How many . . . ?
all	all/every
most	most
much	many
a great deal	a large number
a lot/lots	a lot/lots
some	some
	several
a little	a few
little	few
no/none	
not . . . any	

3 **A little** and **a few** express a *positive* concept.
Take a little of this medicine every day and you'll be fine.

Little and **few** express a negative concept.
Few people understand the whole problem. It's too complex.

Grammar reference: page 116.

CONTROLLED PRACTICE

Expressing quantity

1 **Some** and **any**
Complete the following sentences with **some** or **any**.
a. Would you like _____ more cake?
b. Could you give me _____ information about train times?
c. If you have _____ trouble, just give me a ring.
d. Have you seen _____ good films recently?
e. I tried to buy _____ boots, but I couldn't find _____ .

2 Compounds with **some-**, **any-**, **no-** and **every-**.
Complete the following sentences with a combination of

some	one
any	body
no	+ thing
every	where

a. It was a wonderful party. _____ had a good time.

b. I've looked _____ for my glasses, but I can't find them _____ .
c. 'Was there any post this morning?' 'No, _____ .'
d. I put an advertisement in the paper, but _____ has phoned yet.
e. I've got _____ for you, but I'm not going to tell you what it is.
f. Could you recommend _____ for a quiet weekend break?
g. I haven't spoken to _____ for days.

3 Complete the following sentences in an appropriate way.
a. John's a terrible cook.

Everything _____

_____
b. When I got home, I found the house had been burgled.

Someone _____

c. Fiona, I love you. I've never met

anyone _____

_____
d. I asked lots of people the way,

but no-one _____

_____
e. I'm going shopping. Does anyone

_____ ?

4 **T.19** You will hear eight short conversations of people buying things in different shops.
Listen carefully and decide what sort of shop it is.
a. _____   e. _____
b. _____   f. _____
c. _____   g. _____
d. _____   h. _____

5 **Few**, **a few**, **little**, **a little**
Complete the following sentences with one of the above.
a. I can't play tennis today. I have _____ jobs to do around the house.
b. Help yourself to a whisky. There's still _____ left.
c. Nowadays _____ people have servants in their house.

d. I had _____ time to catch the train, but I just made it.
e. I have _____ friends that I can trust, but not many.

6 **A great deal**, **a large number**, **a lot**, **lots**

A great deal (of) and *a large number (of)* are a more formal, written style.
A lot (of) is neutral style.
Lots (of) is informal.
Make the following sentences positive in three ways.

Example
I don't have many friends.

I have a large number of friends.
I have a lot of friends.
I have lots of friends.

a. He didn't do much work.
b. I haven't made much progress.
c. They didn't invite many people.
d. There wasn't much snow last winter.
e. Not many animals die of starvation in winter.
f. I don't read many books, because I don't have much free time.

7 Work in pairs.
One of you is feeling very depressed about life.
The other is trying to cheer her/him up!
Write a short dialogue together, beginning like this:
A I'm so unhappy. I haven't got any friends.
B Yes, you have! You've got quite a few.
A But nobody ever invites me anywhere.
B But lots of people really like you.
A And . . .

Write about . . . money, work, boyfriends, girlfriends, health, holidays . . .

REVISION

Modal verbs

1 Work in groups of three.
What is the meaning of the *modal verbs* in the following sentences?
Example
He **can** play the piano really well.
***can** = ability*

a. **Can** you lend me five pounds until tomorrow?
b. When you've finished, you **can** go home.
c. You **can't** smoke in here. It's not allowed.
d. **Will** you give me a lift tomorrow? My car's at the garage.
e. You **don't have** to come. It's up to you.

2 Read the review of modal verbs.

Concept	Modal verb
Request	1 could
	2 can
	3 would
	4 will
Offer	5 will
	6 shall
Intention	7 will
Obligation (strong)	8 have to
	9 must
Obligation (mild)	10 should
	11 ought to
Prohibition	12 mustn't
	13 can't
No obligation	14 don't have to
Ability	15 can
	16 could
Permission	17 can
	18 may
	19 could

This list does not include modal verbs of *certainty* and *uncertainty*. See Units 7 and 9.

3 Put the correct numbers from exercise 2 by the following sentences, according to modal verb and concept.
Example
15 *She can dance, but she can't sing.*

☐ a. Could you do something for me? I have a problem.
☐ b. I think you should write and apologize.
☐ c. What time do you have to start work?
☐ d. She could read when she was three.
☐ e. Will you lend me some money?
☐ f. I'll pay you back tomorrow.
☐ g. Could I use your phone for a moment?
☐ h. You must hold it carefully. It's very fragile.
☐ i. You mustn't drive if you've been drinking.
☐ j. Give me your suitcase. I'll take it to the car.

4 Work in pairs.
Write short dialogues for some of the following situations.
Include some modal verbs.
Example
At the doctor's
A *I've got a cough, and I **can't** sleep at night.*
B *Well, you **should** stop smoking. **I'll** give you a prescription for some cough medicine, and you **must** take it three times a day.*
A *Thank you doctor. **Shall I** come back if it doesn't clear up?*
B *Only if absolutely necessary.*

– in a hotel reception
– in a travel agent's
– in a restaurant
– at work
– a parent/teachers' meeting at a school

Future forms

What does the future hold?

● Discussion point

In 1932 an English writer, Aldous Huxley, wrote a book called *Brave New World*. In it, he envisaged life six hundred years into the future. Later in his life, he said that if he rewrote the book, he would place the same vision only one hundred years into the future, because so many of his prophecies had already come true.

This is the vision of the future that *Brave New World* describes. Which aspects . . .
– have already come true?
– will come true soon?
– might come true some time?
– couldn't possibly come true ever?

World

The world is controlled centrally, following a nine-year war between super powers which led to economic collapse.

There is total social stability. World population is maintained at two thousand million. English is the only language, all others are dead. There is no religion. History and literature are censored.

People

Everyone is happy. Babies are born in test-tubes, and by careful use of chemicals and conditioning (babies are taught in their sleep), people are designed to perform certain functions in life. There are five classes of people. There is no illness or disease, but there is also no emotion or privacy. Everyone looks young until they are sixty, when they are sent to hospital to die.

Entertainment

People go to the feelies, where they not only see pictures, but also feel and smell them. There is no love or marriage, and sex is an important form of entertainment.

Everyone takes a drug called soma, in the evenings with friends and for sleep holidays that last two weeks.

The economy

Everybody works seven and a half hours a day, not because this is necessary (they have the technology to allow no-one to work) but because people like their work and would otherwise have too much free time.

It is a throwaway, consumer society.

Travel

The better classes travel everywhere by helicopter, and go on weekend holidays to the other side of the world. Rockets can go from London to America in six and half hours, travelling at 1,250 kilometres per hour.

Pre-reading task

1 How many capital cities have you
  been to?
  Which do you like the most/the
  least?
  Why?
2 Work in two groups.
  Group A Make a list of the
  advantages and disadvantages of
  living in cities.
  Group B Make a list of the
  advantages and disadvantages of
  living in the country.
  When you have finished, compare
  your lists.

Reading and predicting

Read the introduction to a magazine
article and answer the questions.

1 The introduction refers to the
  shanty town as 'nameless'. Why?
2 What are some of the problems
  facing this imaginary city?
3 What is meant by 'high-rise islands
  of power and wealth'?
4 In what parts of the world might
  this city be?
5 Which of the following topics do
  you expect the article to discuss?
- the need for better urban planning
- the need for birth control
  programmes in the Third World
- western governments should give
  more money to poor countries
- why cities are becoming
  overcrowded
- which cities are becoming
  overcrowded
- the arms race
- the success stories of certain cities.
Scan the article quickly to see which
of the above topics are discussed.
Then read it in more detail.

Nightmare of the Monster Cities

BY SPENCER REISS

It is a sweltering afternoon in the year
2000, in the biggest city ever seen on
earth. Twenty-eight million people swarm
about an 80-mile-wide mass of smoky
5 slums, surrounding high-rise islands of
power and wealth.

One-third of the city's work-force is
unemployed. Many of the poor have never
seen the city centre. In a nameless, open-
10 sewer shanty town, the victims of yet
another cholera epidemic are dying
slowly, without any medical attention. And
from the parched countryside a thousand
more hungry peasants a day pour into
15 what they think is their city of hope.

That nightmare of the not-too-distant future could be Cairo or Jakarta or any of a dozen other urban monsters that loom just over the demographic horizon.

20 Already Mexico City, Sao Paulo, and Shanghai are among the largest, most congested cities on earth. Over the next two decades, they — and many others — are expected almost to double in size,

25 generating economic and social problems that will far outstrip all previous experience.

Just 30 years ago some 700 million people lived in cities. Today the number stands at 1,800 million, and by the end of

30 the century it will top 3,000 million — more than half the world's estimated population.

The flood of 'urbanites' is engulfing not the richest countries, but the poorest. By the year 2000 an estimated 650 million

35 people will crowd into 60 cities of five million or more — three-quarters of them in the developing world. Only a single First World city — metropolitan Tokyo, which will have 24 million people — is expected

40 to be among the global top five; London, ranked second in 1950 with ten million people, will not even make 2000's top 25.*

In places where rates of natural population increase exceed three per cent annually

45 — meaning much of the Third World — that alone is enough to double a city's population within 20 years. But equally powerful are the streams of hopeful migrants from the countryside. More often

50 than not, even the most appalling urban living conditions are an improvement on whatever those who suffer them have left behind.

What confronts and confounds urban

55 planners is the enormity of these trends. There have never been cities of 30 million people, let alone ones dependent on roads, sewer and water supplies barely adequate for urban areas a tenth that size.

60 The great urban industrial booms of Europe and America in the nineteenth and twentieth centuries sustained the cities that they helped to spawn. But in today's swelling Third World cities, the

65 flood of new arrivals far outstrips the supply of jobs — particularly as modern industries put a premium on technology rather than manpower. So it will be virtually impossible to find permanent employment

70 for 30 to 40 per cent of the 1,000 million new city dwellers expected by the year 2000.

Optimists maintain that runaway urban growth can be stemmed by making rural or small-town life more attractive. Some

75 say that the trend is self-correcting, since conditions will eventually get bad enough to convince people that city life is no improvement after all. But pessimists see a gloomier correction: epidemics,

80 starvation and revolution. In the end, both sides agree that the world's biggest cities are mushrooming into the unknown.

*Figures are based on United Nations estimates and projections.

85 **Survival Course.** Yet some cities still manage to cope.

Seoul, riding the crest of South Korea's economic boom, is currently building a £2,500 million underground railway

90 system that should ease some of the worst traffic problems in the world. Over the last decade Tokyo has cleared up much of its legendary smog.

Hong Kong has rehoused 1.3 million

95 people in new high-rise towns such as Sha Tin. Built on land reclaimed from the sea and paddyfields, Sha Tin and its sister towns are totally self-contained, down to playgrounds, industrial areas and a

100 railway line into the colony's main business district.

The essence of the larger problem is that despite the dreadful conditions that urban squatters face, their numbers are growing

105 at rates as much as twice that of the cities themselves — and every step taken to improve living conditions in the slums only attracts more migrants.

One solution is to ban migration into the

110 cities. Both China and the Soviet Union use internal passports or residence permits to try to control urban growth, the Russians with rather more success.

Mexico City planners are already gamely

115 laying plans for a metropolitan region of 36 million people by the year 2000. If nothing else, there is a kind of New World bravery in that.

CONDENSED FROM *NEWSWEEK* INTERNATIONAL (OCTOBER 31, 1983) 1983 *NEWSWEEK*, INC. NEW YORK, NY ILLUSTRATION: ROBERTO INNOCENTI

(Reader's Digest July 1984)

Comprehension check

Work in pairs.
Decide whether the following statements are true T or false F.

1 ☐ The number of people living in cities has more than doubled in the last thirty years.

2 ☐ Over 3,000 million people will be living in cities in the year 2000.

3 ☐ The majority of the large cities will be in First World countries.

4 ☐ For the hopeful migrants, conditions in the cities are worse than in the countryside.

5 ☐ Approximately a third of them will not get a permanent job.

6 ☐ Experts are divided over what the best solution is.

7 ☐ Some people say that death and revolution is a possible solution.

8 ☐ Tokyo no longer suffers from smog.

9 ☐ Often there is no point in improving the conditions in slums.

10 ☐ The Russians have succeeded in controlling urban growth.

What do you think?

1 The article refers to First World countries and Third World (or developing) countries.
Give some examples of both.

2 Why isn't urban growth such a problem for many First World countries?

3 'Modern industries put a premium on technology rather than manpower.' (paragraph 6) What is meant by this?
Give some examples of industries that no longer need a large work force.

4 Explain the play on words in the last line of the article.

5 What are the problems facing the capital cities that you know?
What is being done about these problems?

Topic sentences

Most paragraphs have a *key sentence* (or part of a sentence) that summarizes the essential meaning of the whole paragraph. This is called the *topic sentence*. It is usually the first sentence of the paragraph, but not always.

Work in groups of three.

1 Do you think that the following are the topic sentences for the first six paragraphs?
If not, which is the topic sentence?

para. 1 Over the next two decades, they – and many others – are expected almost to double in size . . .

para. 2 Just 30 years ago some 700 million people lived in cities.

para. 3 The flood of 'urbanites' is engulfing not the richest countries, but the poorest.

para. 4 But equally powerful are the streams of hopeful migrants from the countryside.

para. 5 There have never been cities of 30 million people . . .

para. 6 So it will be virtually impossible to find permanent employment . . . for the new city dwellers . . .

2 Underline what you think are the topic sentences for paragraphs 7 to 12.

Guessing meaning

Work in pairs.
Guess the meaning of the following words from the article.

(22) congested   (58) barely adequate
(26) outstrip   (60) booms
(32) urbanites   (68) virtually
(48) streams   (72) runaway
(50) appalling   (86) to cope

▶ Language focus

Read the *Language review* on page 64.
Do the *Controlled practice* exercises 1–5.

● Vocabulary 1

Nouns and verbs

These lines appeared in the article *Nightmare of the Monster Cities*.

'. . . by the end of the century (the number) will *top* 3,000 million . . .

. . . people will *crowd* into 60 cities . . .

. . . cities are *mushrooming* . . .'

You probably know the words in italics as nouns, but here they are used as verbs.

1 The following list of words are all verbs. Which can also be used as nouns? If they aren't the same, what *is* the noun?

answer	notice
arrive	solve
hurry	revolt
turn	agree
design	reply
improve	coach
paint	cheat

2 The following list of words are all nouns. Which can also be used as verbs? If they aren't the same, what is the verb?

butter	advice
question	nurse
experiment	judge
glue	plan
experience	food
public	arm
practice	service

3 Work in pairs.
Look carefully at the stress and the phonemic script of the following words, and practise saying them aloud.

con·vict¹ /kən'vɪkt/ *vt* [VP6A,14] ~ *sb (of sth)* **1** cause (sb) to be certain that he has done wrong, made a mistake: *to ~ sb of his errors; to be ~ed of sin.* ⇨ convince. **2** (of a jury or a judge) declare in a law court that (sb) is guilty (*of* crime): *He was ~ed of murder.*
con·vict² /'kɒnvɪkt/ *n* person convicted of crime and undergoing punishment.

ex·port¹ /'ekspɔːt/ *n* **1** [U] (business of) exporting: *a ban on the ~ of gold;* (attrib) *the* '~ *trade;* '~ *duties.* **2** [C] sth exported: *Last year ~s exceeded imports in value. What are the chief ~s of your country?*
ex·port² /ɪk'spɔːt/ *vt* [VP6A] send (goods) to another country for purposes of trade: ~ *cotton goods.* ~**er** *n* trader who ~s goods. ~**·able** /-əbl/

in·crease¹ /'ɪŋkriːs/ *n* [U] ~ *(in),* increasing; growth; [C] amount by which sth ~s: *I~ in population made emigration necessary. There was a steady ~ in population.* **on the ~,** growing: *Is the consumption of beer still on the ~?*

in·crease² /ɪn'kriːs/ *vt,vi* [VP6A,2A] make or become greater in size, number, degree, etc: *The population has ~d by 200000 to 50000000. The driver ~d speed. Our difficulties are increasing.* **in-**

in·sult /ɪn'sʌlt/ *vt* [VP6A] speak or act in a way that hurts or is intended to hurt a person's feelings or dignity. □ *n* /'ɪnsʌlt/ [C,U] remark or action that ~s. ~**·ing** *adj* ~**·ing·ly** *adv*

pres·ent² /'preznt/ *n* gift: 'birthday ~s; *I'm buying it for a ~ (= as a gift), so please wrap it up nicely.* **make sb a ~ of sth,** give sb sth: *I'll make you a ~ of my old car.*

pre·sent³ /prɪ'zent/ *vt* **1** [VP14,15A] ~ *sth to sb;* ~ *sb with sth,* give; offer; put forward; submit: ~ *the village with a bus-shelter/~ a bus-shelter to the village; the clock that was ~ed to me when I retired; ~ a petition to the Governor; ~ a cheque at the bank,* ie for payment; ~ *one's compliments/greetings, etc to sb,* (polite phrase). **2** [VP6A,14,15A] ~ *sb to sb,* introduce formally.

rec·ord¹ /'rekɔːd *US:* 'rekərd/ *n* **1** [C] written account of facts, events, etc: *a ~ of school attendances/of road accidents; the (,Public) 'R~*
re·cord² /rɪ'kɔːd/ *vt* [VP6A] **1** set down in writing for reference; preserve for use, by writing or in other ways, eg on a disc, magnetic tape, video-tape, film, etc: *This volume ~s the history of the regiment. The programme was ~ed.* Cf *a 'live' broadcast. The tape-recorder has ~ed his voice and the camera has ~ed his features.* ~**ing angel,**

re·fund /rɪ'fʌnd/ *vt* [VP6A] pay back (money to sb): ~ *the cost of postage.* □ *n* /'riːfʌnd/ [C,U] repayment: *obtain a ~ of a deposit.*

When the word is a noun, where is the stress?
When it is a verb, where is the stress?
Practise saying the examples in the dictionary entries.

4 There is a group of such words with variable stress in English. Be careful! Sometimes the meaning changes when the stress changes.

de·sert¹ /dɪ'zɜːt/ *vt,vi* **1** [VP6A] leave; go away from: *The village had been hurriedly ~ed, perhaps because bandits were in the district. The streets were ~ed,* no people were to be seen.

de·sert² /'dezət/ *n* [C,U] (large area of) barren land, waterless and treeless, often sand-covered: *the Sahara D~.* □ *adj* **1** barren; uncultivated: *the ~ areas of N Africa.* **2** uninhabited: *wrecked on a ~ island.*

Check the following words in your dictionary and practise saying the examples. Read the definitions to see which ones change meaning when the stress changes.

import	suspect	refuse
object	contract	protest
progress	produce	addict
decrease	reject	permit

5 **T.20** You will hear twelve unfinished sentences.
Use one of the words from exercises 3 and 4 to complete the sentence appropriately.

Example

The Government is worried because the number of serious crimes *has increased over the past five years*.

● Listening

Pre-listening task

Read the dictionary entry for **ecology**.

ecol·ogy /iːˈkɒlədʒɪ/ *n* [U] branch of biology that deals with the habits of living things, esp their relation to their environment. **eco·logi·cal** /ˌiːkəˈlɒdʒɪkl/ *adj* of ~: *the ecological effects of industry*, eg the pollution of the atmosphere, of rivers, etc. **eco·logi·cally** /-klɪ/ *adv*. **ecol·ogist** /iːˈkɒlədʒɪst/ *n* student of, expert in, ~. **eco·system** /ˈiːkəʊ-/ = ecological system.

What do you understand by the 'Green Movement'?
What are their aims and objectives?

Listening for information

T.21 You will hear an interview with Jonathon Porritt, the Director of 'Friends of the Earth' in the United Kingdom.
'Friends of the Earth' is an environmental pressure group.
Listen to the interview in four parts, and answer the questions at the end of each part.

Comprehension check

Part one
1 How did Jonathon Porritt become interested in the environment?
2 Why do you think he says that 'you can't really talk about ecology as a science, you have to consider ecology within a social and political context'?
3 He says economics is 'the key to it all . . .'
Do you agree?

Part two
4 Why does he call himself a constructive pessimist?
5 He refers to four crucial problems that the planet faces.
Write in the chart what the problems are, and add some notes on each.

Problems	Notes
1	
2	
3	
4	

6 He says that these problems have the same roots, that is, the belief that 'the only way we can increase human wealth is by producing more and consuming more, even if we destroy the planet in the process'.
Do you agree?

Part three
7 He gives three reasons for optimism.
Write in the chart what the reasons are, and add some notes on each.

Reasons	Notes
1	
2	
3	

Part four
8 He refers to the 'dark bits' and the 'points of light' in his job.
What examples does he give of each?

Summary

Summarize each part of the interview in two or three sentences.

▶ **Language focus**

Do the *Controlled practice* exercises 6 and 7.

● Speaking

Discussion

Work in two groups.
Group A Make a list of some of the problems faced by people living in previous centuries that are not such problems now.
Group B Make a list of some of the problems we face in the twentieth century that didn't exist before.

Roleplay

Work in pairs.
Discuss the problems that **Group B** listed. What will happen in the future? One of you is an optimist, and thinks that all the problems will be solved. The other is a pessimist, and expects the worst to happen.

Where the Third World is first

There are plenty of grim statistics about childhood in the Third World, showing that the (1)_____ for survival is long and hard. But in the rich world, children can (2)_____ from a different kind of poverty — of the spirit. For instance, one Western country alone now sees 14,000 attempted suicides every year by children under 15, and one child in five needs professional psychiatric (3)_____.

There are many good things about childhood in the Third World. Take the close and constant (4)_____ between children and their parents, relatives and neighbours. In the West, the very nature of work puts distance between adults and children. But in most Third World villages mother and father do not go miles away each day to do abstract work in offices, shuffling paper to make money mysteriously appear in banks. Instead, the child sees mother and father, relations and neighbours working (5)_____, and often shares in that work.

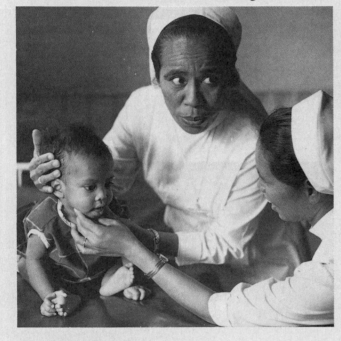

A child growing up in this way learns his or her role through (6)_____ in the community's work: helping to dig or build, plant or water, tend to animals or look after babies — (7)_____ than through playing with water and sand in kindergarten, collecting for nature trays, building with construction toys, keeping pets or playing with dolls.

These children may grow up with a less oppressive (8)_____ of space and time than their Western counterparts. Set days and times are few and self-explanatory, (9)_____ mostly by the rhythm of the seasons and the different jobs they bring. A child in the rich world, on the other hand, is (10)_____ with a wrist-watch as one of the earliest (11)_____ of growing up, so that he or she can worry along with their parents about being late for school times, meal times, clinic times, bed times, the times of TV shows . . .

Third World children are not usually cooped up (12)_____, still less in highrise apartments. Instead of fenced-off play areas, dangerous roads, 'keep off the grass' signs and 'don't speak to strangers', there is often a sense of freedom to (13)_____ and play. Parents can see their children outside rather than observe them anxiously from ten (14)_____ up. And other adults in the community can usually be (15)_____ on to be caring rather than indifferent or threatening.

Of course twelve million children under five still die every year through malnutrition and disease. But childhood in the Third World is not all bad.

(This article appeared in a *Christian Aid* publication.)

● Vocabulary 2

Gap filling

Read the text about children in the Third World. There are fifteen gaps. Work in pairs to find *one* suitable word to fill each gap.

Compare the words you put into the gaps with another pair of students.

Discussion

If you were brought up in the West, was your childhood like the one described in the article?

● Writing

Presenting an argument

1 Joining contrasting ideas

Join a sentence in **A** with a linking device in **B** and a sentence in **C**.

A	B	C
I tried to ring you yesterday,	*although*	I am afraid I cannot come.
We had a good game of tennis	*However,*	the rain.
Thank you for your invitation.	*but*	he continued to compose music.
I went to work	*Nevertheless,*	you weren't in.
Beethoven was deaf from the age of forty.	*despite*	I was not feeling well.

2 Complete the following sentences in an appropriate way.
a. I wanted to go on holiday, but . . .
b. I had always wanted to be a doctor. However, . . .
c. The holiday was enjoyable despite . . .
d. He passed the exam although . . .
e. The prisoner was kept under tight security. Nevertheless, . . .

3 **Comparisons and contrasts**
Write one or two sentences about the following pairs of words, saying in what ways they are *similar* and in what ways they are *different*.

Example
hotel   hostel

Both hotels and hostels are places where you can stay the night, but hostels are often for students and are quite cheap, while hotels are more luxurious and can be very expensive.

teacher – professor
restaurant – snack bar
church – mosque
beer – wine
salary – wage
doctor – surgeon

4 **Discourse markers**
Put one of the following markers into each gap.

what is more	personally
that is why	obviously
generally speaking	

a. Many people like pets, but _____ I cannot bear them.
b. _____ I have not got any in my house.
c. _____, people have pets for companionship.
d. _____, they need to be looked after very carefully.
e. I find them noisy and smelly. _____, they can be very expensive.

5 **Writing an essay**
Look at the first paragraph, and the possible organization of the other paragraphs, for an essay entitled 'Newspapers or television? – Which is better for finding out what is happening in the world?'

para. 1 *Introduction*	We are living in a world of mass communication, and it is now possible to know what is happening in every corner of the world. Every day we are bombarded with the news from many sources. The most important of these are newspapers and television.
para. 2 *Good and bad points of television*	Television has several advantages . . .
para. 3 *Good and bad points of newspapers*	Newspapers, however . . .
para. 4 *Your personal opinions*	Personally, I . . .
para. 5 *Conclusion*	Finally, . . .

6 You have a choice. Either complete the above essay, or write an essay with a similar organization on one of the following subjects:
– 'The advantages and disadvantages of military service.'
– 'Capital punishment – is there ever a case for it?'
– 'Is money the best contribution that the First World can give to the Third World?'
– 'The car is the curse of the twentieth century.' (Churchill)
– 'Which is better – the book, or the film of the book?'

63

Future time

There are several forms that refer to *future time* in English. The choice of which form depends on *how* the speaker sees the event, and not on its certainty or nearness to the present. The most common forms are listed here in order of their frequency.

1 **Will** Prediction or spontaneous intention
It'll rain tomorrow.
I'll give you my phone number.

2 **Going to** Intention or evidence
He's going to be a pilot in the Air Force.
Look at those clouds. It's going to rain any minute.

3 **Present Continuous** Arrangement
We're getting married in the spring.
I'm seeing the doctor this afternoon.

4 **Present Simple** Timetable future
The train leaves at 11.00.
The match starts at 3.00.

5 **Future Continuous**
I'll be having dinner at 8.00.

6 **Future Perfect**
By the year 2000, the population of the world will have reached six billion.

The last two uses can be be expressed in a diagram.

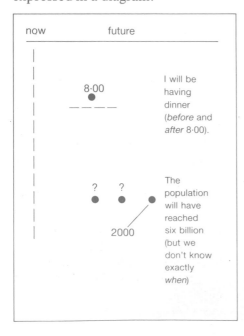

Degrees of certainty about the future

We are predicting a *future event*, and saying how *probable* it is.

Certainty	She **will**	
		come tomorrow.
Possibility	She **might**	
	She **may**	
	She **could**	*be coming tomorrow.*
Certainty	She **won't**	

▶ **Grammar reference:** page 117.

CONTROLLED PRACTICE
Future forms

1 Recognizing the forms

Match a sentence from **A** with a sentence from **B** according to the form and use of the structure. Say which use the two sentences express.

A
1 Your plane arrives at 14.05.
2 What will you be doing this time next week?
3 Take the medicine. You'll soon feel better.
4 What are you going to do while you're on holiday?
5 I'm having lunch with the director tomorrow.
6 I'll have mended your shoes by Friday.
7 Mind the baby! She's going to touch the fire!
8 Ring me tonight. I'll give you my number. 4782115.

B
a. It will remain cold and there will be snow on the hills.
b. Don't phone at 8.00 because I'll be having dinner.
c. He looks pale. I think he's going to faint.
d. What are you doing this afternoon?
e. They're going to knock down that old building. Isn't it a shame?
f. Don't worry about the mess. I'll tidy up.
g. Next term begins on October 1.
h. When do you think you'll have finished?

1 _____	5 _____
2 _____	6 _____
3 _____	7 _____
4 _____	8 _____

2 Compare the use of tenses in the following pairs of sentences.
Say *which tense* is used and *why*.

a. Sorry about the vase. I'll buy you a new one, I promise.
I'm going to buy some new shoes this afternoon.
b. I'll watch the TV programme and tell you about it.
Don't phone at 8.00 – I'll be watching my favourite TV programme.
c. What do you do at the week-end?
What are you doing this week-end?
d. I'll do it tonight.
I'll have done it by tonight.
e. She's been married for three years.
At the end of the month, they will have been married for ten years.

3 Future possibilities

Work in pairs.
Ask and answer about the possibility of the following *future* events in your life.

Example
A *Do you think you'll (ever) write a book?*
B *Yes, I'm sure I will./Well, I suppose I might one day./It's possible, but I doubt it./No, I'm sure I won't.*
Actually, I have done already.

fly in Concorde/go round the world/go to the North Pole/have grandchildren/start smoking/stop smoking/speak perfect English/start your own business/retire before you're fifty/have a lot of money

4 Arranging to meet

Work in groups of three.
You are all business associates working in different parts of the country. You need to meet sometime next week to discuss some important business.
Work together. Quickly decide which parts of the country you all work in.

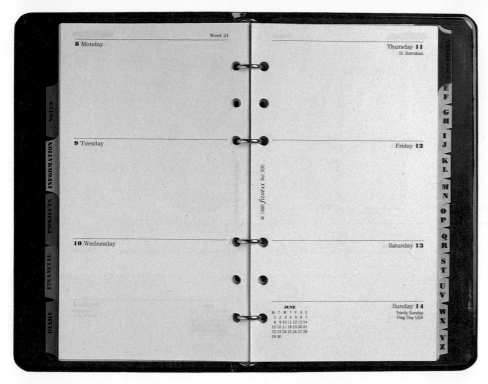

Work alone.
Write in the diary what you're
doing next week.
Leave some spaces free, naturally.
Decide which day would be the
most convenient for you to meet.
Do you want the meeting to be at
your office, or don't you mind
travelling?
If you have to travel, will you go
by car, train or plane?
What time should the meeting
start and end?

Work in pairs.

Student A Phone **Student B**.   Try to
arrange a time and place to meet.
Student B Phone **Student C** to see
if the arrangements suit her/him.
Student C Phone **Student A** to
confirm the day, time and place of
the meeting.

5 [T.22] Listen to the telephone
conversation.
It is similar to the conversation
between **Student C** and **Student A**.

Sally Beecham is phoning Henry
Adams to confirm arrangements
for a meeting between themselves
and a colleague called Jeremy.

Listen to the conversation and
compare it to your own.
Look at the tapescript on page 131.
Notice the use of *future tenses*.

6 **Future Perfect**

Complete the following sentences
with a verb in the *Future Perfect*.

Example
By the year 2000, many cities *will
have doubled in size*.

a. By the year 2000, world
population _____ to about six
billion.
b. We _____ (use up) many of the
world's natural resources.
c. Hopefully, we _____
alternative sources of energy.
d. Robots _____ (replace) people
for many boring jobs.
e. Perhaps we _____ a way to
secure world peace.

In the article on page 58, it said
that planners in Mexico City are
already planning for a city of
thirty-six million people.
What will they have done by the
year 2000?

7 **Future Continuous**

Look again quickly at the text on
page 49.
Imagine the man's name is Jack. It
takes him an hour to get to work,
and he starts work at 9.00.
Tomorrow his day will be the
same.
In pairs, ask and answer questions
about what he will be doing at the
following times tomorrow.

Example
What will Jack be doing at 7.00?
He'll be getting up.

7.05   7.30   7.45   8.30   8.55
9.10   1.15   4.00   6.00
What will *you* be doing at these
times tomorrow?

REVISION

Short answers after verbs of opinion

1 Study the following charts:
A Is Peter coming to the party?

B

I	think hope believe expect	so.

A Is Angela coming too?

B

I don't	think believe expect	so.

I	hope believe	not.

2 Work in pairs.
Which of the above expressions
could be used in answer to the
following questions?
Add a reason to support your
opinion.

Example
A *Have we met before?*
B *I think so. Weren't we both at
Ann's party last week?*

a. Is it going to be a nice day?
b. Are you going out tonight?
c. Do you think you'll ever go on a
cruise around the world?
d. Will there ever be a world
government?
e. Will we ever find life on other
planets?
f. Do you think there'll ever be a
cure for cancer?

3 Work in pairs.
Ask and answer questions about
any plans for your personal
future, for example in connection
with travel, family life, work, and
holidays.
Use short answers where
appropriate.

65

UNIT **8**

Description

Our colourful world

Discussion point

1 Look at the photographs.
   In which country do you think
   they were taken?
   What time of year is it?

2 Work in pairs.
   Choose one of the photographs.
   It is a postcard of where you are
   on holiday.
   Write the postcard to a friend,
   giving some information about the
   countryside, what you're doing,
   the weather, the food, and where
   you're staying.
   Begin like this:
   Dear _____
   We're having a lovely time in . . .

Reading

Somerset Maugham (pronounced /mɔːm/) was an English writer famous for his plays and short stories. He travelled widely, and much of his work is set in exotic locations. A recurring theme in his writing is the boredom of working life and some people's attempts to escape from it.

The following extracts come from *The Lotus Eater*.

In Greek mythology, a lotus eater was a person who lived a life of pleasure and indulgence, drugged by the fruit of the lotus plant.

The Lotus Eater

The story takes place on the island of Capri, and is about a man called Thomas Wilson who has 'boldly taken the course of his own life into his own hands'. At the beginning of the story, we do not quite know in what way he has done this. The writer describes his first impressions of Wilson.

Read Extract 1

Though his teeth were not very good his smile was attractive. It was gentle and kindly. He was dressed in a blue cotton shirt and a pair of grey trousers, much creased and none too clean, of a thin canvas, and on his feet he wore a pair of very old espadrilles. The get-
5 up was picturesque, and very suitable to the place and the weather, but it did not at all go with his face. It was a lined, long face, deeply sunburned, thin-lipped, with small grey eyes rather close together and tight, neat features. The grey hair was carefully brushed. It was not a plain face, indeed in his youth Wilson might have been good-
10 looking. He wore the blue shirt, open at the neck, and the grey canvas trousers, not as though they belonged to him, but as though, shipwrecked in his pyjamas, he had been fitted out with odd garments by compassionate strangers. Notwithstanding this careless attire he looked like the manager of a branch office in an insurance
15 company, who should by rights be wearing a black coat with pepper-and-salt trousers, a white collar and an unobjectionable tie.

Extract 1

We climbed the mountain, admired the spacious view, and got back to the inn as night was falling, hot, hungry and thirsty. We had ordered our dinner beforehand. The food was good, for Antonio was
20 an excellent cook, and the wine came from his own vineyard. It was so light that you felt you could drink it like water and we finished the first bottle with our macaroni. By the time we had finished the second we felt that there was nothing much wrong with life. We sat in a little garden under a great vine laden with grapes. The air was
25 exquisitely soft. The night was still and we were alone. The maid brought us *bel paese* cheese and a plate of figs. I ordered coffee and strega, which is the best liqueur they make in Italy. Wilson would not have a cigar, but lit his pipe.

'We've got plenty of time before we need start,' he said, 'the moon
30 won't be over the hill for another hour.'

'Moon or no moon,' I said briskly, 'of course we've got plenty of time. That's one of the delights of Capri, that there's never any hurry.'

'Leisure,' he said. 'If people only knew! It's the most priceless thing a man can have and they're such fools they don't even know it's
35 something to aim at. Work? They work for work's sake. They haven't got the brains to realize that the only object of work is to obtain leisure.'

Wine has the effect on some people of making them indulge in general reflections. These remarks were true, but no one could have
40 claimed that they were original. I did not say anything, but struck a match to light my cigar.

'It was full moon the first time I came to Capri,' he went on reflectively. 'It might be the same moon as tonight.'

'It was, you know,' I smiled.
45 He grinned. The only light in the garden was what came from an oil lamp that hung over our heads. It had been scanty to eat by, but it was good now for confidences.

Extract 2

Comprehension check

1 What aspects of Wilson does the writer describe?
Is it a sympathetic description?
2 Do you think Wilson is a visitor to Capri, or has he been there for a long time?
3 Draw a sketch of Wilson, following the description.

The writer gets to know Wilson better. Wilson tells him how he fell in love with Capri when he first saw it. He has been there for fifteen years, and will stay for another ten. But what is he going to do after that? The writer does not tell us yet. They have planned to have an evening meal together and then go for a walk in the moonlight.

Read extract 2

Comprehension check

4 Describe the setting of the meal.
What time of day is it?
What sort of inn is it?
What is the food and wine like?
What is the atmosphere of the scene?
5 Why do they feel that 'there was nothing much wrong with life'?
6 What is Wilson's attitude to work and life?
7 'It might be the same moon as tonight', says Wilson.
What does he mean?
Explain the writer's joke in reply.
8 Explain the comment about the light in line 46/7.

What do you expect to happen next?

Wilson goes on to tell his story. He had been a bank manager in London; his wife and daughter had died. He decided he wanted to spend the rest of his life on Capri. He didn't have a lot of money, but he had enough to buy an annuity (a sort of pension) which would give him a small income for twenty-five years. That was fifteen years ago. When his pension runs out in ten years' time, he's going to commit suicide. The writer couldn't stop a little shiver running down his spine at the thought. He describes Wilson's life style.

Read extract 3

Comprehension check

9 In what ways is Wilson special, and in what ways is he 'commonplace'?

10 Why do you think the writer is interested in this character?

The writer had been on Capri on holiday, and had to leave at the end of his stay. It was thirteen years later that he went back. What had happened to Wilson? Had he committed suicide? When the time came, 'after twenty-five years of complete happiness', he had lacked the strength to leave the life he loved so much. He had no money. He half-heartedly tried to kill himself, but his mental powers were disturbed. He was reduced to living in a hut, working as a slave for scraps of food. He was like a 'hunted animal'.

Read extract 4

What do you think?

1 'He brought it on himself', says the writer's friend just before the end of the story. 'After all, he's only got what he deserved.' Do you agree?

2 The writer replies 'I think on the whole we all get what we deserve.' Do you agree?

3 What do you think is Somerset Maugham's attitude to Wilson and the life he chose for himself?

4 If you could escape from the pressures of your life, where would you escape to? What would you be escaping from?

His only passion was for the beauty of nature and he sought felicity in the simple and natural things that life offers to everyone.
50 You may say that it was a grossly selfish existence. It was. He was of no use to anybody, but on the other hand he did nobody any harm. His only object was his own happiness, and it looked as though he had attained it. Very few people know where to look for happiness; fewer still find it. I don't know whether he was a fool or a wise man. He was
55 certainly a man who knew his own mind. The odd thing about him to me was that he was so immensely commonplace. I should never have given him a second thought but for what I knew, that on a certain day, ten years from then, unless a chance illness cut the thread before, he must deliberately take leave of the world he loved so well.

Extract 3

60 He died last year. He had endured that life for six years. He was found one morning on the mountainside lying quite peacefully as though he had died in his sleep. From where he lay he had been able to see those two great rocks called the Faraglioni which stand out of the sea. It was full moon and he must have gone to see them by
65 moonlight. Perhaps he died of the beauty of that sight.

Extract 4

▶ **Language focus**

Read the *Language review* on relative clauses and participles on page 73.
Do the *Controlled practice* exercises 1–4.

● **Vocabulary 1**

Describing people

1 Find a word or expression in the extracts from *The Lotus Eater* that means the same as the following.

Clothes
not ironed
not buttoned up
attractive and colourful

Face
a soft smile
wrinkled
brown
ordinary

Hair
neat

Character
thinking of oneself
having experience and knowledge
ordinary

2 **Compound adjectives**

Put the following *compound adjectives* into the right group, according to what they describe.

good-looking	blue-eyed
well-dressed	self-centred
left-handed	bad-tempered
clean-shaven	narrow-minded
straight-haired	easy-going
well-behaved	broad-shouldered

Character _____

_____

_____

Clothes _____

_____

_____

Face _____

_____

_____

Body _____

_____

_____

69

3 Expressing negative qualities

Somerset Maugham says that Wilson's teeth were 'not very good'. We often avoid a negative adjective by saying *not very + the opposite adjective* because it is more tactful.

Make the following statements more tactful.

a. He's small.
b. Her hair is a mess.
c. She looks miserable.
d. He's rude.
e. He's got a horrible complexion.
f. She's badly dressed.
g. I think he looks stupid. (Careful!)

4 T.23 Work in pairs.

Listen to the tape. Two people are discussing the group of people in the photograph. As you listen, write the names of the people in the spaces.

a. _____ e. _____

b. _____ f. _____

c. _____ g. _____

d. _____ h. _____

5 Work in four groups.

Choose one of the pictures, and describe the person in as much detail as you can.
Begin with your general impressions (age, build, height) and then describe her/his face, hair and clothes. What sort of person does he/she seem to be?

Speaking

Lecturettes

Each student should prepare to talk to the rest of the class for three or four minutes on one of the following subjects.

- a description of a person that you know
- a memorable meal
- a place (town/house/view) that is important to you

Prepare some notes but don't just read them aloud.
The rest of the class should ask questions at the end.

● Listening

Pre-listening task

- In your country, how many seasons are there?
- What characterizes each season?
- Is the climate mild or extreme?
- What is your favourite season? Why?
- What do you like doing in the different seasons?

Listening for gist

T.24 You will hear a man called John, talking about a journey he made in spring on the island of Corsica.

As you listen, take notes.

Comprehension check

1 Look at the following pictures. What part do they play in the story?

2 Retell the story in your own words.

► Language focus

On the tape there are several *modifiers*.

Listen to the tape again and complete the gaps with the modifier used.

1 it's _____ hot in summer
2 the winters are either mild or _____ severe
3 the interior is _____ wild and mountainous
4 I was _____ puzzled
5 it had been snowing _____ heavily
6 it was getting dark, and _____ cold
7 my jaw was _____ frozen solid
8 it's _____ true, I assure you

Read the *Language review* on modifiers on page 74.
Do the *Controlled practice* exercise 5.

● Vocabulary 2

Describing objects

1 Divide the following words into three groups: shape, material, and colour.

circular	purple
gold	oval
grey	triangular
rubber	round
cotton	crimson
cylindrical	rectangular
nylon	silver
straight	iron
glass	navy blue
wooden	square
metal	maroon
scarlet	turquoise

2 Look at the objects in the room around you.
Can you see something with the shapes and colours, and made of the materials above?

3 Work in pairs.
Describe an everyday object without saying what it is.
Read out the description. Can the others guess what it is?
If necessary, tell them also what it is for.

● Writing

Look at the following two descriptions of Cardiff and answer the questions.

Questions

1 What is the purpose of each text? Where are they taken from?
– an encyclopaedia?
– a tourist guide?
– a history book?
– publicity from the Welsh Development Agency?

2 Which description is more factual? How would you describe the style of the other text?

3 In the first text, what is the purpose of each paragraph?

4 In the second text, underline with a solid line _____ what is fact, and with a broken line _ _ _ _ _ what is opinion.

Cardiff is the capital and largest city of Wales, and it is also the country's main economic, industrial and cultural centre. It is situated on the southeast coast of Wales, and three rivers, the Taff, the Ely and the Rhymney flow through it into the Bristol Channel.

A large area of parkland lies near the centre of Cardiff, and many of the city's major commercial buildings are found around Cathays Park. The Civic Centre is also situated here, and this includes the Law Courts, the National Museum of Wales and the University College. Nearby there are many fashionable shops and modern hotels, and Cardiff Castle, which was built in 1090. Factories in Cardiff produce parts for cars, chemicals, electronic equipment, engineering products, processed food and tobacco. Modern rail and road communications link Cardiff with the rest of Great Britain, and an airport lies outside the edge of the city.

In about AD 75, Roman soldiers built a fort on the site of what is now Cardiff — the name itself means *fort on the Taff*. Normans settled the area around 1050, building the Castle, and a walled town grew up around the Castle. By the early 1800's it was still a small town. Then, when Wales became a major centre of coal mining and iron and steel production, Cardiff served as the shipping centre for these products and grew rapidly. By 1890 it had become known as the *Coal Metropolis of the World*, but the industry declined after the First World War. Since the mid-1940's Cardiff has grown steadily as the administrative and commerical centre of Wales. Its current population is approximately 300,000.

Wales has a reputation for giving its guests a warm welcome, and nowhere is this more true than in Cardiff, which has all the advantages of a capital city together with the friendly atmosphere that is rarely found elsewhere. Cardiff is a city of contrasts. The castle, with 1900 years of history, stands alongside a modern shopping centre and one of the world's great civic centres. Hundreds of acres of beautiful parkland reach into the very heart of the city. Castles abound in and around Cardiff — a reminder that for centuries this was turbulent frontier land.

CAER

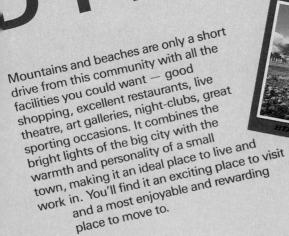

Cardiff Castle

Roman
Norman
Medieval
Civil War
Victorian...

1900 Years of History

Getting around Cardiff

Under One Roof

DYDD

South Wales
BRITAIN
Cardiff - Wales
Europe's youngest capital city!
CARDIFF

Mountains and beaches are only a short drive from this community with all the facilities you could want — good shopping, excellent restaurants, live theatre, art galleries, night-clubs, great sporting occasions. It combines the bright lights of the big city with the warmth and personality of a small town, making it an ideal place to live and work in. You'll find it an exciting place to visit and a most enjoyable and rewarding place to move to.

Write two descriptions of a town that you know.
The first should be factual. Organize it into paragraphs, as in the first text. The second should try to sell the town, either as a tourist attraction or as a place for industry to move to.

● Language review

Relative clauses

Relative clauses are like *adjectives*. They give us more information about nouns and pronouns.

Adjectives
*Show me an **interesting** book.*
*The **Indian** doctor lives next door.*

Relative clauses
*Show me a book **that has pictures**.*
*The doctor **that I go to** lives next door.*

We leave out relative pronouns whenever possible, especially in spoken English.

The author I like best is Conrad.
The house we finally bought was perfect.

Notice the word order in the relative clause when the verb has a preposition (*apply **for**, stay **at**; speak **to***).

I didn't get the job I applied for.
That's the hotel he stayed at.
The woman I spoke to was most helpful.

Participles

Present and *Past Participles* can be used as adjectives.
a fascinating story
a broken cup
When participles come after a noun, they are like reduced relative clauses.

| *I met a woman* | *riding a donkey.* |
| | *who was riding a donkey.* |

| *I had a drink* | *made of five different fruits.* |
| | *which was made of five different fruits.* |

◄ Look again at the extracts from *The Lotus Eater*.
Find the examples of relative clauses and participles.

► **Grammar reference:** page 118.

Modifiers

Very, absolutely, quite
Modifiers make adjectives more or less extreme.
There are three kinds. Look at the chart opposite.

▶ **Grammar reference:** page 119.

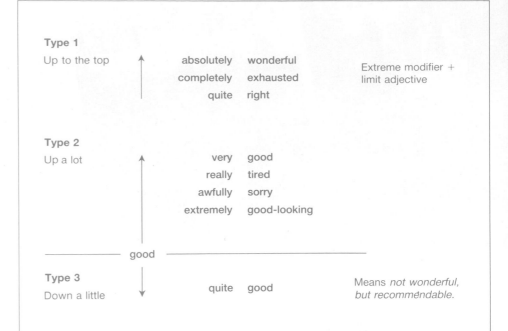

Type 1				
Up to the top		absolutely	wonderful	Extreme modifier + limit adjective
		completely	exhausted	
		quite	right	

Type 2				
Up a lot		very	good	
		really	tired	
		awfully	sorry	
		extremely	good-looking	

good

Type 3				
Down a little		quite	good	Means *not wonderful, but recommendable.*

CONTROLLED PRACTICE
Describing

1 Relative clauses

Add *who*, *that*, *whose* or *where* to complete the sentences.
If *who* or *that* is not necessary, add nothing.

a. Somerset Maugham was a writer _____ wrote short stories.
b. He travelled to the Far East, _____ he got ideas for his books.
c. The story _____ we read is called *The Lotus Eater*.
d. It is about a man called Wilson, _____ gave up work.
e. Wilson, _____ wife and daughter both died, wanted to live a life of leisure.
f. He had a pension _____ provided him with a small income.
g. For years he lived a life _____ was very pleasurable.
h. One evening, he and the writer went to a restaurant, _____ they had a wonderful meal.
i. The wine _____ they drank came from the cook's own vineyard.
j. The man _____ the writer spoke to thought Wilson got what he deserved.

2 Relative clauses and participles

Join the following sentences in two ways.

Example
Look at the man. He's talking to your wife.

Look at the man who's talking to your wife.
Look at the man talking to your wife.

Be careful with word order in f, g and h.

a. I read a book. It was written by a friend of yours.
b. A man got on the bus. He was carrying a monkey in a box.
c. In the street there were several people. They were waiting for the shop to open.
d. Britain imports many cars. They are made in Japan.
e. There are a lot of people in your office. They want to talk to you.
f. The cowboy fell off his horse. He had been wounded by an arrow.
g. Most of the people recovered quickly. They were injured in the crash.
h. John looked anxiously at his watch. He wished he hadn't come to the party.

3 Sentence building

Make one sentence, incorporating the extra information into the base sentence. Make any necessary changes and additions.

Example
A lady was sitting in her garden.
grey-haired/shawl around her shoulders/she watched the sun/the sun was setting.

A grey-haired lady, with a shawl around her shoulders, was sitting in her garden watching the setting sun.

a. Peter has a house.
he works in London/he works for a company/the company sells computers/three-bedroomed/the house overlooks the Thames.
b. A man walked along the road.
elderly/a wrinkled face/an old raincoat/slowly/dusty/tree-lined.
c. Ann Cross was seen in a restaurant.
the actress/she won an Oscar for a film/the film was made last year/she was having dinner with a man/his company recently went bankrupt.

4 Divide into five groups.
Choose one of the following base sentences each.
See which group can make the longest sentence!

a. The General inspected the soldiers.
b. The cowboy rode off into the sunset.
c. James Bolan is getting married to Angela Duffy.
d. The Prime Minister had lunch with the President.
e. The girl sat in front of the fire.

5 Modifiers

Work in pairs.
Make up some short dialogues, using the pairs of adjectives and appropriate modifiers.

Example

A *That painting's **rather valuable** isn't it?*

B *Valuable! You're joking! It's **absolutely priceless**!*

cold – freezing
big – enormous
good – marvellous
wet – soaked
frightened – terrified
bad – revolting
difficult – impossible
hungry – starving

REVISION

Get

1 The verb **get** is very common in spoken English, and it has many different meanings.
In the following sentences replace the word **get** by one of the verbs below.

a. We got home after midnight.
b. While you're at the shops, could you get something for supper?
c. Can we stop for a while? I'm getting tired.
d. I'm getting the ten o'clock train.
e. She gets three hundred pounds a week.
f. Could you get my slippers for me? They're upstairs.
g. We can get something to eat on the train.
h. Did you get my last letter?

fetch   earn   receive   arrive
catch   buy   become   have

2 **Get + adverb/preposition** is also commonly used to express some kind of *movement*.
Put the correct adverb or preposition in column **A** to mean the same as the verb in column **B**.

	A	**B**
a.	to get ___	to return
b.	to get ___	to enter
c.	to get ___	to escape
d.	to get ___	to pass with difficulty (e.g. a person)
e.	to get ___	to climb (e.g. a wall)
f.	to get ___	to remove (e.g. a stain)
g.	to get ___	to leave (e.g. a train, a bus)
h.	to get ___	to make contact (e.g. on the phone)

3 Complete the following sentences using **get + adverb/preposition**.

a. My house was burgled yesterday. The burglar managed to ___ .
b. The police were called, but the burglar ___ .
c. We were in the capital when war broke out. Naturally we ___ .
d. The journey was terrible. We didn't ___ until three in the morning.
e. Someone spilt wine on the carpet, but I ___ .
f. I've been trying ___ to you for ages, but you're always engaged.

4 **Multi-word verbs (1)**

Many verbs in English are followed by a preposition or an adverb. These are called *multi-word verbs*. (They are also referred to as *prepositional* and *phrasal verbs*.)
In many **verb + adverb/preposition** combinations, both parts are used quite literally.
Put one of the following adverbs or prepositions into each gap.

away   out   on   down   off
up   in

a. I'd better write your telephone number ___ . I've got a terrible memory.
b. Don't run ___ . Come here! I want to talk to you!
c. The bird's cage wasn't closed properly. It managed to get ___ , and unfortunately it flew ___ . We haven't seen it since.
d. When Mrs Johnson died, she didn't have a penny. She'd given all her money ___ to charity.
e. I don't feel like cooking tonight. Shall we eat ___ ?
f. The soup doesn't taste very nice. If I were you, I'd put some more salt ___ .
g. A button has come ___ my shirt. Could you sew it back ___ for me?
h. It has just started to rain, and the washing is hanging outside. Could you help me to bring it ___ ?
i. Hello. It's Peter, isn't it? I hardly recognized you! You've shaved ___ your beard.
j. Kate's having a birthday party this afternoon. Could you help us to blow ___ some balloons?
k. I fell ___ my horse and dislocated my shoulder.
l. And my wife fell ___ stairs! One disaster after another!
m. The wind was very strong last night. It blew ___ a tree in our garden.
n. **A** Where are you going?
B Henry's taking me ___ to the theatre.
A Lucky you! Have a nice time!

Modal verbs of deduction

Sunday February 1st
There was a lot of shouting late last night.
The kitchen bin was knocked over and the back door
kept being slammed. I wish my parents would be a
bit more thoughtful. I have been through an
emotional time and I need my sleep. Still, I don't
expect them to understand what it is like being
in love. They have been married for 14 ½ years.

Relationships

● Discussion point

1 How do you think the people in the photograph are related? Which relative took the photograph?
2 Look at the texts. Where do you think they are from? A magazine? A book? A newspaper? Who wrote them? Why? What sort of relationship is being described?

I ___ take thee ___ to my wedded wife, to have and to hold from this day forward, for better for worse, for richer for poorer, in sickness and in health, to love and to cherish, till death us do part, according to God's holy ordinance; and thereto I plight thee my troth.

I ___ take thee ___ to my wedded husband, to have and to hold from this day forward, for better for worse, for richer for poorer, in sickness and in health, to love, cherish, and to obey, till death us do part, according to God's holy ordinance; and thereto I give thee my troth.

We've been married three years but my husband's thoughtlessness gets me down. He never lets me know when he's coming home, and sometimes I'll have dinner waiting and he simply doesn't turn up. He always says he met a friend and they got talking in the bar, or he had to work late. We have endless rows about it and I end up in tears. Most of the weekend he's out with his hobbies and I get a bit lonely. I'm starting to feel he's a complete stranger to me.

Mr M.J. Fothergill-Smythe and Miss P.L. Howard-Thompson

The engagement is announced between Malcolm James, youngest son of Captain C.G.E. Fothergill-Smythe and the late Mrs Laura Fothergill-Smythe, of Fothergill Hall, Buntingford, Hertfordshire, and Penelope Lesley, younger daughter of Major H.C. Howard-Thompson and the late Mrs Rosemary Howard-Thompson, of Dunromin the Water Mill, Little Chalfont, Buckinghamshire.

Pre-reading task

Divide into two groups, those with children and those without. Discuss the following questions.

Group A People with children
1 Who do your children look like? Who do they take after in character?
2 Have you brought up your children similarly to the way your parents brought *you* up? Are you more/less strict? More/less indulgent?
3 In what ways do you hope your children's life will be better than yours?

Group B People without children
1 Who do you most take after, your mother or your father? Who do you look like? Who are you like in character?
2 How much of a generation gap is there/was there between you and your parents?
3 Would you want to bring up your children similarly to the way your parents brought *you* up?

Jigsaw reading

There is a feature in a magazine in which members of the same family describe their relationship.
You will read about James Mitford, an actor, and his daughter Amy.

Group A Read James Mitford's description of their relationship.

Group B Read Amy Mitford's description of their relationship.

As you are reading, try to answer the questions.
You won't be able to answer them all, so try to guess the answer if you're not sure.

Family Matters

Relative Values

Two points of view on a family relationship

My Daughter

James Mitford: My wife and I only had the one child. It might have been nice to have a son, but we didn't plan a family, we just had Amy.

5 I see her as my best friend. I think she'd always come to me first if she had a problem. We have the same sense of humour, and share interests. I don't mind animals, but she's completely obsessed with them, and she has always had dogs, cats, horses, and goldfish in her life.

We were closest when she was about four, which I think
10 is a lovely age for a child. They know the parents best, and don't have the outside contacts. She must have grown up suddenly when she went to school, because I remember her growing away from her family slightly. Any father who has a teenager daughter comes across an extraordinary collection of
15 people, and there seemed to be an endless stream of strange young men coming through our house. By the time I'd learned their names they'd gone away and I had to start learning a new lot. I remember I told her off once in front of her friends and she didn't talk to me for days afterwards.

20 I wanted more than anything else for her to be happy in what she was doing, and I was prepared to pull strings to help her on her way. She went to a good school, but that didn't work out. She must have upset somebody. When she left she decided she wanted to become an actress so I got her into
25 drama school. It wasn't to her liking so she joined a theatre group and began doings bits and pieces in films. She was doing well, but then gave it up. She probably found it boring. Then she took up social work, and finally went to work for a designer and he became her husband. And that's really the
30 story of her life. She must be happy with him — they're always together.

We have the same tastes in books and music, but it takes me a while to get used to new pop songs. I used to take her to see the opera, which is my big passion, but I don't think
35 she likes it very much, she doesn't come with me any more.

I don't think she's a big television watcher. She knows when I'm on, and she might watch, but I don't know. It's not the kind of thing she tells me.

We're very grateful for Amy. She's a good daughter as
40 daughters go. We're looking forward to being grandparents. I'm sure she'll have a son.

My Father

Amy Mitford: I don't really know my father. He isn't easy to get on with. He's quite self-centred, and a little bit vain, I think, and in some ways quite unapproachable. The public

45 must think he's very easy-going, but at home he keeps himself to himself.

He can't have been at home much when I was a child, because I don't remember much about him. He's always been slightly out of touch with family life. His work always came

50 first, and he was always off somewhere acting or rehearsing. He loves being asked for his autograph, he loves to be recognized. He has won several awards, and he's very proud of that. He was given the Member of the British Empire, and we had to go to Buckingham Palace to get the medal. It was

55 incredibly boring — there were hundreds of other people getting the same thing, and you had to sit there for hours. He shows off his awards to whoever comes to the house.

I went to public school, and because of my total lack of interest and non-attendance I was asked to leave. I didn't want

60 to go there in the first place. I was taken away from all my friends. He must have been very pleased to get me into the school, but in the end it was a complete waste of money. I let him down quite badly, I suppose. I tried several jobs but I couldn't settle down in them. They just weren't challenging

65 enough. Then I realized that what I really wanted to do was live in the country and look after animals, so that's what I now do.

As a family, we're not that close, either emotionally or geographically. We don't see much of each other these days.

70 My father and I are totally different, like chalk and cheese. My interests have always been the country, but he's into books, music and above all, opera, which I hate. If they do come to see us, they're in completely the wrong clothes for the country — mink coats, nice little leather shoes, not exactly

75 ideal for long walks across the fields.

He was totally opposed to me getting married. He was hoping we would break up. Gerald's too humble, I suppose. He must have wanted me to marry someone famous, but I didn't, and that's all there is to it. We don't want children, but

80 my father keeps on and on talking about wanting grandchildren. You can't make someone have children just because you want grandchildren.

I never watch him on television. I'm not that interested, and anyway he usually forgets to tell me when he's on.

Comprehension check

In questions 1–3, there is not necessarily one correct answer only.

1 How would you describe their relationship?
a. It was closer when Amy was a child.
b. They get on well, and agree on most things.
c. He has more respect for her than she does for him.
d. They don't have very much in common.

2 How would you describe James Mitford?
a. He has done all that a father can for his daughter.
b. He isn't very aware of how she really feels.
c. He's more interested in himself than his family.

3 How would you describe Amy?
a. She is selfish and spoilt.
b. It took her a long time to decide what she wanted to do in life.
c. She found happiness in marriage that she didn't have in childhood.

4 What did he think of her friends when she was a teenager?
5 Why did she leave school?
6 Why did she give up her jobs?
7 What does he think of her husband?
8 Is she interested in his career?
9 Is she going to have children?
10 How often do they see each other?

When you have answered as many questions as you can, find a partner from the other group.
Compare your answers and swap information.

What do you think?

Who has the more realistic view of the relationship?
Why?

▶ **Language focus**

Read the *Language review* on page 81.
Do the *Controlled practice* exercises 1 and 2.

Vocabulary 1

Multi-word verbs (2)

1 On page 75, we saw that many *multi-word verbs* are used literally. Work in pairs.
Your teacher will ask you some questions, and you must reply using a verb + adverb/preposition used literally. Write down your replies.

Example
What does a dentist do to a bad tooth?
He/she pulls it out.

2 In other multi-word verbs, the verb is used literally and the adverb/preposition serves to intensify the verb meaning.

Example
Could you tidy up your room, please?
We could also say *Could you tidy your room, please?*, but English likes using prepositions!

Put one of the following adverbs or prepositions into each gap.
down   up   out

a. Come on! Eat _____ your soup before it gets cold!
b. We put fifty pounds a month into our deposit account. We're saving _____ to buy a new car.
c. (At a petrol station) Could you fill it _____ for me?
d. I'm tired _____. I've been working all day.
e. Everybody thought old Mr Jones had no money. It was only after he died that we found _____ he was in fact a millionaire.
f. It's pouring _____ with rain. You can't possibly go out.
g. John! You're driving much too fast! Slow _____ .
h. Could you wrap the jumper _____ for me? It's a present.
i. **A** How do you spell your name? Is it M-A-L-C-O-M?
   B No. You've missed _____ an L. It's M-A-L-C-O-L-M.
j. We can't finish the decorating because we've used _____ all the paint.
k. **A** Help! I've lost my purse!
   B Don't be silly! Just calm _____ ! I'm sure we'll find it.
l. No wonder you haven't got any money. If you added _____ the amount of money you spend on cigarettes and beer, you'd realize where you spent it all.

3 Work in groups of four.
Compare the use of *multi-word verbs* in the following sentences.
a. He *looked up* the chimney, but couldn't see anything.
   He *looked* the word *up* in the dictionary.
b. She *put out* the cat, locked the door and went to bed.
   She *put out* her cigarette in the ash-tray.
c. She *looked after* the baby for me.
   She *looked after* him for me.
d. The plane *took off*.
   He *took off* his coat.
e. She *came across* the room and gave me a kiss.
   I *came across* this old photograph while I was tidying out my desk.

The sentences illustrate some of the problems of form and use.
In which of the sentences are the parts (verb + adverb/preposition) used quite literally?
In which sentences can the adverb move position?

▶ **Grammar reference:** page 120.

4 In the texts about the Mitfords there are a number of *multi-word verbs* with non-literal meanings. Replace the words in italics in the following sentences with a *multi-word verb* from the texts.
a. He *started playing* golf because he needed the exercise.
b. I *unexpectedly met* an old school friend last week.
c. Have you heard? Jane and Andrew have *separated*.
d. *What sort of relationship* do you *have* with your parents?
e. I can't stand her. She's always *boasting* about her wonderful children.
f. Are you beginning to *get established* in your new flat?
g. Tennis was taking up too much of my time, so I *stopped doing* it.
h. Don't *disappoint* me. I'm relying on you to help me.
i. She was *reprimanded* for getting her new clothes dirty.
j. It was a good plan in theory but it *wasn't successful* in practice.

5 Complete the following dialogues with one of the same *multi-word verbs* in the correct form.
a. **A** I saw Bernard and Mary last night. You don't like them very much, do you?
   B Well, I quite like Bernard, but I've never been able . . .
b. **A** I was in Manchester yesterday, at the College of Art.
   B Really? That's where Alan works. Did you . . .
c. **A** You're getting fat.
   B Yes. I think I'll . . .
d. **A** How's the old car of yours? Still going, is it?
   B Don't say that about my car. It's never once . . .
e. **A** Paul seems to lose his temper with the children very easily.
   B Yes. He's always . . .

Listening

Pre-listening task

You will hear an interview with an Indian lady, Rajkumari Kejriwal, known to her family and friends as Raj.
In the interview she talks about her arranged marriage, and the day she was introduced to her future husband.
Work in pairs.
Write questions. What information would you like to learn?

Intensive listening

T.25 Listen to the interview, and see if your questions are answered.

Comprehension check

1 How did Raj's father find the two men?
2 Was it difficult to find a husband for Raj?
3 Describe the day that Raj met the two men.
4 Why did her father choose Shyam?
5 What happened between that day and their marriage?

Summary

In the following summary there are some factual mistakes and some gaps.
Correct the mistakes and complete the gaps.

Raj's father arranged her marriage when she was still at school. He chose her husband by _____. In Raj's case, this didn't take long, but sometimes _____. Two men were introduced to Raj and her family, and together they decided _____. The men were of similar background, but one of them _____, and this was the one _____. Raj didn't agree with her father, but she had no choice. She has now been married for twenty-two years, and in fact _____. Most marriages in India are still _____, and the usual age _____.

What do you think?

1 What was Raj's attitude to her arranged marriage?
  Did she accept it or resent it?
2 How do you think she felt on the day she met the two men?
3 Raj says that her husband's family wasn't wealthy, but they owned a village and were like princes.
  What does this tell us about Raj?
4 What else would you like to know, either about Raj's marriage, or about arranged marriages?
5 What advantages does she see to arranged marriages?

In groups, list other advantages and disadvantages.
Can you think of any interest points that are neither good or bad, but are results of the idea?

▶ **Language focus**

Do the *Controlled practice* exercises 3 and 4.

● Vocabulary 2

Idiomatic expressions

1 The meaning of an *idiomatic expression* cannot usually be guessed from the individual words.
  To find an *idiomatic expression* in the dictionary, you must decide what is the key word.
  The idiom *to pull strings* appeared in the text about the Mitfords.

Notice how the dictionary refers you to the correct entry if you have looked up the wrong word.

> **pull²** /pʊl/ *vt, vi*
>   For other uses with *nn*, ⇨ the *n* entries, eg
> ~ a face/faces; ~ sb's leg; ~ one's punches;
> ~ strings; ~ wires; ~ the 'wool over sb's eyes.

Idiomatic expressions are always printed in **bold italic** type.

> **string¹** /strɪŋ/ *n* 1 [C,U] (piece or length of) fine cord for tying things, keeping things in place, etc;
>   **pull ~s**, exert a (hidden) influence: *pull ~s to get sb a job/to have sb dismissed.*

2 Here are some idiomatic expressions to do with relationships between people.
  Work in pairs.
  Decide what is the key word. Find the idiom in your dictionary.
  Rewrite the sentences in non-idiomatic English.

  Example
  We're like chalk and cheese.
  We're completely different.

a. Patrick and Jenny get on like a house on fire.
b. It was love at first sight.
c. She really gets on my nerves.
d. He's tied to his mother's apron strings.
e. They're head over heels in love.
f. We're not on speaking terms any more.

g. They don't see eye to eye on anything.
h. She wears the trousers.

● Speaking

The Murder Game

Four men are sitting in the library of a country house. Suddenly one of the men drops dead.
Who did it?

Your teacher will give you cards with information about the murder and the people. Work together to solve the murder. You can't show your card to anyone else, but you can of course say what is on it.
The best way to solve the murder is by organization, cooperation, and knowing when to speak and when to listen. If you work together well, you can solve the murder in about twenty minutes. If you don't work together, you'll never solve it!

When you have finished, discuss the following questions:
1 How did you organize yourselves?
  Was everybody involved?
  Did one person dominate?
2 How could you have solved the murder more quickly?
  What should you have done?

● Writing

Reporting conversations

1 Work in groups.
  Look at the *direct speech* and the two different ways of *reporting* it. Which do you think is better? Why?

a. 'I'm terribly sorry. I really won't do it again.'
  1 *She said that she was terribly sorry, and that she really wouldn't do it again.*
  2 *She apologized, and promised not to do it again.*
b. 'I couldn't come yesterday. I had to stay at home.'
  1 *He said that he hadn't been able to come the previous day because he'd had to stay at home.*
  2 *He explained why he hadn't come the day before.*

2 Report the following direct speech, using one of the verbs below. Notice how they are used.

complain announce insist agree explain	that + clause

explain	what why + clause how

refuse offer	to + infinitive

suggest that + person + should + infinitive (*I suggested that he should go to bed.*)

Make the sentences quite short. Remember to report the essence of the direct speech, not every word.

a. 'I'll give you a lift to the station, if you like. It's no trouble at all,' he said to me.
b. 'Listen, everybody. Anita and I have something to tell you. We're getting engaged,' said Jeremy.
c. 'Now then, Peter. If I were you, I'd start revising for that exam,' said the tutor.
d. 'I think you're right, Annie. Your solution is best,' said Johnny.
e. 'It's not fair!' said Beth. 'I always have to do twice as much work as Philip. He hardly does anything!'
f. 'There's no way you can have the car tonight, my boy. I need it myself,' said James to his son.
g. 'Thanks for the invitation,' said Stephanie, 'But we can't come, I'm afraid. Joseph's got the flu, you see. I hope the party goes well.'
h. 'I must make the point quite strongly,' she said, 'that I did my best to help.'

3 **T.26** Listen to the conversation on tape. The Prime Minister is being interviewed about a proposed pay increase for politicians of thirty-five per cent. Report the conversation. The following verbs might help.

explain   insist   refuse

point out go on to say deny	that . . .

tell someone that . . .

Begin like this.
The Prime Minister began by saying that he had the situation under control, and that there was no crisis. He was asked . . .

● Language review

Modal verbs of deduction

1 Expressing **degree of certainty** about the *present*.
We are deducing and supposing about a present event.

Certainty	He **must**	
Possibility	He **might**	be in love.
	He **may**	live near here.
	He **could**	be earning a lot of money.
Certainty	He **can't**	

2 Expressing **degrees of certainty** about the *past*.
We are deducing and supposing *now* about an event in the *past*.

Certainty	He **must**		
Possibility	He **might**		been ill.
	He **may**	have	gone home.
	He **could**		been going to work.
Certainty	He **can't**		

For degrees of certainty about the future, see page 64.

'Good luck, Minister – and when you lie remember to look straight into the cameras!'

◄ Look again at the texts on pages 77 and 78.
Find the examples of modal verbs of deduction.

► **Grammar reference: page 120.**

CONTROLLED PRACTICE
Past and present deductions

1 Rewrite these sentences using a
modal verb of deduction.
Add a reason to support your
deduction.

Example
I'm sure Amy likes animals very
much.

*Amy must like animals very much.
She's always had them around her.*

a. I'm sure she doesn't like children
   very much.
b. I'm sure James is a famous actor.
c. Perhaps she has a farm.
d. I'm sure she didn't work very
   hard at school.
e. Perhaps James has won an Oscar.
f. I'm sure she had a lot of friends
   when she was young.
g. He probably didn't want her to
   marry Gerald.
h. He probably wanted her to marry
   someone famous.
i. I'm sure they're not very close to
   each other.
j. Perhaps she gets on better with
   her mother.

2 Work in pairs.
What can you deduce from the
following situations?

Example
Alice is on her hands and knees.

*She must be looking for something.
She might have dropped a contact
lens.*

a. The neighbours are making a lot
   of noise.
b. It's the beginning of your lesson,
   and your teacher isn't here.
c. Penny's phone bill is enormous.
d. John's lost a lot of weight
   recently.
e. A car is found crashed into a tree,
   with the driver unconscious at the
   wheel.

3 Here are photographs of four
different weddings.
Which country do you think they
are from?
What role do the various people
play in the wedding?

4 Work in pairs.
You will hear one half of two
telephone conversations.
Listen carefully.
a. What is the relationship
   between the two people?
   What are they talking about?
b. Choose one of the dialogues.
   Look at the tapescript on page
   133.
   On a separate piece of paper
   write down what you think is
   the other half of the
   conversation.
   Compare your dialogue with
   another pair of students.

REVISION
Words commonly confused

Work in groups.
The following words are often
confused.
For each word write a sentence
which illustrates the difference.

rob	steal
expect	wait for
lend	borrow
lie	lay
check	control
fit	suit
rise	raise
remind	remember
actually	at the moment
loose	lose
invent	discover
sensible	sensitive
take	pass/fail (exams)

Compare your sentences with other
students'.

UNIT 10

Expressing habit

Vice and virtue

● Discussion point

1 What are Andy Capp's vices?

2 Work in pairs.
Are the following descriptions of people *positive* or *negative*?
a. She'll always give you what you need.
b. She's got a very high opinion of herself.
c. I never know whether to believe him.
d. He eats like a pig.
e. He says what he means, and he means what he says.
f. He's always trying to pick a fight.
g. She won't let her husband out of her sight.
h. He wouldn't give you yesterday's newspaper.
i. You can always depend on him.
j. Once she's made up her mind, she won't change it.

3 Match one of the sentences in 2 with a vice or virtue listed below. Write in the adjective.

Vices	
aggression	*aggressive*
pride	_____
obstinacy	_____
meanness	_____
greed	_____
jealousy	_____
deceit	_____

Virtues	
sincerity	_____
reliability	_____
generosity	_____

– What qualities do you most admire in people?
– What characteristics most annoy you in people?

● Reading

1 Look at the newspaper article on page 84 quickly, and decide what you think is the best title.

a. **A statistical survey of the habits of mean people**

b. **Home economics – how to save around the house**

c. **Scrooge is alive and well**

d. **The vices of a nation**

83

1.

We all know about Paul Getty I, the richest man in the world. He's the one who, in his 72-bedroomed country mansion, used to have a pay-phone for his guests. He's also the one who refused to pay the ransom for the release of Paul Getty III, his grandson, until the poor boy's ear was cut off — and even then, the money paid was a loan to Paul Getty II at an interest rate of four per cent.

2.

A magazine recently asked its readers to write in with their tales of miserliness done to or by them. Obviously, this is a subject close to many people's hearts. Many readers said they could hardly bear to remember the tight-fisted habits of their parents, while others reported that years of stinginess had either broken up their marriages or had made their lives a misery.

3.

One man bought his wife a dustpan for a Christmas present. When his workmates asked him about the brush to go with it, he replied, 'Oh, she's getting that for her birthday.'

4.

Every year on her birthday her husband would give her the same birthday card, until one year she hit upon the idea of burning it (one wonders what took her so long). What did her husband do? He bought the cheapest substitute he could find, which happened to be a card for belated birthday greetings, so his wife suffered the added insult of receiving the card late.

5.

There's the woman who for birthdays gives delightful home-made cards, with the message written on a separate piece of paper. With the card she'll enclose a short note asking for the card back in a few days' time.

6.

His wife wrote, 'He's always charging the family for the things he does around the house. He grows vegetables in the back garden, but I have to pay for them out of my house-keeping money. When he gives our daughter a lift to work, he'll ask her for the bus fare and a little bit more because it's a door-to-door service.'

7.

Putting out the pilot light on gas cookers and fires is commonplace. Some people refuse to let others open the freezer without their permission. One man unashamedly wrote in to say how he cuts down on his heating bill. His wife never has the central heating on during the day while he's out at work because he's told her that gas is twice as expensive in the day-time — so the heating conveniently comes on at six o'clock in time for his return.

8.

You might marvel at the man — a Frenchman at that — who ordered half a bottle of wine and eight glasses, or shake your head at the couple who boasted they could make a tin of beans last a week, but there is something very upsetting about putting bacon rashers end to end so that each portion can be measured to the nearest millimetre.

9.

She has decreed that family and friends must limit themselves to three sheets of paper per visit to the lavatory.

10.

There were tales of people who scrape salt from dirty plates back into the salt-cellar, retrieve cloves from eaten apple pies, save lemon slices from dirty glasses and preserve them in water to be re-used later, or put used paper tissues to dry on the radiator. Life with a Scrooge is not a lot of fun.

2 The *topic sentences* (in this case, the first sentence of each paragraph) have been removed. They are listed here.
Match them with the correct paragraph. Write the corresponding paragraph number in the box by the topic sentence.

- [ ] a. When it comes to counting the pennies, how about this charming man?
- [ ] b. Many of the stories were to do with the giving of presents.
- [ ] c. Incidentally, the woman who used to measure the bacon so carefully, rations other aspects of her family's life.
- [ ] d. The meanness of the rich is legendary.
- [ ] e. One woman's attempts to reform her husband's meanness were a complete failure.
- [ ] f. Common ideas of hospitality do not inhibit mean people, then, and nor do considerations of hygiene.
- [ ] g. Fuel economies are a wide-spread form of penny-pinching.
- [ ] h. Stories about stinginess over food were plenty.
- [ ] i. But the meanness of more humble people is no less breathtaking.
- [ ] j. Giving with one hand and taking with the other is a common trick.

Comprehension check/language work

Here are the answers to some questions about the article.
Work out the questions.

1 So that he wouldn't have to pay for his guests' phone calls.
2 Yes, but it was a loan. His son had to repay the money.
3 Because it was the cheapest one he could find.
4 No, he waited until a few days afterwards.
5 So that she can send the card to someone else.
6 No, he *sells* them to her.
7 Because her husband has told her that it would be too expensive.

What do you think?

1 Which person seems to you the meanest?

2 Work in pairs.
Choose one of the stories from the article.

Student A Imagine that the mean person described in the story is your aunt or uncle. Tell **Student B** about her/him.
Student B React, and ask questions to get more information about this mean person.

Begin like this.

Student A *Have I ever told you about my aunt/uncle?*
Student B *No, what's he/she like?*
Student A *Well, he/she's one of the meanest people I've ever met actually.*
Student B *Why . . . ?*

▶ Language focus

Read the *Language review* on page 89 about *present* and *past habit*.
Do the *Controlled practice* exercises 1–5.

● Vocabulary 1

Money

1 Work in groups.
Discuss these two sayings.
Money is the root of all evil.
Money makes the world go round.
Do you agree?

What examples can you think of to prove or disprove them?

2 Here is a list of words and expressions to do with money. Use your dictionary and divide them into the following categories:
- borrowing money
- saving and investing money
- having a personal bank account
  Sometimes the same word will fit different categories.
- to withdraw money
- a building society
- a current account
- a loan at 15% interest
- a cheque card
- a mortgage
- to cash a cheque
- to buy shares in a company
- a credit card
- a monthly statement
- a deposit account
- to earn 10% interest
- monthly repayments
- to put money in
- the Stock Market
- a piggy bank

3 Work in pairs.
How would you feel in the following situations?
Say why.
Would you be pleased, sorry or angry if . . . ?
a. you picked up a bargain in the sales?
b. you paid next to nothing for something?
c. you were overcharged in a restaurant?
d. you were overdrawn at the bank?
e. you were well off?
f. you were broke?
g. you were hard up?
h. you lost a quid and found a fiver?

Underline the idiomatic expressions and the examples of slang.

4 Work in groups.
   Discuss the following questions.
a. What do sensible people do with
    their money?
    What do foolish people do with
    their money?
    Are you sensible or foolish with
    your money?
b. What are the different ways of
    buying things?

    Think of the following:
    a house   a television   a meal
    a car   clothes

● Listening

Pre-listening task

Discuss the following questions in
groups.

1 Have you got a pet?
   Did you have a pet when you were
   younger?
   What is/was it?
   What is/was it like?
   What habits does/did it have?

2 What can animals do better than
   people?
   Think of birds, cats and dogs.

3 You will hear a talk by Johnny
   Morris, a popular expert on
   animals and their behaviour, who
   has made many television and
   radio programmes.

He talks about the following
subjects.
– animals compared to people
– the benefits of having animals in
  our lives
– pets in Ancient Rome and Egypt
– a difficult animal he has known

Make guesses about the content
before you listen.

Listening and note taking

T.28 Listen to the talk and make
notes under the headings above.
When you have finished, compare
your notes with another student's.

What do you think

1 Do you agree with Johnny Morris
   when he says that in many respects
   human beings are inferior to
   animals?

2 How many ways can you think of in which we use animals?
How are the animals suited to this particular task?
Example
Eskimos use huskies to pull their sledges. Huskies are very strong, have a thick coat, and seem to enjoy working together.
3 Which animals make good pets? Why?
Which animals don't make good pets? Why?
4 What animals are popular in your country?

▶ **Language focus**

Read the *Language review* on page 89 about **be used to**.
Do the *Controlled practice* exercises 6 and 7.

● Vocabulary 2

Words with similar meaning

1 In the article on page 84, and the topic sentences on page 85, find words with similar meaning to the following:

meanness   stories   common

2 Words with similar meaning are sometimes interchangeable and sometimes not.

Example

to hire to rent	a car

to rent	a room
	a flat
	a television

not to hire

| to hire | a boat |
| | a suit |

not to rent

To *rent* is for a longer period of time.
We usually *hire* something for a relatively short period of time.

3 Which words in column **A** can combine with words from column **B**?

A	B
tall high	person
	tree
	mountain
	wall
	building
	price

	noise
heavy strong loud	traffic
	smoker
	drink
	wind
	music
	rain

	your temper
	a bus
to lose to miss	a football match
	weight
	an opportunity
	a TV programme
	your parents

	New Year!
Happy Merry	Birthday!
	Christmas!
	Anniversary!

	an appointment
	sure
	a lot of damage
	up your mind
to do to make	your homework
	a mess
	your best
	an excuse
	sense

● Speaking

Castaways

In 1980 an advertisement appeared in a London magazine, beginning 'Writer seeks companion for a year on a tropical island.'

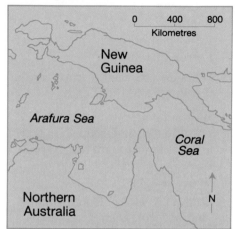

1 Work in two groups.

Group A You are the writer. Talk together to decide what sort of person you are looking for. List qualities under these headings, and add headings of your own.

– Abilities
– Interests/hobbies
– Personality

What do you want the companion to do on the island?

Group B You have answered the advertisement.
Talk together to decide why you think *you* should be the one who is chosen.

List qualities under these headings, and add headings of your own.

- Abilities
- Interests/hobbies
- Personality

What do you want to know about the writer and the island?

2 Work in pairs.
A student from **Group A** interviews a student from **Group B**.
Begin like this:

Student A Hello. Could you tell me why you answered the advertisement?
Student B Well, ...
Student A What makes you think you could live on a desert island for a year?
Student B ...

3 After a while, change partners.

4 **Student A** Have you found a suitable person?
Why/why not?
Student B Are you still interested in going to the desert island?
Why/why not?

⬤ Writing

Jumbled texts
Work in pairs.
Here are two newspaper articles, but they have been mixed up.
Look at the headlines, and read the paragraphs quickly to decide which paragraphs go with which story.
Then put them in the right order.

Divorce
1 _____ 2 _____ 3 _____ 4 _____
5 _____ 6 _____ 7 _____ 8 _____

Marriage
1 _____ 2 _____ 3 _____ 4 _____
5 _____ 6 _____ 7 _____

Litter wrecked untidy handyman's marriage

Bride No. 26 – a record for Mr Wolfe

a. She also complained that there were piles of hardcore, bricks and old cars in the garden. And, when she attempted to clear a space, her husband would fill it with more rubbish.

b. The judge, sitting in the High Court Family Division said Mr White, a 'moody, aggressive and difficult' man, took on too many jobs in the home.
He accepted the complaints of Mrs White, a 'highly-strung' woman, that for many years her kitchen was left 'in disarray' and she found it difficult to work in.

c. THE ways of a handyman husband who started jobs, but seldom finished them, finally became too much for his wife.

d. Yesterday Mr Justice EWBANK ruled that she need not put up with her home in disarray and a garden full of builder's materials any longer.
He awarded Mrs LUCY WHITE, 40, a decree nisi because of the unreasonable behaviour of her husband PAUL, 41.

e. **AMERICA'S most married man has broken his own record by marrying wife No. 26.**

f. 'I just don't know, but I feel good about this one.
'Anyway, getting married is better than living in adultery. Everyone should get married instead of living together,' he insisted.

g. As he left the wedding chapel in Las Vegas 75-year-old Glynn Wolfe confessed: 'Marriage is the greatest adventure in the world, next to death. It's fun.'
He said he had always been married. 'The faces just change.'

h. Tools were left all over the house, except for the bathroom. Apparently the husband did not leave them there because they would get rusty.

i. **Followed wife**
Mr Justice Ewbank said Mr White was also moody, sometimes for weeks at a time and jealous. At one stage he took to following his wife when she went out.

j. The couple married in 1966 and have two daughters, aged 12 and 10.

k. Christine refused to comment as her new husband criticised her eating habits.
The latest Mrs Wolfe, a divorcee with a grown-up daughter, has known her husband for 10 years. The couple do not plan to have a family.

l. Mr Wolfe, father of 40, admitted that he did not know how long his latest bride would last.
His longest marriage was four years, his shortest only 19 days.

m. He also complained about her visiting a woman neighbour, saying all she did there was to 'yacketty yak' and the proper place for her was at home with him and the family.

n. He had a word of warning for his 38-year-old wife, Christine. 'The only thing I don't like is that she eats sunflower seeds in bed.'

o. Mr Wolfe's other brides were aged from 17 to 72.
Four of his marriages involved two women whom he married, divorced, and remarried.

(Standard 30 January 1984 and Daily Telegraph 2 November 1984)

2 Write one of the following.

a. A dialogue between Lucy White and Paul White before their divorce. He has just begun to decorate the living-room.

b. A letter to the Agony Page of a magazine, asking for advice about your husband/wife/son/ daughter.
Compare her/his past behaviour with the present.

c. Argue the case for and against divorce.
Look at page 63 again to remind you how to present an argument.

● Language review

Present habit

1 **Present Simple**
The Present Simple is the most common tense for expressing *present habit*. It is often used with an adverb of frequency.
*He **always buys** me flowers on my birthday.*
*We **hardly ever go out** in the evening.*

2 **Present Continuous**
The *Present Continuous*, used with **always**, **continually** or **forever**, expresses an *annoying habit*.
*She's **always asking** people for money.*
*He's **forever losing** things. It makes me mad!*

3 **Will**
Will expresses *typical behaviour*, something that is to be expected from someone.
She'll get so interested in a book that she'll sit reading it all day.
He'll often begin a sentence and then forget what he's talking about.
In this use, **will** is not stressed when spoken, and can be contracted when written.

Past habit

1 **Used to + infinitive**
Used to expresses *habitual actions in the past* which do not happen now.
*We **used to** go to the same place for our holidays every year.*
Used to can be used to express past states and actions.
*Before he went to prison, he **used to** live in a large house.* (= a state)
*He **used to** have a lot of money.* (= a state)
*He **used to** gamble a lot.* (= an action)

2 **Would**
Would is the past form of **will** above.
It expresses *typical behaviour*.
*My grandfather **would** sit in his rocking chair for hours, looking into the fire and smoking his pipe.*
Would cannot be used to express a past state.
NOT
He'd live in a large house.
He'd have a lot of money.

◄ Look again at the article on page 84.
Find the examples of *present* and *past habit*.

► Grammar reference: page 122.

| Be/get used to | + gerund |
| | + noun |

This is completely different from **used to + infinitive**.
Here, **used** is an adjective, and means **accustomed**.

| *He's a builder, so he's **used** to* | *working in bad weather.* |
| | *physical work.* |

*When I arrived, it took me a long time to get **used** to the noise – but I'll never get **used** to the food!*

◄ Look at the tapescript on page 133-4.
Find the examples of **used to = accustomed to**.

► Grammar reference: page 122.

CONTROLLED PRACTICE

1 **Present Simple and expressions of frequency**
How often do you think the actions a.–h. happen?
Example
I always brush my teeth after a meal.
I brush my teeth three times a day.
Give your answers by using these expressions.

once	a day
twice	a week
three times	a month
	a year
every	day
	Sunday morning
	six months

a. We often go to the cinema.
b. We hardly ever eat out.
c. He goes to church regularly.
d. She occasionally plays tennis.
e. She often buys new clothes.
f. I go to the dentist regularly.
g. We usually have a bottle of wine with our supper.
h. I have my hair cut regularly.

2 Work in pairs.
Ask and answer questions about how often you do the actions in exercise 1.
Example
How often do you brush your teeth?
Twice a day, usually.

3 Present Continuous for annoying habits

Add a reason to each of the following statements, using a verb in the *Present Continuous*.

Example
You just can't trust Tim. *He's always letting you down.*

a. Peter's very absent-minded.
b. My flate-mate is impossible to live with.
c. Alice really gets on my nerves.
d. Andy is so embarrassing when he's had too much to drink.
e. Our teacher is awful!

4 Used to and would for past habits

Look at the following text.

As a boy, I *liked* going for long walks, especially on summer mornings. We *lived* in the country, and the hills behind our house were beautiful. I *got up* early, and without waking my parents, I *crept* out of the house. Once I *walked* for twenty miles, and my parents *got* very worried. We *had* a dog called Rex, and together we *climbed* the hills while the rest of the world was sleeping. I *loved* those days, so innocent, so carefree. I *went* back there last year; but it wasn't the same.

Which of the verbs in italics . . .
a. can take *would* or *used to*?
b. can take only *used to*?
c. must stay in the *Past Simple*?

Example
I liked going for long walks.
(b.) *I used to like going for long walks.*
because **like** is a state verb.

Now retell the story, using the *Past Simple*, *used to* or *would*.

5 **T.29** Listen to four people talking about their relationship with their parents.
As you listen, decide
a. if they are talking about the present or the past.
b. if the relationship was good or not.
How did you use to get on with your parents when you were younger?

6 Answer the following questions, using either **used to do** or **be/get used to**. Use short answers where appropriate.

Example
Do you play in the street with your friends?
No, but I used to.

Do you mind getting up at 6.00?
No, I'm used to it.

a. Where did you go on holiday when you were young?

b. Why do English people always stand in queues?

c. How did you find driving in England when you first arrived?

d. Does your mother read you a story before you go to bed?

e. Does Britain still have an empire?

f. It must be horrible to be a famous film star and have photographers following you everywhere.

g. What hobbies did you have when you were a child?

h. I wonder how people adapt to retirement after working all their lives.

7 Work in pairs.
Write a short dialogue.
Student A You have been living and working in New York for six months.
Student B You want to know how he/she has settled down.
Ask about accommodation/ work/travel/food/people.
Begin like this.
Student B How do you find living in New York? Do you like it?
Student A Yes, generally I do. At first . . .

REVISION

Time expressions

1 Imagine that today is Wednesday the 15th.

S	M	T	W	T	F	S
			1	2	3	4
5	6	7	8	9	10	11
12	13	14	(15)	16	17	18
19	20	21	22	23	24	25
26	27	28	29	30	31	

Give the day and the date for the following times:

a. the day before yesterday
b. the day after tomorrow
c. in a fortnight's time
d. a fortnight ago
e. this time next week
f. next weekend
g. the Friday after next
h. this time last week
i. a week last Thursday
j. a week tomorrow
k. by the end of the week.

2 Write a sentence to illustrate the meaning of the following:

– in time
– on time
– two times two
– from time to time
– Take your time!
– a waste of time
– in record time.

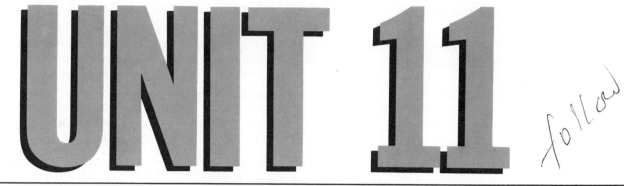

Hypothesis

It's easy to be wise after the event

● Discussion point

1 The following extracts are taken from the *Book of Heroic Failures*. What were the criminals' mistakes?
What should/shouldn't they have done?
Why?

The Least Successful Mugging   1

In 1978 Sussex police launched a hunt for a 'six-foot, dark-haired youth of about 20' who failed to mug a five-foot, 74-year-old grandmother.

The youth sprang upon Mrs Ethel West while she was walking through Chichester Cathedral cloisters. The result should have been a foregone conclusion. Surprisingly, however, when Mrs West grabbed the mugger's wrist, he cried, 'Oh God! Oh no! Stop!'

Encouraged by these pleas, she put him in an arm lock at which the mugger cried, 'Oh no, Oh Christ!' and ran away.

'If I hadn't been carrying my shopping, I would really have put him on his back,' said Mrs West who took a course in judo when younger.

'Before my husband died I used to practise throwing him at Christmas,' she explained.

The Worst Bank Robbers   2

In August 1975 three men were on their way in to rob the Royal Bank of Scotland at Rothesay, when they got stuck in the revolving doors. They had to be helped free by the staff and, after thanking everyone, sheepishly left the building.

A few minutes later they returned and announced their intention of robbing the bank, but none of the staff believed them. When, at first, they demanded £5,000, the head cashier laughed at them, convinced that it was a practical joke.

Considerably disheartened by this, the gang leader reduced his demand first to £500 then to £50 and ultimately to 50 pence. By this stage the cashier could barely control herself for laughter.

Then one of the men jumped over the counter and fell awkwardly on the floor, clutching at his ankle. The other two made their getaway, but got trapped in the revolving doors for a second time, desperately pushing the wrong way.

The Least Successful Bank Robber   3

Not wishing to attract attention to himself, a bank robber in 1969 at Portland, Oregon, wrote all his instructions on a piece of paper rather than shout.

'This is a hold-up and I've got a gun,' he wrote and then held the paper up for the cashier to read.

The bemused bank official waited while he wrote out, 'Put all the money in a paper bag.'

This message was pushed through the grille. The cashier read it and then wrote on the bottom, 'I don't have a paper bag,' and passed it back.

The robber fled.

The Least Alert Burglar   4

A Parisian villain broke into a house at the village of Lachelle in 1964. Once inside he began to feel decidedly peckish and so went in search of the icebox. There he found his favourite cheese which it would have been a shame not to try.

He then found some Bath Oliver biscuits and three bottles of champagne.

After a while he began to feel sleepy and decided that he would lie down and digest his meal in comfort. He was arrested next morning fast asleep upstairs in the spare bedroom.

The Worst Hijacker   5

We shall never know the identity of the man who in 1976 made the most unsuccessful hijack attempt ever. On a flight across America, he rose from his seat, drew a gun and took the stewardess hostage.

'Take me to Detroit,' he said.

'We're already going to Detroit,' she replied.

'Oh . . . good,' he said, and sat down again.

2 Work in groups.
Discuss the following questions.
Which story is funniest?

Which criminal was . . .
– the most stupid?
– the worst prepared?
– the most cowardly?
– the most unprofessional?

What do you think of the way the victims of the crimes behaved?

What would you have done if you had been the cashier/the old lady/ the stewardess?

Reading

Pre-reading task

Work in groups.
What do you think the following people might regret about their lives?

– someone who left school at 15
– a boy doing National Service
– a workaholic
– a millionaire

Reading and inferring

In the *Sunday Express Magazine*, there used to be a feature called *Things I wish I'd known at 18*, in which famous people were invited to look back on their life and comment on their successes and failures.
In this article, there is some quite colloquial language.

written off   dismissed

an oddball   a strange person who doesn't fit in

a back-to-back   a terraced house for working class people

daft   stupid, mad

nowt but a lad   just a young man

As you read the article about Jack Higgins, answer the following questions.

1 Was he happy when he was . . . 15? 18? 31? 42 (in 1971)?
Why? Why not?

2 Is he happy now? Why? Why not?

Glossary

Room at the Top
This, and another play by John Osborne called *Look Back in Anger*, is about the rebellion of youth against society and its conventions.

repertory company
a theatrical company that performs different kinds of plays, musicals, comedies, etc., usually at its own theatre.

an ego trip
(informal) something a person does, purely out of self-interest, to make himself/herself important.

IQ
intelligence quotient, a measure of an individual's intelligence, derived from a series of tests.

Mensa
a society for the exceptionally intelligent. You need to have an IQ of at least 150 to join.

THINGS I WISH I'D KNOWN AT 18

Jack Higgins left school at 15, later became a teacher, then a university tutor before succeeding as a writer and becoming a millionaire. *The Eagle Has Landed* appears next month in its original unabridged form. A new hardback, *Touch the Devil*, comes out in October. Higgins also writes under his real name, Harry Patterson. He lives, in much luxury, in Jersey. Here he talks to Pamela Coleman.

JACK HIGGINS

I WISH I HAD known at 18 somebody like I am now at 53, an older person with hard-won wisdom to whom I could have gone for advice.

As a teenager, I was written off as an oddball. Coming from the docks of Belfast and living in a back-to-back in Leeds I was thought of as 'Daft Harry' because of my obsession about becoming a writer. I had pretensions to being a kind of Ernest Hemingway. I wish I'd known my limitations.

I wish I had known that you are capable of anything at 18. I was a teenager in the days before teenagers were invented — when it was a handicap to be young. You were 'nowt but a lad', held back because you were only 18, 20 or whatever. There were no pop singers speaking for younger people then. It was before John Braine, who's a friend of mine, wrote *Room at the Top*, before the Angry Young Man thing took off.

Getting a safe job, earning a steady wage — that was the philosophy of life. It was a philosophy based on parents' attitudes. So I went into a succession of boring clerical jobs. I wish I hadn't wasted my energies in so many directions before I finally got to grips with writing.

I wish, for instance, I'd had the guts to try to become an actor. I was quite good, I used to act at the Civic Theatre in Leeds as an amateur and longed to try my luck with a seaside repertory company. But when I talked about it to friends — who were all office workers, factory workers, shop workers — they'd say: 'Ooh no.'

I wish I'd known at 18 that other people's opinions were nothing like as important as I thought they were. For me it's what I think that's important, and I don't mean that in an arrogant way. In writing, for example, I had to learn to trust my own judgment. For years I earned modest sums and my first real break didn't come till 1971, with a thriller called *The Savage Day*, based on the Irish Troubles. Everyone I told thought it was a terrible idea for a book, but I went ahead and wrote it. It got to number ten in the best-seller list without any fanfare of publicity.

When I suggested writing about Winston Churchill spending a quiet weekend in the country when German paratroopers drop in to kidnap him, my publisher said it was the worst idea he'd ever heard. I was terribly shaken. But I was so hooked on the idea, I persisted. That was *The Eagle Has Landed*, which created publishing history.

Because I left school at 15 with no School Certificate I thought I was a failure, but I think now that being a school drop-out was probably a good thing. It made me an instinctive writer. I think too much education can be a disadvantage. Universities are full of professors and academics who want to write but can't. I wish I'd known that at 18. When I pulled Dostoevsky's *The House of the Dead* off a library shelf as a lad I read it simply because I enjoyed the story, not because I'd been told to read it.

But at 18 I longed for a piece of paper that said I was intelligent. I got it eventually when I was 31 after taking a double honours degree through night-school and correspondence courses. It didn't mean much, apart from improving my career prospects. I became a lecturer in a polytechnic and finally a tutor at Leeds University. It was an ego trip more than anything else. Recently I had my IQ tested — it's 147, just short of Mensa. I realised that the truth was, I always was a clever idiot who didn't fit into the system and whom the system didn't recognise.

At 18 I went into the Horse Guards on National Service and was stationed in Berlin. The Cold War had just started and we had to patrol the borders. Occasionally a shot was fired — a close friend of mine was shot in the stomach and died at my side.

For me life has been a disappointment in general terms, which may sound surprising. I thank God for my wife, Amy, and four marvellous kids, but life is life, in spite of success. The total sales of my books are now well over 100 million. When *Eagle* was number one in England and number one in America, I never thought my success would continue. Since then I've had six more number ones. I've climbed my personal Everest. And so what? I realise I've been driven by a terrible desire to achieve. That desire made me a workaholic. I didn't have time for hobbies, so now that I do I find there's nothing I really want to do. I tried karate for a year and thought 'What am I doing this for?' Then I tried being very healthy and running everywhere and weight-lifting.

These days I get invited to Buckingham Palace garden parties and lunch with Princess Margaret and to talk to Prime Ministers. I feel as though it's all a mistake.

So what? is a phrase that has figured rather largely in my life. I'm glad I didn't know at 18 that when you've got to the top of the peak you're left with an emptiness.

(Sunday Express 29 August 1982)

Comprehension check

1 Put the following events of Jack Higgins' life into chronological order.
You will have to guess when some of the events happened.

He ☐ was a tutor at university.
☐ became a millionaire.
☐ lived in Belfast.
☐ did several clerical jobs.
☐ started writing.
☐ acted in Leeds.
☐ wrote *The Eagle Has Landed*.
☐ got a degree.
☐ did National Service.

2 What are some of the things he wishes he had done/he hadn't done/he had known when he was younger?

What do you think?

1 Work in groups.
Explain what he means by the following:
line 15   I was a teenager in the days before teenagers were invented.
line 48   In writing . . . I had to learn to trust my own judgement.
line 66   *The Eagle Has Landed* created publishing history.
line 80   I read (*The House of the Dead*) simply because I enjoyed the story, not because I'd been told to read it.
line 88   It didn't mean much.
line 111 . . . life is life, in spite of success.
line 117 I've climbed my personal Everest.
line 132 I feel as though it's all a mistake.
line 134 So what? is a phrase that has figured rather largely in my life.

2 Which of the following adjectives describe Jack Higgins?

arrogant   home-loving
snobbish   disillusioned
self-confident boastful
hard-working   self-made
wise   cynical
proud

3 Find a word or expression in the article that means the same as the following.

para. 2 a persistent idea
para. 3 a disadvantage
para. 4 worked hard at and was successful in
para. 5 had the courage
         wanted very much
para. 6 lucky opportunity
         shocked, troubled
         obsessed by, addicted to
para. 7 a person who does not finish a course of study
para. 8 chances of professional advancement

▶ **Language focus**

Read the *Language review* on **should have** and **wish** on page 97.
Do the *Controlled practice* exercises 1–3.

Speaking

Paradoxes

1 Work in groups.
Jack Higgins is a millionaire who lives in great luxury.
Which aspects of his life do you envy?
Do you wish you could stop work for ever?

2 Make two lists.
What are the advantages and disadvantages of being rich and famous?

Advantages

Disadvantages

3 Jack Higgins is an example of someone who is very rich, but also in a way, he is poor.
Explain the following paradoxes.

Is it possible . . .
– for a poor person to be rich?
– for a wise man to be a fool?
– for a genius to be slightly mad?
– for a child to express a great truth?
– to feel free in prison?
– to feel imprisoned when you're not in prison?
– to feel lonely in a crowd of people?
– to be kind by being cruel?
– to be cruel by being kind?
– to love someone, but not to like them?
– to not lie, but not tell the truth?

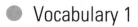

Vocabulary 1

Driving

1 Work in pairs.
Write down all the instructions for starting a car and moving off.
Begin like this.
Unlock the door and get in.
Put the key in the ignition and . . .

2 Read your instructions to another student.
He/she must mime the actions.

3 Look at the picture.
How many traffic offences are being committed?

4 What kinds of road are the following?
What can/can't you do on them?
  a dual carriageway
  a one-way street
  a cul-de-sac
  a by-pass
  a flyover

5 When driving, why would you . . .
– dip your lights?
– flash your lights?
– do a U-turn?
– sound your horn?
– swerve?
– slam on your brakes?

Listening

Pre-listening task

Discuss the following questions in groups.
What does the driving test consist of in your country?
Is there a written test?
What manoeuvres do you have to carry out in the test?
Do people often pass first time?

Listening and form filling

T.30 You will hear a conversation between Jill, who has just taken her driving test, and her husband Bob. Jill failed the test.
As you listen, complete the form as the examiner would do.
Put ✕ in the relevant boxes and underline the relevant phrases.

Example
4 ✕ *Make proper use of/*
accelerator/clutch/gears/
footbrake/handbrake/steering.

Department of Transport Road Traffic Act 1972   Test Centre: _____

Statement of Failure to Pass Test of Competence to Drive

Name _____

has this day been examined and has failed to pass the test of competence to drive prescribed for the purposes of section 85 of the Road Traffic Act 1972.

Date _____

Authorised by the Minister of Transport to conduct tests

Examiners have regard to the items listed below in deciding whether a candidate is competent to drive. The matters needing special attention are marked for your information and assistance and should be studied in detail.

1. ☐ Comply with the requirements of the eyesight test.
2. ☐ Know the Highway Code.
3. ☐ Take proper precautions before starting the engine.
4. ☐ Make proper use of/accelerator/clutch/gears/footbrake/handbrake/steering.
5. ☐ Move away/safely/under control.
6. ☐ Stop the vehicle in an emergency/promptly/under control/making proper use of front brake.
7. ☐ Reverse into a limited opening either to the right or left/under control/with due regard for other road users.
8. ☐ Turn round by means of forward and reverse gears/under control/with due regard for other road users.
9. ☐ Make effective use of mirror(s) and take effective rear observation well before signalling/changing direction/slowing down or stopping.
10. ☐ Give signals/where necessary/correctly/in good time.
11. ☐ Take prompt and appropriate action on all/traffic signs/road markings/traffic lights/signals given by traffic controllers/other road users.
12. ☐ Exercise proper care in the use of speed.
13. ☐ Make progress by/driving at a speed appropriate to the road and traffic conditions/avoiding undue hesitancy.
14. ☐ Act properly at road junctions: —
  – regulate speed correctly on approach;
  – take effective observation before emerging;
  – position the vehicle correctly/before turning right/before turning left;
  – avoid cutting right-hand corners.
15. ☐ Overtake/meet/cross the path of/other vehicles safely.
16. ☐ Position the vehicle correctly during normal driving.
17. ☐ Allow adequate clearance to stationary vehicles.
18. ☐ Take appropriate action at pedestrian crossings.
19. ☐ Select a safe position for normal stops.
20. ☐ Show awareness and anticipation of the actions of/pedestrians/cyclists/drivers.

What do you think?

1 Do you think Jill deserved to pass? Why/why not?
2 What advice would you give her for her next test?
3 Did you pass your driving test first time? Second time?
  If you failed, what went wrong?

▶ **Language focus**

Read the *Language review* on **Third conditional** sentences on page 97. Do the *Controlled practice* exercises 4–7.

● Vocabulary 2

Formal style

1 The *Statement of Failure* to pass a driving test is written in formal language.
  This is how some of the sentences might be spoken in a more neutral style. Match them to the correct number of the *Statement*.
  Example
  [1] You have to have good eyesight.
  a. ☐ When you're backing, look to see if there's anybody in your way.
  b. ☐ Look behind you.
  c. ☐ Don't drive too fast.
  d. ☐ You should slow down when you get near a junction.
  e. ☐ You should look in both directions before pulling out.
  f. ☐ Don't go too close to parked cars.
  g. ☐ Keep your eyes on other people around you.

2 For the following examples of formal style, say
  – what the context is.
  – how it might be expressed in a more neutral style.
  a. Diners are requested to refrain from smoking in this section of the restaurant.
  b. Please vacate this seat should an elderly or infirm person require it.
  c. Should the goods not meet with your entire satisfaction, please

return them stating date and place of purchase, and we will gladly refund you.
  d. In the event of fire, proceed to the nearest exit point.
  e. In a recent correspondence, I drew your attention to the fact that your current account was overdrawn by £520.57p, and you were requested to draw no more cheques on this account. In your reply, you suggested that you were attempting to restore your account to credit.

  It was with some surprise, therefore, that I find you have used your cash card, when you are fully aware that you have no funds in your account to meet it.

  I should be grateful if you would refrain from using this and from drawing cheques until this situation has been regularized.

3 Work in pairs.
  Student A You received the above letter from your bank manager. You have come to talk to her/him. Explain the situation, and what you intend to do about it.
  Student B You are Student A's bank manager. You sent her/him the above letter.
  Explain how the bank can help, and the bank's requirements.

● Writing

Sentence combination

Combine the following sentences to form a coherent biography of Ernest Hemingway. Reorder the information if necessary. Divide it into paragraphs.

Ernest Hemingway was born in 1899.
He was born in Illinois.
Illinois is a suburb of Chicago.
He had a middle-class upbringing.
His father was a doctor.
All his life Ernest Hemingway rebelled against the morals of his parents.
He rebelled against the conventions of life in Chicago.
He graduated from High School in 1917.

He didn't go to college.
He was impatient for a less sheltered environment.
He went to Kansas City.
He was employed as a reporter.
He was a reporter for the *Star*.
The *Star* was a leading newspaper.
Working for the *Star* gave him invaluable vocational training.
He wanted to be a soldier.
He was rejected for military service.
He had poor eyesight.
He became an ambulance driver for the American Red Cross.
He was injured in World War I.
He was decorated for heroism.
He was fascinated by war.
He worked as a war correspondent.
He reported wars in Spain, China and Europe.
Many of his books were about war.
For Whom the Bell Tolls was written in 1940.
It was his most successful book.
It was about a volunteer American soldier in the Spanish Civil War.
It dealt with the comradeship of war.
A Farewell to Arms is about the pointlessness of war.
He won the Nobel prize for literature in 1954.
He suffered from depression towards the end of his life.
He loved life, but was obsessed with death.
He committed suicide in 1961.

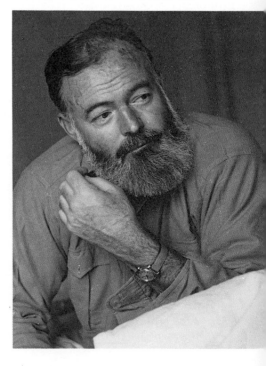

Language review
Hypothesis

Should + perfect infinitive

Should have done expresses *advice*, *obligation* or *criticism* about a past action.

*You **should have worked** harder for the exam.*
*You **shouldn't have said** that. It wasn't true.*
*She **should have been helping** me, instead of lying in bed.*

Wish

What we wish is always contrary to existing facts.
To show this unreality, the verb moves *one tense back*.
See the chart opposite.

◄ Look again at the article on page 93.
Find the examples of **wish**.

Third conditional sentences

Third conditional sentences express *imaginary situations about the past*. Like **wish**, they are contrary to the facts.

Fact
I didn't work hard.
I failed the exam.

Imaginary past
If I had worked hard, . . .
. . . I would have passed the exam.

*She **would have felt** more relaxed if the examiner **had been** nicer.*
*If she **had driven** more carefully, she **might have** passed.*

◄ Look at the tapescript on page 134. Find the examples of the *third conditional*.

► **Grammar reference:** page 123.

Fact	Wish
I'm fat.	*I wish I **wasn't** fat.*
I don't have any friends.	*I wish I **had** some friends.*
I didn't work for the exam.	*I wish I **had worked** for the exam.*
I can't swim.	*I wish I **could** swim.*
I've lost my pen.	*I wish I **hadn't lost** my pen.*
He won't help me.	*I wish **he'd help** me.*

CONTROLLED PRACTICE

1 Wish
The following sentences express some of Jack Higgins' regrets about his past and present life. Rewrite them using **I wish**.

Example
I listened to other people's advice.
I wish I hadn't listened to other people's advice.

a. My parents made me get a safe job.
b. I didn't try to become a professional actor.
c. I wasn't encouraged to be a writer.
d. I had to do National Service.
e. I'm a workaholic.
f. I find life disappointing.
g. I don't have any hobbies.
h. I can't be a member of Mensa.

2 Wish and **should have**
Write one sentence with **I wish** and one sentence with **should/ shouldn't have** for the following situations.

Example
I've got no job and no qualifications.
I wish I had a job.
I should have worked harder at school.

a. I've got a terrible hangover this morning.
b. And I crashed the car last night.
c. I've got to go to court next week because I forgot to pay a parking fine.
d. My wife has left me.
e. And I'm late for work.

3 Dialogues
Work in pairs to write a dialogue.

Student A Life is getting too much for you. Nothing is going right. Share your troubles with **Student B**.

Student B Lend a sympathetic ear to **Student A** and offer some advice.

4 Third conditional sentences
Re-arrange the following words to form *third conditional sentences*.

a. If/more/she/been/would/ confident/have/had/she/passed.
b. If/she/nervous/been/hadn't/ would/let/the/remembered/ handbrake/to/she/have/off.
c. She/skidded/lost/have/control/ hadn't/wouldn't/if/she.
d. If/names/had/she/the/number-plate/have/read/the/cars/known/ could/she/of/the.
e. The/put/wouldn't/brakes/ examiner/more/had/if/have/ been/she/paying/on/attention/ the.

5 Here are some facts about the past.
Use your imagination to say how things would/could/might have been different.

Example
I didn't get the job.
If I'd answered the questions better, I would have got the job.
If I'd been smartly dressed, I might have got it.

a. President Kennedy was assassinated in Dallas.
b. I wasn't staying in the hotel where the bomb went off.

c. I met my wife at a party.
d. I lost the tennis match.
e. Luckily, she wasn't on the hijacked aircraft.

6 What would you have done in the following situations?

Example
Yesterday a man came home to find a burglar in his house. He attacked the burglar, who hit him over the head and fractured his skull.
I wouldn't have attacked him. I'd have let him go.
I wouldn't. I'd have made a noise to frighten him.
I'd have phoned the police and tried to lock him in the house.

a. A man found a wallet with £1,000 in it in the back of a taxi. He put it all on a horse and lost.
b. A mother found drugs in her son's pockets. She told the police, who arrested the son. The son was sent to prison.
c. A boy died in a fire at his home, as he tried to rescue his pet dog.
d. A man was served in a restaurant by a very rude waiter, but he didn't complain. He just didn't leave a tip.
e. A fifty-year old man was made redundant. He tried for six months to find another job, but he couldn't. He felt so ashamed that he committed suicide.

7 **Gap filling**
T.31   Listen to the conversation of a couple in a restaurant, and fill in the gaps.

A Did you enjoy that, darling?

B Yes, not bad. _____, and I don't think the pastry was quite cooked enough.

A Well, you _____. The chicken was lovely. And that dessert, the Chef's surprise, was delicious. You really _____, Gerald.

B Don't nag, please. My _____. I wish _____ pudding. Talking

of surprises, I'm dreading what _____. Did you look at the prices?

A Gerald, this is our _____. Of course I didn't. You _____ we came in.

B Could we have the bill, please?

C Certainly, sir.

A There's no point in worrying about the bill now. It _____ if we'd _____ a house wine, but no, you had to have champagne.

C Your bill, sir.

B Thank you. Oh no! I _____ .

REVISION

Sentence stress

1 In the following dialogues, mark where the main stress is in B's replies.

Example
A *You look tired.*
B *I am tired.*

a. A Did you give Peter his book back?
   B I thought you'd given it to him.
b. A I sold my old tennis racket to Peter.
   B I thought you'd given it to him.
c. A That's Sylvia over there. She's French.
   B I thought she was French.
d. A What a brilliant idea of mine this is!
   B I thought of it first.
e. A Do you work for Jeremy?
   B No, he works for me.
f. A What was Jeremy doing in your office?
   B He works for me.
g. A Did you enjoy your steak and chips?
   B The chips were nice.

2 **Emphatic/do/does/did**
Look at the dialogue.

A You don't love me any more.
B I *do* love you!

Notice that in the *Present Simple* and *Past Simple*, **do/does/did** is added for *emphasis*. Other tenses already have auxiliary verbs which are stressed.
Reply to the following sentences.

a. You don't work very hard, do you?
b. Why didn't you do your homework last night?
c. Your teacher never arrives on time.
d. Why doesn't the teacher correct your homework?
e. You'd learn quickly if you spoke English in class.

3 **Correcting people**
T.32   You will hear a tape about Jack Higgins that contains factual mistakes.
When your hear one, tell your teacher to stop the tape.
Correct the mistake.

Example
Jack Higgins lives in New York.

*He doesn't live in **New York**.*

*He lives in **Jersey**.*

He doesn't write novels.

*He **does** write novels*

4 Write some sentences that contain factual mistakes about people in your class.
Read them out for the other students to correct.

UNIT 12

Articles

Time

● Discussion point

HOW'S YOUR TIMING?

Answer the questions to see how efficiently you use your time. Circle a. b. c. or d.

1 **How would you describe the pace of your life in general?**
a. Natural. I just let things happen.
b. Quite fast, but I do stop to smell the flowers.
c. Sometimes frantic, sometimes relaxed.
d. Demanding, sometimes non-stop, but I like it that way.

2 **How do you deal with what you have to do every day?**
a. I do first what attracts me most.
b. I do the most important things and put off the rest.
c. There always seems to be too much or too little. I do what's really urgent.
d. I deal with things in order of importance.

3 **Which of the following is nearest to your philosophy on life?**
a. Go where life takes you.
b. Life is not a dress rehearsal.
c. To everything there is a season.
d. Do it now.

4 **What do you feel about punctuality?**
a. I don't waste energy worrying about being on time.
b. Being on time is polite and efficient, and I try to be that way.
c. I'd love to arrive on time in theory, but I don't often manage it.
d. I'm always on time, and I get furious with people who are late.

Based on copyright material by Celia Brayfield

5 **How many things have you begun and not finished in the last few years?**
a. Lots of things. I have sudden enthusiasms and then drop them.
b. One or two minor things, but not too many.
c. Quite a few. I always seem to get distracted.
d. There are no uncompleted projects in my life — I have always finished things.

6 **How do you like to spend your leisure time?**
a. I don't know what to do with my time off — it just slips away.
b. I relax and recharge my batteries, and maybe follow a sport or interest.
c. I do one or two little jobs, but nothing very energetic. This is my most enjoyable occupation.
d. I don't have any leisure time. All my time is put to good use.

Interpretation

Mostly a. answers

You're a daydreamer. Did you actually manage to finish the quiz? You have little control over your life. Chaos is your natural habitat. Perhaps you tell yourself that this is creative, but the truth is you hate discipline and you are frightened of it. Your abilities remain untested and your dreams unfulfilled.

Mostly b. answers

You represent balance. Your ability to manage time is impressive, but you respect yourself enough to know when to relax, and you are clever enough to know that the best decisions are never made in an atmosphere of pressure. Deadlines don't worry you, and your work seldom puts unbearable demands on you. You look ahead and make sure crises don't happen.

Mostly c. answers

You're like Cinderella waiting for a fairy godmother who's going to make time for all your dreams and so make everything alright for you. 'I'll get round to it,' you tell yourself. What you don't tell yourself is that you alone can provide the time you need to start those dreams happening. You are an expert at putting things off for the best reasons. Your excuses are endless. Forget them. The right time is *now*.

Mostly d. answers

You are an achiever. Superman/superwoman is your middle name. You certainly know how to get a job done, and you are proud of your management of time. You are compulsive about using every second of the day to good effect, and you get irritable with people who take life at a slower pace. Relax a little. Stress is a killer, remember?

Based on copyright material by Celia Brayfield

100

Reading

Pre-reading task

What ideas do the following graffiti express?

Reading and predicting

The following article by Ray Connolly appeared in a London newspaper. Read the first two paragraphs.

Which of the following ideas and topics do you expect the article to mention?

a. You should take up a sport before it is too late.
b. Graffiti.
c. Interpreting your dreams.
d. Enjoy life now.
e. How to use your time creatively.
f. Don't put off till tomorrow what you can do today.
g. Don't do today what you can put off till tomorrow.
h. Life is short and sad.
i. Buying a house.

As you read the rest of the article, answer the true/false questions. Put T or F into the boxes.

1 ☐ According to the author, we don't live for the present.
2 ☐ The author has learned to live life for today.
3 ☐ People don't live for the present because they are afraid of failure.
4 ☐ Real Life begins when you have a home and family.
5 ☐ The author likes the American saying 'Have a nice day'.
6 ☐ The journalist left the *Daily Telegraph* for a better paid job.
7 ☐ His life was richer as a result.
8 ☐ The author is very envious of this man.
9 ☐ The author thinks that life goes by very quickly.

What do you think?

1 Look again at the interpretation of the quiz on page 100.
What sort of person does Ray Connolly think most people are?
What sort of person does he suggest we should be?
2 What does the journalist who left the *Daily Telegraph* have in common with Thomas Wilson, the character in Somerset Maugham's story *The Lotus Eater*?

Pipe dreams. . . . Will you really take up that pastime when you "get promotion"?

It isn't a rehearsal, you know

Returning with a message for dreamers . . .

SEVERAL YEARS ago while sheltering from a typhoon in a sleazy motel in Cincinnati I came across a tattered beer-stained notice pinned to a wall above a public telephone. It read simply:
5 'This isn't a rehearsal. This is Life. don't miss it.'

It was a message which has ghosted through my life ever since. How many of us can honestly claim not to have mortgaged our lives to some future dream, a
10 dream which as likely as not will never be realised?

We live life on the never-never: telling ourselves that just as soon as we have got past this or that particularly onerous chore or stage we will be able to devote our energies to what we really want to do.
15 I must admit to being a master of the art of the never-never. Daily I say to myself that as soon as I have finished this or that script, or article or paid off my overdraft, then I will really start to live.

It is, I believe, a delusion I share with the great
20 hopeful majority, and a delusion it is dangerous to harbour, because each of us knows that tomorrow never comes.

Ambition

For some I suspect that this life-long planning for the future is a way of procrastinating: a get-out for not
25 having the will, talent or nerve for trying something new and discovering oneself to be a failure.

How many people have I met who have told me about the book they have been planning to write but have never yet found the time? Far too many.
30 This is Life, all right, but we do treat it like a rehearsal and, unhappily, we do miss so many of its best moments.

We take jobs to stay alive and provide homes for our families always convincing ourselves that this style of
35 life is merely a temporary state of affairs along the road to what we really want to do. Then, at 60 or 65,

we are suddenly presented with a clock and a couple of grandchildren and we look back and realise that all those years waiting for Real Life to come along were
40 in fact real life.

In America they have a saying much ridiculed by the English: 'Have a nice day' they intone in their shops, hotels and sandwich bars. I think it is a wonderful phrase, reminding us, in effect, to enjoy
45 the moment: to appreciate this very day.

How often do we say to ourselves, 'I'll take up horse-riding (or golf, or sailing) as soon as I get promotion,' only to do none of those things when promotion comes.
50 When I first became a journalist I knew a man who gave up a very well paid responsible job at the Daily Telegraph to go and edit a small weekly newspaper. At the time I was astonished by what appeared to me to be his complete mental aberration. How could
55 anyone turn his back on Fleet Street for the parish pump? I wanted to know.

Now I am a little older and possibly wiser, I see the sense in it. In Fleet Street the man was under continual pressure. He lived in an unattractive
60 London suburb and he spent much of his life sitting on Southern Region trains.

Lucky

In Kent he became his own boss, lived within minutes of the office in a very pretty village and found his life enriched tenfold. His ambition for
65 advancement in his career had been smothered by his enjoyment of the life he was leading. His life had stopped being a rehearsal and become the real thing.

I am not suggesting that this would suit every one of us. Unhappily it would not suit me. But in many ways
70 I consider that man in Kent to be one of the luckiest chaps I know.

I am not advocating that one should live for the minute in any hedonistic sense. That isn't the answer. But it is, I hope, an exhortation to some degree of self-
75 fulfilment. Whatever you want to do, do it now: because, no matter how old you are, it's later than you think.

(Standard 14 May 1984)

101

3 What is the difference between *Real Life* (with capital letters) and *real life*? Go back to the paragraph to read the context.

4 Read the article again and mark it like this.
✓ I agree. This is true for me.
✗ I don't agree. I'm not like this.
? I don't understand the point he's making.

5 What are your short-term and long-term ambitions?
Do you think they stop you enjoying real life?

6 What is your motto for life?

Summary

Work in pairs to complete the following summary.

The author's main point is that _____

_____

_____

_____

He thinks we fail to live for the

present because _____

_____

_____

_____

When we are old, we suddenly

realize that _____

_____

_____

_____

He quotes the example of a man who

_____

_____

_____

_____

_____

▶ **Language focus**

Read the *Language review* on page 107.
Do the *Controlled practice* exercises.

● Vocabulary 1

Multi-word verbs (3)
Replace the words in italics in the following sentences with a word from column **A** combined with a word from column **B**. Put the verb in the correct tense.

A	B
come	over
break	off
take	up
cut	back
hold	down
build	away

a. Talks between both sides of the lorry drivers' strike *ended in failure* yesterday.
b. Janet Mannering *returned* to the London stage last night, and gave a wonderful performance as Desdemona.
c. Ford, the American motor company, have *bought* the British motorcycle company, Hansards, in a fifty million pound deal.
d. The waiter *removed* the dirty plates.
e. The aeroplane *left the ground* smoothly.
f. The Government is *reducing* the number of people employed in the Health Service.
g. The Super Powers are *increasing* their stocks of nuclear weapons.
h. Sorry we're late. We were *delayed* in the traffic.

Nouns from multi-word verbs
There are many *nouns* which are formed with a verb + adverb/ preposition.

Example
There was a **break-in** *at the factory last night, and some money was stolen.*
Harold Minter won the fight with a **knock-out** *in the second round.*

The majority of these words are joined with a hyphen. Some are one word.

Example
The robbers escaped to a secret **hideaway** *in the country.*

The stress is always on the first word.

Complete the following sentences with a noun formed from the multi-word verbs in columns A & B.

a. Most plane crashes occur during _____ or landing.
b. At the age of 35, Frank Haggler made a _____ last night, and regained the heavyweight championship of the world at Wembley Stadium.
c. Shall we eat out tonight or get a Chinese _____ ?
d. If you have a _____ while driving on a motorway, it can be very expensive to get your car repaired.
e. _____ in teaching staff have meant that the student-teacher ratio has increased.
f. There was a _____ on the Underground yesterday because of a temporary power failure.
g. The City pages of daily newspapers are full of stories about company mergers and

_____ .

h. Before the war broke out, there was a steady _____ of tension, as each side accused the other of atrocities.

● Speaking

Periods in world history

1 Work in groups.
Look at the pictures opposite. Match the pictures with a period or event in history.

2 If time travel were possible, which period of world history would you like to return to? Why? How far into the future would you like to travel?
What would you hope to see?

3 On your time travels, you can take five objects to show people what life is like towards the end of the twentieth century.
What five objects would you take? Try to agree as a class on five objects that typify this period in world history.

PERIODS IN
WORLD HISTORY

2000 BC

500 BC → 0 → 476

BIRTH OF JESUS CHRIST

BIRTH OF MUHAMMAD, FOUNDER OF ISLAM

DISCOVERY OF AMERICA BY
CHRISTOPHER COLUMBUS

ANCIENT CHINESE CIVILIZATION

ROMAN EMPIRE

EGYPTIAN EMPIRE

BRITISH EMPIRE

NAPOLEONIC ERA

COLONIZATION OF AFRICA BY
EUROPEAN COUNTRIES

COLONIZATION OF SOUTH AMERICA BY
EUROPEAN COUNTRIES

RUSSIAN REVOLUTION

3000 BC

570

1492

1917

16TH CENTURY

18/19TH CENTURY

Listening

Pre-listening task

You will hear an interview with Margaret Thatcher, who became leader of the Conservative Party in Britain in 1975, and who became Britain's first woman Prime Minister. In the interview she talks about her interest in Victorian times.

Work in two groups.

Group A

Complete the chart with some facts and opinions about Mrs Thatcher.

Facts

Opinions

Group B

Complete the chart with some facts and opinions about Victorian times in Britain.

Facts

Opinions

When you have finished, swap your information.

Listening for information

T.33 Listen to the interview. Are any of the points you listed mentioned in the interview?

Comprehension check

1 What are the Victorian values that Mrs Thatcher admires?
2 What aspects of Victorian times does the interviewer mention?
3 Mrs Thatcher believes in private enterprise, and the non-intervention of the state. What examples from Victorian times does she quote that support this view?
4 What are the advantages that Mrs Thatcher sees in home ownership?
5 What, according to the interviewer, is it that the 'have-nots' cannot do?

What do you think?

1 From what Mrs Thatcher says, what do you think her attitude is to the following issues?
– the National Health Service
– law and order
– borrowing money
– unemployment
– inflation
2 What are the views and policies of the main political parties in your country?

● Writing

1 **Linking devices**
Put one of the following *linking devices* into each gap.
There are sixteen words, but only twelve gaps!

first	until
during	still
next	while
finally	at last
meanwhile	instead
actually	afterwards
at first	after
naturally	fortunately

The day we moved house was one of the busiest days of my life. It was in December. (a) _____, we had been packing for a long time, but there was (b) _____ an awful lot of work to do on the actual day. (c) _____, everything went smoothly. The removal men arrived and began loading their van. (d) _____ they were emptying room after room, my wife and I were trying to clean up. We hardly noticed the fact that it had begun to snow. Then things began to go wrong. (e) _____ a valuable table was dropped and its leg broke. (f) _____ we lost the baby, and it was not (g) _____ she started to cry that we realized she had been put into the van by mistake. We worked hard all morning, and by midday our old house was empty. (h) _____, it continued to snow. We set off on the journey to our new house, driving slowly to avoid skidding in the icy conditions. We (i) _____ arrived at four o'clock, by which time it was dark, and three feet of snow covered the ground. (j) _____, we had quite a few people to help us unload, and by six o'clock we were in. (k) _____, we wondered how we had managed to do everything. I'll never forget that day. (l) _____, I still have nightmares about it!

2 Write an essay about a time in your life that is important to you. The time might be significant for any reason – because you liked or hated it; because of your profession; because of a relationship; or because it was a turning point in your life.

● Vocabulary 2

The words practised in the following two exercises are contained in a poem you will read.

1 When you look up a word in the dictionary, you sometimes might not be able to understand the definition. The example provided in the dictionary entry can help you.

Work in pairs.
Look at the words and the examples. Try to work out the meanings, then check in the dictionary to see if you were right.

stiff — have a stiff leg/back; feel stiff after a long walk.

clay — clay soil; clay pipe: bricks made of clay.

root — pull up a plant by the roots; the roots go deep into the soil.

frost — on winter mornings, car windows can be covered in frost.

faded — the strong sunlight had faded the curtains. Will the colour in this material fade?

stuff — What's the stuff on the floor? I can't get all my stuff in this bag.

fit — The food was not fit to eat; a meal fit for a king.

itch — **1** scratch where it itches. Are your mosquito bites itching? **2** The boys were itching for the lesson to end.

scold — scold a child for being lazy; he was scolded by his mother because he was late.

snare — to snare a rabbit in a trap.

2 Divide the following words into three categories – health, food, or household chores.

to sweep	a trout
sores	greens
a hare	to sew
pains	to baste
a cure	sprains
a herb	to dust

E. Nesbit
1858–1924

The Things That Matter

Now that I've nearly done my days,
    And grown too stiff to sweep or sew,
I sit and think, till I'm amaze,
    About what lots of things I know:
5 Things as I've found out one by one—
    And when I'm fast down in the clay,
My knowing things and how they're done
    Will all be lost and thrown away.

There's things, I know, as won't be lost,
10   Things as folks write and talk about:
The way to keep your roots from frost,
    And how to get your ink spots out.
What medicine's good for sores and sprains,
    What way to salt your butter down,
15 What charms will cure your different pains,
    And what will bright your faded gown.

But more important things than these,
    They can't be written in a book:
How fast to boil your greens and peas,
20   And how good bacon ought to look;
The feel of real good wearing stuff,
    The kind of apple as will keep,
The look of bread that's rose enough,
    And how to get a child asleep.

25 Whether the jam is fit to pot,
    Whether the milk is going to turn,
Whether a hen will lay or not,
    Is things as some folks never learn.
I know the weather by the sky,
30   I know what herbs grow in what lane;
And if sick men are going to die,
    Or if they'll get about again.

Young wives come in, a-smiling, grave,
    With secrets that they itch to tell:
35 I know what sort of times they'll have,
    And if they'll have a boy or gell.
And if a lad is ill to bind,
    Or some young maid is hard to lead,
I know when you should speak 'em kind,
40   And when it's scolding as they need.

I used to know where birds ud set,
    And likely spots for trout or hare,
And God may want me to forget
    The way to set a line or snare;
45 But not the way to truss a chick,
    To fry a fish, or baste a roast,
Nor how to tell, when folks are sick,
    What kind of herb will ease them most!

Forgetting seems such silly waste!
50   I know so many little things,
And now the Angels will make haste
    To dust it all away with wings!
O God, you made me like to know,
    You kept the things straight in my head,
55 Please God, if you can make it so,
    Let me know *something* when I'm dead.

106

Comprehension check

T.34 Read the poem and answer the questions.

1 Which of the following best summarizes the poem?
a. She is afraid of death and wants to hold on to life.
b. She would like her knowledge to be passed on, and not lost when she dies.
c. She wonders what her life was for, if, in death, she forgets everything she has learned.
d. She thinks it would be a waste if her knowledge was lost when she dies.

2 Read the poem again and mark it like this.
   A References to food and cooking
   B References to health care
   C References to looking after a house

3 Many of the old lady's chores were to do with food and its preparation. Which of them are still commonly done by people nowadays?

4 Her knowledge of health care seems to rest on *old wives' tales*. What popular cures for illnesses exist in your country?

5 What impression do you have of the old lady?
   How do you envisage her appearance?
   Where does she live?
   What is her way of life like?
   Was your grandparents' life like hers in any way?

6 The old lady would appear to have no fear of death, and complete faith in God.
   Compare the life that she led, and the values that people held in those days, with today's consumer, 'throw-away' society. Have we lost a certain innocence with the knowledge that we now possess?

● Language review
Articles

Indefinite article

A/an is used:
1 when we mention a singular, countable noun for the first time.
   I bought a jumper and a tie this afternoon.
   Have you seen a black dog with white spots? I've lost him.
2 with professions.
   She's a doctor.
3 in exclamations with singular countable nouns.
   What a nice day!
4 in certain numerical expressions.
   fifty pence a pound; sixty miles an hour

Definite article

The is used:
1 when the speaker and the listener both know which noun is referred to.
   I bought the jumper for Alice, and the tie is to go with my suit.
   Have you seen the dog? (Our dog – we have only one.)
   Shut the door.
2 when the noun referred to is unique in the world.
   the sun, the Alps, the Thames, the Pope
3 when the noun is defined and clearly specified.
   the wines of France, the girls sitting over there
4 with certain adjectives to refer to general classes of people.
   the rich, the unemployed, the Welsh, the Germans
5 with certain public places.
   I went to the pub/cinema/opera/theatre last night.
   First I went to the bank, then the post office.
   Which pub/cinema, etc. is not important.

Zero article

No article is used:
1 in general statements.
   Dogs make very good pets.
   Sugar is bad for your teeth.

2 with certain categories of nouns.
   He's playing tennis. (Games)
   He studies physics. (Academic subjects)
   Have you had lunch? (Meals)
   Love is eternal. (Abstract nouns)
3 in certain common prepositional phrases.
   at home   in bed
   at university   in hospital
   to work   at night   by bus
4 in exclamations with uncountable nouns and plural nouns.
   What lovely weather we're having!
   What beautiful eyes you've got!

▶ Grammar reference: page 123.

CONTROLLED PRACTICE
Articles

1 Work in pairs.
   In the following sentences, explain the use (or absence) of the article.
a. I met an interesting chap at a party last night.
b. Why are you still in bed? You should be at school.
c. Life is full of surprises.
d. I'm researching the life of Mozart.
e. The Amazon is the longest river in the world.
f. My mortgage costs three hundred pounds a month.
g. Did you remember to go to the bank?
h. Do you like the flowers I gave you?
i. Birds migrate in winter.

2 Decide if the articles are used correctly in the following sentences.
   Correct the mistakes.
a. What did you have for the breakfast?
b. We had a lovely lunch in a small restaurant.
c. My sister lives in United States.
d. Accommodation is difficult to find in big cities.
e. I saw very good programme on television last night.
f. Do you come to the school by bus?

g. We have small house by the sea.
h. The Italian food isn't as fattening as people think.
i. I'm studying the history of Europe in the eighteenth century.

3 Put **a**, **the**, or nothing into each gap.
a. She was sent to _____ prison for _____ murder of her husband.
b. 'Is your father at _____ work?' 'No, he's in _____ hospital having _____ operation. _____ doctor said he should be home soon.'
c. _____ lunch Sally served was excellent. We had _____ soup with _____ garlic bread, then _____ lovely Mexican dish with _____ rice, followed by _____ most delicious ice-cream I've ever tasted.
d. I've got _____ degree in _____ modern languages. I studied _____ French language and literature at _____ Bristol University.
e. I met Barbara Simmons, _____ actress, in _____ Oxford Street yesterday. She won _____ Oscar last year for her performance in Shakespeare's _____ *Taming of* _____ *Shrew*.
f. _____ beauty is in _____ eye of _____ beholder.
g. _____ cats are _____ interesting creatures. During _____ day they sleep, and at _____ night they go out hunting.
h. Turn out _____ lights and keep _____ doors shut. We're wasting _____ energy. If we're not careful, _____ electricity bill will be enormous.

4 **'Just a minute'**
This is a popular radio programme in Britain. You must take it in turns to talk about one of the subjects below.
The other students can interrupt if . . .
– you repeat yourself
– you hesitate for too long

– you use articles incorrectly.
If your teacher agrees with the person who interrupts, he or she must continue talking. The person talking at the end of sixty seconds scores five points!

Air travel   Vegetarians
Capital cities   Horses
Graffiti   Cheese
Housework   Astrology
Camping holidays
The Royal Family
Learning languages
The restaurants in your town

5 Compare the following sentences. How does the use of the article change the meaning?
a. I left the key under the mat.
   I left a key under the mat.
b. Few people have read the book.
   A few people have read the book.
c. The solicitor is now in prison.
   The solicitor is now in the prison.
d. Mr Smith is on the phone for you.
   A Mr Smith is on the phone for you.
e. We all went on holiday in a caravan.
   We all went on holiday in one caravan.

Countable or uncountable nouns?

1 Correct the following sentences.
a. Can you give me an information about train times?
b. He couldn't give me any good advices.
c. There was an interesting news on the radio this morning.
d. Spain grows a lot of fruits, many of which are exported.
e. My luggages are in the car.

2 The following words can be *both* countable and uncountable, but the meaning changes.
Example
hair
She has straight, blonde hair.
Waiter! There's a hair in my soup.

Write sentences to illustrate the two meanings.

wood	time
experience	custom
glass	chocolate
rubber	arm
cake	paper
iron	minute

REVISION

Singular or plural nouns?

Make sentences from the chart. You must decide which nouns are *singular*, which are *plural*, and which can be *both*.

A	B	C	D
The *or* no article	news police trousers government politics team scissors mathematics staff people	is are	boring. interesting. coming. winning. a difficult subject. sharp. awful. trying hard at the moment. unhappy at the decision.

Grammar section

UNIT 1

The tense system

Introduction

There are three classes of verbs in English:

1 Auxiliary verbs

The verbs **do**, **be** and **have** are used as auxiliary verbs to form different tenses.

Do

a. **Do** as an auxiliary is used to form negative and question forms of the *Present Simple* and **did** is used in the *Past Simple*:

	Present Simple	Past Simple
Negative	*I **don't** understand.*	*I **didn't** agree.*
	*They **don't** like it.*	*He **didn't** pass.*
	*She **doesn't** eat meat.*	*They **didn't** like it.*
Question	*Do they like it?*	***Did** they enjoy it?*
	*What **does** he want?*	*When **did** they arrive?*
	***Don't** you want to come?*	***Didn't** we go to the same school?*
	***Doesn't** she know him?*	

b. **Do** is only used in the positive to give *emphasis* to a verb:

	Present Simple	Past Simple
	*She isn't lazy. She **does** try hard.*	*I **did** try to phone, but there was no answer.*

c. **Do** is used in tag questions and short answers:

	Present Simple	Past Simple
	*You think it'll work, **don't** you?*	*It worked, **didn't** it?*
	*He knows I'm here, **doesn't** he?*	
	*A You don't want to go, **do** you?*	*A Who made the cake?*
	*B I **do**.*	*B Jack **did**.*

Be

a. **Be** as an auxiliary + present participle (**-ing**) is used to form *continuous* tenses:

*Alice **is writing** a book.*
*We **were going** for a walk.*
*I've **been trying** to get hold of you for a week.*
*We'll **be leaving** soon.*

b. **Be** + past participle (**-ed** etc.) is used to form *passive* sentences:

*Paper **is made** from wood.*
*My car **is being repaired** at the moment.*
*He **was injured** in a car accident.*
*It'll **be finished** soon.*
*They've **been robbed**.*

Have

Have as an auxiliary + past participle (**-ed** etc.) is used to form *perfect* tenses:

*I've never **been** there before.*
*By the time we arrived they **had left**.*
*Will you **have finished** by lunch time?*

2 Modal auxiliary verbs

Modal auxiliary verbs are auxiliary because they 'help' other verbs, but unlike **do**, **be** and **have** (which only help to form tenses) modal auxiliaries have their own meanings. They express certainty, ability, possibility, and advice, etc.

*He **must** be at least sixty.* (certainty)
*I **can't** swim.* (ability)
*It **might** rain this afternoon.* (possibility)
*You **should** rest for a few days.* (advice)

The modal auxiliary verbs are: **can, could, may, might, will, would, shall, should, must, ought, need.** They are dealt with in greater detail in Units 6, 7, 9, 10, and 11.

3 Full verbs

Full verbs are all the other verbs in the language, for example, **go, walk, think, help, eat.**
The tense chart on page 8 shows all the tenses of full verbs.

English tense usage

English tenses have two elements of meaning:

TIME – Is the verb action present, past or future?
ASPECT – How does the speaker see the verb action?

Examples

She's talking on the phone.
TIME – present
ASPECT – activity in progress now

I saw a good film last night.
TIME – past
ASPECT – action completed at a specific time

Have you ever seen 'Gone with the Wind'?
TIME – before now
ASPECT – the exact time *when* is not important. The question asks about an experience *at any time* in the past.

I'll give you my phone number.
TIME – immediate future
ASPECT – spontaneous intention

I'm going to give Helen a plant for her birthday.
TIME – future
ASPECT – planned intention

There are two *aspects* in the English tense system: they are called *continuous* and *perfect*.

Continuous aspect

1 The continuous aspect expresses the following ideas:

a. activity in progress.
   *Don't interrupt me. **I'm thinking**. Why **aren't you working**?*
   ***I was going** out of the hotel when someone tapped me on the shoulder.*
   *Don't phone her at 8.00. **She'll be having** dinner.*
   *Why don't you stop reading now? **You've been reading** all day.*

b. temporary activity.
   ***We're living** in a hotel until we can find a house to buy.*
   ***You're being** very silly today. Usually you're so sensible.*

c. possibly incomplete activity.
   ***Who's been eating** my sandwich?*
   (Compare ***Who's eaten** my sandwich?*)
   ***I was writing** the report on the plane.*
   (Compare ***I wrote** the report on the plane.*)

2 There are four main groups of state verbs that are rarely used in continuous tenses. This is because they have the idea of permanency and completeness, which conflicts with 'b' and 'c' above.

   Verbs of the mind and thinking:

   believe think assume consider understand suppose expect agree know remember forget

   Verbs of emotion:

   like love detest envy hate hope prefer wish want

   Verbs of having and being:

   belong own depend contain cost seem appear need have

   Verbs of the senses:

   see hear taste smell

3 Some of these verbs can be used in continuous tenses when the verb expresses an *activity*, not a *state*. However, the meaning changes slightly.
   Compare the use of simple and continuous tenses in the following pairs of sentences:

   ***I think** it's a great idea.* ('think' as opinion, i.e. a *state*)
   ***He's thinking** of emigrating.* ('think' as mental process, i.e. an *activity*)

   ***I see** what you mean.* ('see' meaning 'understand')
   ***I'm seeing** Jenny this afternoon.* ('see' meaning 'meet')

   ***The soup tastes** delicious.* (a state)
   ***I'm tasting** the soup to see if it needs more salt.* (an activity)

I expect you'd like something to eat. ('expect' meaning 'suppose')
She's expecting a baby. (She's pregnant.)

Perfect aspect

The perfect aspect expresses the following ideas:

a. The exact time of the verb action is not important.
   ***I've bought** a new car.*
   ***Have you seen** my wallet anywhere? **I've lost** it.*

b. The action is completed *before* another time.
   ***Have you ever been** to America?* (some time before now)
   *When I arrived, **he had already left**.* (some time before I arrived)
   ***I'll have finished** the report by tonight.* (some time before tonight)

The *Present Perfect*, *Past Perfect* and *Future Perfect* could perhaps be renamed 'Before-present', 'Before-past', and 'Before-future' to give a more accurate description.
Perfect tenses are dealt with in Units 2, 5, and 7.

Active and passive

1 When we make active sentences passive, the focus of the sentence moves. The object of an active sentence becomes the subject in a passive sentence.

   This might be because:

a. the agent is unknown.
   ***My car** was stolen yesterday.*
b. the agent is unimportant.
   ***Houses** are built using a variety of materials.*
c. the agent is understood.
   ***He** will be arrested if he tries to leave the country.*
d. the object is important and needs to be emphasized.
   ***The results of the enquiry** were published in the newspaper.*

2 Many verbs have two objects.
   *She gave **me a book**.*

   In the passive, it is more usual for the person to be the subject.
   *I was given **a book**.*
   (Compare *A book was given to **me**.*)

   Other verbs like this are **show**, **tell**, **send**, **offer**.

   ***We** were shown **our room**.*
   ***I** was told **the news** this morning.*
   ***You** were sent **the information** by post.*
   *If **I** am offered **the job**, I'll take it.*

3 *People say he's a millionaire.*

   Notice how this sentence can be expressed using a passive + infinitive.
   *He **is said to be** a millionaire.*

   Other verbs like this are **believe**, **consider**, **report**, **know**, **suppose**, **expect**, **think**.

*He **is believed to have left** the country.*
*The Government **is reported to be losing** its fight with
  the unions.*
*You're **supposed to be working**. Why aren't you?*

UNIT 2

The Present Perfect Simple and Continuous

(See page 110 for an introduction to continuous and
perfect tenses.)

The Present Perfect tenses relate *past* actions and
activities to the *present*.

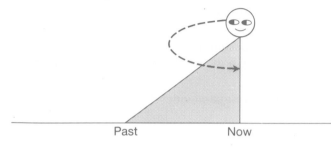

Past   Now

They are used:

a. to express unfinished past.

*He's **worked** here for ten years.*
*Scientists **have been looking** for a solution since the
  problem was discovered.*
***Have** you **been waiting** long?*

The verb action began in the past and still continues.
In this use there is little difference between the simple
and the continuous.

Certain verbs, by definition, suggest duration. The
following are usually found in the continuous:

rain snow learn sit lie wait stay

If the continuous is possible in English, it tends to be
used. However, remember the verbs that are rarely
used in continuous tenses (page 110).

b. to express the present result of a past event. (The past
event is usually recent.)

A *You've changed. What **have** you **done** to yourself?*
B *I've lost a lot of weight. I've **been taking** exercise, and
I've **been watching** my diet.*
*I've just **finished reading** an excellent book.*

In this use, the simple emphasizes the *completed*
action, and the continuous emphasizes the *repeated*
activity.
Certain verbs, by definition, do not suggest duration.
For example:

start begin finish stop find lose break die decide

These verbs are usually found in the simple rather
than the continuous tenses.

c. to express a past experience, the time of which is not
specified.

***Have** you ever **been** in a plane crash? I **have**.*
*I've **heard** this story before.*

(The experience happened sometime in my life, but
exactly when is not important.)
The continuous is unusual in this use.

Compare the use of tenses in the following pairs of
sentences:

I've mended your car. (completed action)
I've been respraying it. (recent activity – 'that's why I'm
  covered in paint.' The action is perhaps finished,
  perhaps not.)

I've cut my finger. (single action)
I've been cutting wood. (repeated action)

She's had four operations. (completed actions)
She's been having problems with her knees. (repeated
  activity)

He's lived here all his life. (permanent)
She's been living here for a few weeks. (temporary)

Where did you put my keys?
Where have you put my keys? (no real difference)

Have you seen the Renoir exhibition? (It is still open.)
Did you see the Renoir exhibition? (It is finished.)

He's been to America. (experience – 'He isn't there
  now.')
He's gone to America. (present result – 'He's there
  now.')

UNIT 3

The gerund

The gerund is used:

a. after prepositions.

***After leaving** school, I went to university.*
*The firemen rescued the lady **by breaking down** the
  door.*
*Is anyone here good **at sewing**?*
*She was accused **of killing** her husband.*

Examples of prepositions frequently followed by the
gerund are:

before after without by about at to of

b. after certain verbs.

*I **enjoy staying** in hotels.*
*I **avoid working** at the weekend.*

Some of the most common verbs which are followed
by the gerund are:

admit avoid deny enjoy finish

c. as the subject or object of a sentence.

Swimming is my favourite sport.
Smoking is bad for your health.
I find working in the garden very relaxing.

d. after certain idiomatic expressions.

It's no use talking to him. He doesn't know anything.
This is an excellent book. It's worth buying.

Other idiomatic expressions are:
There's no point in (waiting all day).
It's no good (pretending that you understand).

e. after certain verbs which are followed by the preposition **to**.

I'm looking forward to visiting you in July.
He can't get used to driving in London.

The infinitive

The infinitive is used:

a. after certain verbs.

I can't afford to pay all my bills.
I hope to see you again soon.

Some of the most common verbs that are followed by the infinitive are:

agree appear attempt choose dare decide expect help learn manage need offer promise refuse seem

You should consult a good dictionary, for example the *Oxford Advanced Learner's Dictionary of Current English*, to see which structures are possible after a particular verb.

b. after certain verbs followed by an object.

He advised me to listen carefully.
They invited her to have lunch with them.

Some of the most common verbs that are normally used with an object and an infinitive are:

allow encourage force order persuade remind teach tell warn

c. after certain verbs which sometimes take an object and sometimes don't.

I want to find out the answer. (no object – 'I find out.')
I want you to find out the answer. ('you' as object – 'You find out.')
I'd like to help you.
I'd like you to give her a message.
NEVER ~~I want that you~~ . . .
        ~~I'd like that you~~ . . .

Other common verbs are:

ask expect

d. after certain adjectives.

It's difficult to explain how to get there. It's possible to walk there.

e. after **make** and **let**.

She made me do the exercise again. (active – without 'to')
I was made to do the exercise again. (passive – with 'to')
He let me borrow the car. (active – without 'to')
I was allowed to borrow the car. ('Let', in the sense of 'allow', is not possible in the passive.)

f. to express purpose.

I came here to learn English.
I need more money to buy the things I want.

g. after certain verbs followed by question words, e.g. **what, where, who**.

I didn't know what to do.
Can you tell me how to get there?
Show me where to put it.
Do you know where to buy it?

After these verbs and others with similar meanings, it is possible to use **how, what, where, when, whether** etc.

ask consider explain wonder find out understand

Forms of the infinitive

1 **The continuous infinitive**

The continuous infinitive is formed with **to be** + present participle.
It expresses activities in progress.

I'd like to be lying in the sun right now.
He seemed to be having financial difficulties.

2 **The perfect infinitive**

The perfect infinitive is formed with **to have** + past participle.

I'd like to have seen his face when you told him.
He seems to have forgotten about the appointment.

3 **The passive infinitive**

The passive infinitive is formed with **to be** + past participle.

I'd like to be promoted to sales manager.
I asked to be informed as soon as there was any news.

Notes

The continuous, perfect, and passive infinitives can also be used with modal auxiliary verbs (see page 109), but with these verbs **to** is omitted.

You should be working, not watching television.
She must have gone home already.
This report must be finished tonight.

The gerund or the infinitive after verbs?

1 Continue, start, begin

Either the gerund or the infinitive can be used.

It started | *to snow.*
| *snowing.*

The infinitive is more common.

2 Love, like, prefer, hate

The meaning changes slightly, depending on whether the gerund or the infinitive is used.

Followed by the gerund, the statement is *general*.

I like swimming.
I love going to parties.
I hate driving in the dark.

Followed by the infinitive, the statement is *more specific*.

I like to read a book before going to sleep at night.
I hate to tell you, but I've lost your coat.

3 Remember, forget, stop, try

The meaning changes greatly depending on whether the gerund or the infinitive is used.

I remember being very unhappy as a teenager. (I know that I was very unhappy as a teenager.)
I'll never forget meeting you. (The day I met you is very clear in my memory.)

The gerund refers to actions and states *in the past*, i.e. *before* the remembering, forgetting, etc. take place.

Remember to put some petrol in the car! (There isn't much petrol in the car and it is important that you buy some.)
Don't forget to post the letter! (The letter is important, so you must remind yourself to post it.)

The infinitive refers to actions that must still be done, i.e. that happen *after* the remembering, forgetting, etc.

I stopped smoking years ago. (previous activity)
I stopped to pick up a hitchhiker. (This tells us *why* I stopped.)

We tried to put out the fire, but it was impossible.
I tried pouring on water, my husband tried covering it with a blanket and my son tried using the fire extinguisher, but in the end we had to call the fire brigade.

Try + infinitive is your goal; it is what you *want* to do.
Try + gerund is the method you use to achieve that goal.

UNIT 4
Question forms

1 Here are some commonly used question forms:

What sort of music do you like?
What kind of car have you got?
There's tomato soup or chicken soup – which one do you want?
How much do you weigh?
How tall are you?
How big is your bedroom?
Whose is this book? It's not mine.
What have you done to your hair? It looks awful.
What have you done with my slippers? I can't find them anywhere.
What did you do that for? (Why did you do that?)
What does 'handle' mean?
How do you spell your surname?
What's your mother like? (Describe her generally.)
How's your mother? (Is she in good health?)
Whereabouts do you live? (In or near what place?)

2 Questions which ask for descriptions

The questions below both ask for descriptions. The first asks for quite objective information, and the second asks for a more personal reaction.

What was the party like?
How was the party?

3 Reported questions

The word order is the same as the statement.
Do/does/did is not added.

A *When did you arrive?*
B *I arrived on Monday.*

He asked me when I arrived.

Here are some more examples:

She wanted to know when I was born.
He wondered why I was going to Germany.
She asked me where my parents lived.

4 Indirect questions

The word order is the same as the statement. Do/does/did is not added.

He lives in Wimbledon.

I don't know where he lives.
(NEVER ~~I don't know where does he live.~~)

Here are some more examples:

I can't remember what time the film starts.
Do you know how many children he's got?
I don't understand where all my money has gone.
I couldn't understand what she was trying to say.
I explained how I wanted the room arranged.

Have

There are four different ways that **have** is used:

1 as an *auxiliary verb* to form *perfect tenses*. (See also page 109.)

Positive	*I've always* **wanted** *to go to America.*
	She **had** *already* **done** *it.*
Negative	*I* **haven't seen** *it.*
Question	**Have** *you* **done** *it yet?*

2 as a *full verb* to refer to an *activity*.

Present Simple

Positive	*I* **have a lesson** *every Monday.*
Negative	*I* **don't have meetings** *very often.*
Question	*How often do you* **have a bath**?

Present Continuous

Positive	*They're* **having an argument** *about money.*
Negative	*I'm not* **having a holiday** *this year.*
Question	*When are you* **having lunch**?

Past Simple

Positive	*I* **had difficulty** *starting the car this morning.*
Negative	*I didn't* **have** *any* **breakfast**.
Question	*What did you* **have** *for* **lunch**?

3 as a *full verb* to refer to a *state*.

Present Simple

Positive	*He* **has a new car.**
	He's **got a new car.**
Negative	*He* **doesn't have any children.**
	He **hasn't got any children.**
Question	*Do you* **have a headache**?
	Have *you* **got a headache**?

British English prefers the forms with **got**, while American English generally uses the other form. However, if there is an idea of repetition or habit, the forms with **got** are not used.
Compare the following sentences:

I've got a headache. It's killing me.
I often have a headache at this time of day.

Present Continuous

It is incorrect to use **have** in the Present Continuous to refer to a possession.

NEVER ~~He's having a new car.~~
~~He's having blue eyes.~~

Past Simple

Positive	*I* **had a bad back** *last week.*
Negative	*I didn't* **have enough money**.
Question	*Did you* **have a bicycle** *when you were young?*

4 as a *modal auxiliary verb* to express *obligation*.

Present Simple

Positive	*I* **have to go** *now.*
Negative	*I don't* **have to work** *terribly hard.*
Question	*Do you* **have to wear** *a uniform?*

When the obligation is on a specific occasion, it is possible to use a form of **have** with **got**.

I've **got to go** *now. Bye-bye.*
Have *you* **got to wear** *that hat? It looks awful.*

When the same obligation often occurs, the forms with **got** are not used.

I never **have to do** *anything at home. My mother does it all.*
Do you **have to go abroad** *much in your job?*

Present Continuous

We're **having to eat** *less meat. It's too expensive.*
She's **having to work** *day and night for her exam.*

The Present Continuous form of **have** above is used to express an external obligation in progress. This use is rare.

Past Simple

Positive	*I* **had to save** *for two years to afford a holiday.*
Negative	*We* **didn't have to wait** *long – only a few minutes.*
Question	*Did you* **have to pay** *interest on the loan?*

UNIT 5
Narrative tenses

Past Simple

The Past Simple is used:

a. to express a completed action at a definite time in the past.

   Shakespeare **died** *in 1616.*

b. to express past habits.

   We always **had** *steak and kidney pie on Saturdays when I was a boy.*
   I **walked** *to school until I was given a bike.*

Past habits can also be expressed with **used to**. See page 122.

Past Continuous

The Past Continuous is used:

a. to express an activity in progress at a time in the past.

   I phoned you at four, but there was no reply. What **were you doing**?

b. to describe a situation or activity.

*Jan looked lovely. She **was wearing** her green velvet gown. Her eyes **were shining** in the light of the candles that **were burning** nearby.*

c. to express the future in the past.

*Maria was in a hurry. She **was catching** the midnight boat to Venice, and did not want to be late. She got into her car and drove as fast as she could to the docks.*

Compare the use of tenses in the following sentences:

*When we **arrived**, she **made** some coffee.* (One action followed another.)

*When we **arrived**, she **was making** some coffee.* (She was in the middle of making the coffee.)

*I **decorated** the dining room yesterday.* (I finished the job.)

*I **was decorating** the dining room yesterday.* (I did part of the job.)

*He **drowned**.* (completed action)

*He **was drowning**, so I jumped in and saved him.* (activity in progress)

*He **kicked** the cat.* (single action)

*He **was kicking** the cat.* (repeated activity)

*The castle **stood** on top of a hill.* (permanent)

*He **was standing** on the corner, waiting for the shop to open.* (temporary activity)

Past Perfect Simple and Continuous

(See page 110 for an introduction to continuous and perfect tenses.)

The Past Perfect relates a past action to the past.

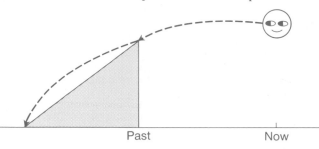

Past   Now

1 The Past Perfect is used to express an action that happened *before* a definite time in the past.

*I arrived at midday to give Peter a lift, but **he had already left** to catch his train.*
*Ann could not hold back her tears any longer. She **had had** a terrible day. She **had been late** for work, she **had lost** her purse, and now she **had burned** the meal.*

2 The Past Perfect Continuous expresses longer activities that had been going on continuously up to a definite time in the past.

*He looked filthy. He **had been sleeping** under bridges for a month, and **had been drinking** far too much.*

Compare this with the use of the Past Perfect Simple in the following sentence:

*He **had lost** his job and his wife **had left** him.*

Compare the use of tenses in the following sentences:

*He couldn't stand up. He'**d been drinking** all day.* (repeated activity)
*He'**d drunk** half a bottle of brandy.* (completed action)
*She was pale. She **had cut** her wrist and **lost** a lot of blood.* (single actions)
*I was tired. I **had been cutting** wood all morning.* (repeated activity)

3 Verbs in the Past Simple tell a story in chronological order.

*John's parents **separated** when he was a boy, and his sister **married** and **emigrated** to Australia. John's wife **died**, and he **sent** his children to stay with their grandmother before the funeral. John **was** alone in the world, and the house **was** silent. He **had** to decide how to rebuild his life.*

By using the Past Perfect, the speaker (or writer) can 'look over their shoulder' to a previous time, and so re-order the material for dramatic effect.

*John **was** alone in the world. His parents **had separated** when he was a boy; his only sister **had married** and **emigrated** to Australia years before, and his wife **had died**. He **had** to decide how to rebuild his life. He **had sent** the children to stay with their grandmother before the funeral, so the house **was** silent.*

4 Time clauses with **when**

Two Past Simple tenses can be used if there is the idea that the second action is the result of the first, and that it happened immediately afterwards.

*When his flight **was announced**, he **went** to the check-in desk.*
*When I **heard** the postman, I **went** to see if there was any mail.*

If it is important to show that the first action was completed *before* the second one began, the Past Perfect must be used for the action that happened first.

*When I **had read** the paper, I **threw** it away.*
*When I **had written** the letter, I **went** to the post office.*

5 Time clauses with **till, until, as soon as, before, after**

As with **when**, two Past Simple tenses can be used unless it is important to show that one action was completed *before* another began.

*I **sat** outside until the sun **went** down.*
*He **didn't leave** the house until he **had checked** that all the windows were closed.*

*As soon as she **saw** the mouse, she **jumped** on a chair.*
*We **left** as soon as we **had finished** dinner.*

6 The Past Perfect is used in reporting speech and thoughts in the past.

*I told him how much I **had enjoyed** meeting him.*
*She said she **had posted** the letter on Monday.*
*I thought I **had bought** a new film, but I couldn't find it.*
*He realized he **had been** a fool.*
*She knew I'**d been lying**, but she didn't say anything.*

UNIT 6
Expressing quantity

1 The following can be used with a noun:

some any no every much many more most
little a little less few a few fewer
several all

some people   *a few days*
no money   *every year*
much progress   *many people*
several years   *little bread*
                        few eggs

Most of them can also be used without a noun. (**No** and **every** cannot.)

*I've got **some**.*   *Don't take them **all**.*
*He didn't take **any**.*   *There's **little** left.*
*There was **a little**.*   *We don't need **much**.*
*I've met **several**.*

2 With **of** + noun phrase

Most of the quantifiers listed above can be used with **of** + noun phrase. (**No** and **every** cannot.)

Some of the people liked it.
He didn't take any of my books.
I didn't like much of the food.
We spent most of the weekend decorating.
I read a few of the books.
I got lots of presents for my birthday.

For **no** and **every**, use **none** and **every one**.

None of the people was interested.
Every one of the hotels was fully booked.

3 **A little/a few** and **little/few**

A little and **a few** express a small amount or number in a *positive* way, generally meaning that although there is only a little or a few, it is probably enough.

*Can you lend me **a little** sugar?*
*I'm meeting **a few** friends at the pub – do you want to join us?*
*There's **a little** cake left – would you like some?*

Little and **few** express a small amount or number in a *negative* way, generally meaning that there is *not* enough.

Few people expect to pass the exam.
*There is **little** hope of finding our cat.*
*There is **little** milk left – we'll have to buy some more.*

4 **Some** and **any**, and the compounds **somebody, anybody** etc.

The general rule is **some** for *positive* sentences, and **any** in *negatives* and *questions*.

*I need **some** help.*
*He doesn't want **any** help.*
*I didn't go **anywhere**. I just stayed at home.*
*Can **anybody** help me?*

But **some** is used in *requests* and *invitations*, or when we expect the answer to be 'yes'.

*Have you got **some** money you could lend me?*
*Would you like **something** to eat?*
*Did **someone** just knock at the door, or did I imagine it?*

Any is used in *positive* sentences that have a *negative meaning*, particularly with words such as **never, hardly, without**.

*He **never** has **any** money.*
*There are **hardly any** mistakes.*
*I made it myself **without any** help.*

Any, and its compounds **anyone, anywhere, anything**, are also used to express 'It doesn't matter which/who/where.'

*Take **any** book you like. I don't mind.*
***Anyone** will tell you how to get to the station.*
*You can sit **anywhere** you like.*
*I eat **anything** – I'm not fussy.*

5 **Nobody, no-one, nowhere, nothing**

These are used as more emphatic forms for **not . . . anybody** etc.

*I did**n't** see **anybody** all week-end.*
*I saw **nobody** all week-end.*

*We had**n't** eaten **anything** the whole day.*
*We'd eaten **nothing** the whole day.*

They are also used at the beginning of a sentence.

No-one was saved.
Nothing can help me now.
Nowhere is safe anymore.

6 **Much, many, a lot of, a great deal of, a large number of, plenty of**

Much and **many** are generally used in *questions* and *negatives*.

*Is there **much** unemployment in your country?*
*I don't have **much** spare time these days.*
*Will there be **many** people there?*
*You don't see **many** snakes in England.*

In positive sentences, the following forms are possible:

Spoken

*There'll be **plenty of** people that you know at the party.*
*We've got **lots of** time. There's no need to hurry.*
*A **lot of** my friends work in advertising.*

Written/more formal

*A **great deal of** money was lost during the strike.*
*A **large number of** strikes are caused by bad
   management.*
***Many** world leaders are over sixty when they reach the
   peak of their careers.*

7 Fewer and less

Fewer is the *comparative* of **few**, and is used before
plural nouns.

***Fewer people** turned up to the party than we expected.*

Less is the comparative of **little** and is used before
uncountable nouns.

*I spend **less time** at home than I do at work.*

UNIT 7

Future forms

We can be quite certain about the past and the present,
but we cannot be so certain about the future. For this
reason, *aspect* (see pages 109–10) is more important
than *time* when discussing the future. This explains why
there are several different ways of expressing future time
in English.

Will (short forms will = 'll, will not = won't)

Will is used:

a. as an *auxiliary* to form the future.
   Will here expresses *future time* only.

   *I'**ll be** thirty in a few days' time.*
   *It **will be** cold and wet tomorrow, I'm afraid.*
   *I'm sure we'**ll have** a lovely time.*
   *We probably **won't be** at home this evening.*

   Will is also common when there is another clause with
   if, **when**, **until**, **as soon as**, **unless**, **before** and **after**.

   *You'**ll break** it **if** you aren't careful.*
   *I **won't leave until** you get here.*
   *We **will start** the meeting **as soon as** he arrives.*
   *I'**ll leave before** it gets too late.*

   Will is the most frequently used form of the future.

b. as a *modal auxiliary* to express a *decision* or *intention*,
   often made at the moment of speaking.

   *I'**ll have** the steak, please, medium rare.*
   *I like the car very much. I'**ll offer** you £900 for it.*
   *She'**ll** probably **come** to see you tonight.*
   NEVER ~~I have the steak, please.~~

c. as a *modal auxiliary* to express *willingness*.

   ***Will** you **help** me?* (request)

   *I'**ll give** you a lift*
   *Rob'**ll do** it for you.*   (offer)
   NEVER ~~I give you a lift.~~

Going to

Going to is used:

a. to express an *intention* that has already been planned
   or decided *before* the moment of speaking.

   *We're saving up because we'**re going to buy** a house.*
   *I'**m going to make** some coffee. Do you want some?*

b. to *predict a future event* for which there is some
   evidence now.

   *I think I'**m going to faint**.* (I already feel ill.)
   *Careful! That glass **is going to fall**!* (It's rolling towards
      the edge of the table.)
   *It looks as though it'**s going to rain**.* (It's very cloudy.)

Present Continuous

The Present Continuous is used to talk about a future
event which is already arranged.

   *He's **meeting** Jane at the theatre tomorrow night.*
   *We're **moving** house on the 13th.*
   *I'm **having** a party on Saturday. Would you like to
      come?*
   ***Are** you **leaving** soon?*

Think of the kind of events that you might put in your
diary. These are the sort of future events for which the
Present Continuous might be used. It commonly occurs
with the following verbs:

come go see leave meet

There is often little difference between a *future intention*
and a *future arrangement*, and often **going to** and the
Present Continuous are interchangeable.

We're going to see | Hamlet *at the Royal Theatre tonight.*
We're seeing

Present Simple

The Present Simple is used to express a future event
which is seen as *certain* because of a timetable or
calendar.

*You **leave** Heathrow at 11.00 and **arrive** in Paris at 12.30.*
*The film **starts** at 7.30.*
*The exam **takes place** on 2 April.*

Future Continuous (will be + -ing)

The Future Continuous is used:

a. to express an activity that will be in progress at a
   specific time in the future.

   *Don't phone at 8.00 – I'**ll be having** supper.*
   *This time tomorrow I'**ll be flying** to New York.*

b. to express events that are *certain* to happen in the future. This use is rather difficult to define. It does *not* express intention or decision, but something that will happen naturally.

> *When **will** you **be moving** into your new house?* (You are going to move some time – when is it?)
> *We'**ll be flying** at 30,000 feet.* (This might be said by the pilot of a plane. He hasn't just decided to fly at that height. 30,000 feet is the normal height.)
> *Where **will** you **be staying** while you are in England?*

Future Perfect (will have + -ed)

(See page 110 for an introduction to perfect tenses.)

The Future Perfect relates a future event to a *definite* time in the future.

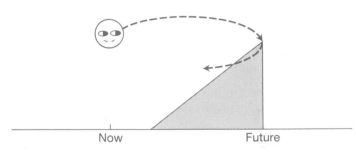

The Future Perfect is used to express an action that will be finished *before a definite time in the future*. We do not know exactly *when* the action will happen; we only know it will happen *before* a certain time.

> *I'**ll have finished** it before you get back.*
> *Many natural resources **will have disappeared** by the end of the century.*
> *She **won't have completed** the job until tomorrow night.*

This tense can be called 'the past in the future'.

UNIT 8
Relative clauses

There are two kinds of relative clauses, *defining* and *non-defining*.

Defining relative clauses are much more common.

Compare the following sentences:

a. *A philatelist is a person **who collects stamps.***
b. *I had a very interesting meeting with Dr Widdows, **who collects stamps and butterflies in his spare time.***

In 'a', the relative clause is *defining*. It tells us what a philatelist is. Without the words in bold, the sentence makes no sense. The relative clause cannot be left out.

In 'b', the relative clause is *non-defining*. It adds extra information of secondary importance and could be left out of the sentence. Non-defining relative clauses are more frequent in written English, where sentences are

carefully constructed. In spoken English, they sound rather formal, and can easily be expressed by simpler sentences.

> *I had a very interesting meeting with Dr Widdows. Did you know he collects stamps and butterflies in his spare time? Well, he does.*

1 Defining relative clauses

	Person	Thing
Subject	who (that)	that (which)
Object	(that)	(that)

The forms in brackets are possible but not as common.

No relative pronoun is necessary when it introduces a relative clause that defines the *object* of the sentence. (See last 3 examples below.)

> *The woman **who is wearing blue shorts** is my wife.* (subject)
> *Fleming? Wasn't he the man **who discovered penicillin?*** (subject)
> *The group **that wins** will represent the school.* (subject)
> *A corkscrew is an instrument **that is used for opening bottles of wine.*** (subject)
> *The man (that) **you met yesterday** was my father.* (object)
> *Have you eaten the chocolate (that) **I bought you?*** (object)
> *The road (that) **we wanted to take** was blocked.* (object)

Notes

There are *no* commas before and after defining relative clauses when written, and *no* pauses when spoken.

That is usually used with superlatives, **all**, **the only** and **it is.**

> *This is **the biggest** plane **that** has ever flown.*
> ***All that's** needed is a little time.*
> ***The only** thing **that** matters is that you're safe.*
> ***It's** the lack of money **that** prevents us moving at the moment.*

2 Non-defining relative clauses

	Person	Thing
Subject	, who . . . ,	, which . . . ,
Object	, who . . . , , whom . . . ,	, which . . . ,

> *Mr Jenkins, **who has written several books,** spoke at the meeting last night.* (subject)
> *My favourite drink is whisky, **which is Britain's biggest export.*** (subject)
> *Peter Wetherington, **who the Prime Minister sacked from the post of Minister of Defence,** has become chairman of the Redland Bank.* (object)
> *I gave him a sandwich, **which he ate greedily.*** (object)

*Mr Jones, **for whom I've been working for 10 years,** got married yesterday.* (object)

Notes

Relative pronouns *cannot* be left out of non-defining relative clauses.

There are *commas* around non-defining relative clauses when written and *pauses* before and after them when spoken.

That is *not* used in non-defining relative clauses.
Which can be used in *non-defining* relative clauses to refer to the whole sentence before.

*He arrived on time, **which surprised everybody.***
*She passed her exams, **which made her parents very proud.***
*The lift doesn't work, **which means we'll have to walk up six flights of stairs.***

3 **Whose**

Whose can be used in *both* defining and non-defining relative clauses.
Whose introduces relative clauses that describe *possession* of people, places, things, etc.

*That's the woman **whose son was killed recently.*** (defining)
*My parents, **whose greatest ambition is to retire to the coast,** have just sold their house.* (non-defining)
*Is that the company **whose accountant has disappeared with thousands of pounds of their money?*** (defining)
*Which is the dog **whose owner recently died leaving it her fortune?*** (defining)

4 **What**

What is used as a relative pronoun instead of **the thing that** in sentences like:

***What** I need to know is where we are meeting.*
*Has she told you **what** is worrying her?*
*I have to do **what** I believe is right.*

5 **Why, when** and **where**

Why, **when** and **where** can be used as *relative pronouns* to introduce defining and non-defining relative clauses.

In *defining relative clauses:*

a. **why** and **when** can be left out.
*Do you remember the reason (**why**) we were arguing?*
*I need to know the exact time (**when**) you expect to arrive.*

b. **where** cannot be left out unless we add a preposition.
*Do you know the hotel **where** we're staying?*
*Do you know the hotel we're staying **at**?*

In *non-defining relative clauses*, we can use **when** or **where** and they can never be left out.

*We go swimming after 5 o'clock, **when** everyone else has gone home.*
*He shops over in Oxford, **where** his sister lives.*

Participles

1 **Participles used as adjectives**

Present participles (**-ing**) describe an action still happening.

*He dived into the sea to save the **drowning** child.*
*She poured **boiling** water into the dish.*
*They watched the **burning** forest helplessly.*

Past participles describe the result of an action that has happened.

*She looked at the **broken** chair, wondering if it could be mended.*
*The **completed** statue looked very lifelike.*
*After the storm the tent was **ruined**.*

2 **Participle clauses**

Participles are often used to describe two actions that happen:

a. at the same time.

*She **sat** by the fire **reading** a book.*
*He **walked** down the road **singing** a song.*
*He **went** to the party **dressed** as a monster.*

b. one after the other:

***Loosening** his tie, he **sat down** in the chair.*
***Opening** his suitcase, he **took out** a thousand pounds in five-pound notes.*

If it is important to show that one action has finished *before* the other begins, the perfect participle is used.

***Having finished** lunch, we **set off**.*
***Having had** a shower, she **got dressed**.*

c. Two actions that happen one because of another:

***Being** a mean person, he **never bought** anything for anybody.* (i.e. Because he was a mean person . . .)
***Not knowing** what else to do, I **waited** patiently.*
***Weakened** by years of bad health, she **could hardly sit up** in bed.*

Notice that in these three uses, the subject of the main verb must be the same as the subject of the participle.

Modifiers

1 It is important to distinguish between *two* kinds of adjective, *limit* and *gradable* adjectives.

Limit adjectives already have very strong meanings.

Exhausted means 'very tired'.
Delicious means 'very tasty'.

For this reason, it sounds odd to say 'very exhausted' or 'very delicious'.

Gradable adjectives express qualities that can exist in different strengths.

A person can be **more** or **less tall**, or **more** or **less attractive**.
A thing can be **more** or **less big**, or **more** or **less dirty**.

So we can use modifiers like **fairly, quite, very, extremely** with gradable adjectives like **tall, attractive, big, dirty, tired**.

Examples

gradable	limit
big	vast huge enormous
dirty	filthy revolting
good	perfect marvellous wonderful
angry	furious
frightened	terrified
difficult	impossible

2 To modify limit adjectives, we need an *extreme* modifier.

absolutely *huge*
completely *terrified*
quite *perfect*
utterly *ridiculous*
totally *blind*

Some modifiers and adjectives go together, and some do not. It takes time and practice to learn which are used together. We can say 'absolutely furious' but not 'completely furious' for example.

The best advice is to start by recognizing the different modifiers when you are listening and reading, and if you are in doubt, use **absolutely**, which can go with all limit adjectives.

3 **Quite**

Quite can be used with *limit adjectives* to mean **absolutely**.

quite | *right*
| *sure*
| *extraordinary*

Quite can also be used with *gradable adjectives*, and its meaning changes according to stress and intonation. Again, practice is needed in hearing and reading these expressions in context to know when to use them.

It's quite 'good. (weak **quite**, stressed **good**)
This is positive. 'I like it.'

It's 'quite 'good. (equal stress)
This is neutral. 'It's moderately good.'

It's 'quite good. (stressed **quite**, weak **good**)
This is negative. 'It's all right, but not wonderful.'

Rather and **pretty** are similar, but again, practice is needed to know how and when to use them.

Notice that when **quite** is followed by a noun, it usually comes before the article.

*That's **quite a clever dog** you've got.*
*I thought it was **quite an interesting film**.*

UNIT 9
Modal verbs of deduction

We use modal verbs of deduction to express *degrees of certainty* about the present and the past – what we *are* or *are not* sure/certain about and what we think *may* or *may not* be true/possible.

1 *To express certainty*, we use **must** in the positive and **can't** in the negative.

*They **must** be in bed. They **can't** be out at this time of night.*
*He **must** have got lost. He **can't** have known the way.*

2 *To express possibility*, we use **may**, **might**, **could** in the positive and **may not**, and **might not** (short forms *not* usual), in the negative.

*She **may** be there already.*
*He **may not** be there yet.*
*It **might not** be John – it **might** be a burglar!*
*He **might not** have been drunk – he **might** have been ill!*
*She **may not** have seen you. She **may** have been looking the other way.*

3 To ask a question about things over which we are uncertain we use **Do you think** . . .?

A *Do you think she's married?*
B *She **can't** be. She hasn't got a ring.*

A *Where **do you think** he's from?*
B *He **might** be French. He smokes French cigarettes.*

A *Do you think they've arrived yet?*
B *They **must** have arrived. Their car's in the drive.*

A *How **do you think** they got here?*
B *Someone **must** have left them here.*

A *Where **do you think** everyone is?*
B *They **could** be at the pub.*

4 *Continuous infinitives* are used *to express activities in progress*. (See page 112)

Compare the following sentences:

A *What do you think he does for a living?*
B *He **might** work in a bank.*

A *There's a light on in his office.*
B *He **must be working** late.*

*He **can't have seen** the other car.* (single action)
*He **must have been driving** too fast.* (activity with duration)

Multi-word verbs

A very important feature of *multi-word verbs* is that many of them have special meanings. They cannot be understood by knowing what the individual parts mean. They must be learnt as a single unit in the same way as one learns an idiomatic phrase.

There are four types of multi-word verbs.

Type 1: verb + adverb (phrasal verb *without* an object)

Look at the examples:

a. *He came into the room and then **went out**.*
b. *I didn't put enough wood on the fire and it **went out**.*

In 'a' the verb and adverb are used literally, and the meaning can easily be worked out.
In 'b' they are not used literally. **To go out** here means 'to stop burning'.

More examples with literal meaning:

*I **sat down**.*
*He **got up**.*
*The soldiers **marched past**.*
*Please **go away**.*

This type is very common with verbs of motion.

go	across
come	away
walk	back
run	past
	in
	out

More examples with non-literal meaning:

*The marriage didn't **work out**.* (succeed)
*He wanted us to **break up**.* (separate)
*The meat has **gone off**.* (gone bad)
*Our plans **fell through**.* (failed)

Type 2: verb + adverb + object (phrasal verb *with* an object)

Look at the examples:

a. *I **put up** the picture. It looked lovely next to the clock.*
    (*I **put** it **up**.* NOT ~~I put up it.~~)
b. *I **put up** my sister for the night.*
    (*I **put** her **up**.* NOT ~~I put up her.~~)

In 'a', the verb and adverb are used literally. The adverb can change position but *not* if the object is a pronoun.

    *I **put** the picture **up**.*
    *I **put up** the picture.*
BUT *I **put** it **up**.*

In 'b', the verb and adverb are not used literally. **To put up** here means 'to provide food and a bed'. The adverb can change position but *not* if the object is a pronoun.

    *I **put** my sister **up** for the night.*
    *I **put up** my sister for the night.*
BUT *I **put** her **up** for the night.*

More examples with literal meaning:

*Waiter! Could you **take away** my plates, please?*   ***Take** them **away**!*
*Don't **throw** that piece of paper **away**. I need it.*   *Don't **throw** it **away**.*

*They're **pulling down** that lovely old building. Isn't it a shame?*   *They're **pulling** it **down**.*
*Please **put** your clothes **away**.*   ***Put** them **away**.*

More examples with non-literal meaning:

*I **put off** the meeting till next week.* (postponed)   *I **put** it **off**.*
*She **told** the cleaning lady **off** for being late.* (reprimanded)   *She **told** her **off**.*
*Don't **let** your parents **down**.* (disappoint)   *Don't **let** them **down**.*
*They **turned** Jim **down** for the job.* (refused)   *They **turned** him **down**.*

Type 3: Verb + preposition + object (prepositional verb)

A prepositional verb always has an object. The object *always* comes *after* the preposition.

Look at the examples:

a. *She **came across** the room.*
b. *She **came across** an old friend while she was out shopping.*

In 'a', the verb and preposition are used literally. The preposition *cannot* change position.

In 'b', the verb and preposition are not used literally. **To come across** here means 'to find by accident'. The preposition *cannot* change position.

This type of multi-word verb is very common with verbs of motion.

go	across	the park
come	over	the hill
walk	past	the church
drive	into	the garage

More examples with literal meaning:

*I'm **looking for** Jane. Have you seen her?*
*He **ran across** the road.*
*We **drove past** the museum.*

Non-literal meaning:

*Who's going to **look after** the cat while we're away?* (care for)
*You **take after** your father.* (resemble)
*I'll **look into** the matter for you.* (investigate)

Type 4: verb + adverb + preposition (phrasal-prepositional verb)

Look at the examples:

a. *Do you **get on with** your boss?*
b. *Do you **get on with** her?*

The preposition *cannot* change position. It must come *before* the object.
Verbs of this kind are not used literally.

More examples:

*I'm **looking forward to** seeing you.* (anticipating with pleasure)
*How can you **put up with** the noise?* (tolerate)
*She **looks down on** the lower classes.* (despises)

UNIT 10
Habit

1 Present Simple + adverbs of frequency

The Present Simple is the most common tense for expressing *present habit*. It is often used with an adverb of frequency.

always   continually   constantly   forever

often   frequently   regularly   usually   normally

sometimes   occasionally

rarely   hardly ever   seldom

never

The normal position for adverbs of frequency is *before* the main verb.

*We **hardly ever go out** anymore.*
*She **frequently forgets** what she's doing.*
*We don't **usually eat** fish.*
*Do you **often eat out**?*

However, they come *after* the verb **to be**.

*She's **always** late. She's **never** on time.*
*They **are usually** in bed by this time.*
*Is he **normally** so bad tempered?*

2 Present Continuous

The Present Continuous can be used to express a habit which happens often and perhaps unexpectedly. It can express a pleasant habit.

*I like Peter. He's always **smiling**.*
*He's always **giving** people things.*

However, there is usually an element of criticism. Contrast the pair of sentences below.

*He always **asks** questions about the lesson.* (Present Simple. A teacher describes a student's habit. We don't know the teacher's attitude.)

*He's always **asking** questions about the lesson.* (Present Continuous. The teacher finds it *annoying*.)

3 Will

Will expresses typical behaviour. It can be used to describe both pleasant and unpleasant habits.

*He'll often **buy** me things, even when it's not my birthday.*

*She'll **tell** lies even when there's no need.*
*The cat **will** often **curl up** by the fire and stay there all evening.*

The negative form of **will** is **won't**.

*He'll **sit** in his chair and he **won't talk** to anyone.*
*She's a good dog. She **won't bite** anyone unless she's provoked.*

4 Used to + infinitive

The structure **used to** + infinitive exists only in the past, and expresses *past actions* and *states* that happened often but do not happen now.

Positive form:

We
They | **used to go out** *a lot.*

Negative form:

I
He | **didn't use to like** *it.*

Question form:

*Where **did*** | *you **use to*** | *go?*
Did | | ***have** holidays abroad?*

More examples:

*When I was a boy, we always **used to go** camping at week-ends.*
*They don't see each other any more, but they **used to do** everything together.*
*Did you **use to go** there often?*
*We never **used to enjoy** ourselves.*

To express *present habit*, use the Present Simple.

*We usually **go** camping at week-ends.*
*They're inseparable. They **do** everything together.*
*I often **go** there.*
*We always **enjoy** ourselves.*

5 Be/get used to + noun or gerund

This expresses an action that was difficult, strange or unusual before, but is no longer so. Used this way, **used to** is an adjective meaning **accustomed to** (something).

*I found it very tiring at first but I'm **used to it** now.*
*You must **be used to reading** bed-time stories if you've got children.*

Notice the use of **get** to express the process of change:

*I'm **getting used to the climate**.*
*I couldn't **get used to eating** with chopsticks.*

UNIT 11
Hypothesis

Should have (done), **wish**, and **would have (done)** all express actions which *didn't* happen (or *aren't* happening), and so are contrary to reality.

I should have worked harder. (But I didn't.)
I wish I hadn't done that. (But I did.)
If I'd been there, I'd have told him. (But I wasn't there, and I didn't tell him.)

1 Should + perfect infinitive (simple or continuous)

Should have (done)/should have been (doing) express *advice*, *obligation*, or *criticism* about a *past* action. Compare the following sentences:

You shouldn't have hit him. (single action)
You should have been watching the road. (activity with duration)

2 Wish

Notice how we express wishes about the present, to say that we would like things to be different from the way they are.

State

Present Simple ⟶ wish + Past Simple

We live in the country.   *I wish we lived in the town.*
I have a cold.   *I wish I didn't have a cold.*

Actions

Present Simple ⟶ wish + would + infinitive

You don't help in the house.   *I wish you'd help in the house.*
You wash your socks in the bath.   *I wish you wouldn't wash your socks in the bath.*

Would here expresses annoying habit or insistence, and implies desire for change in the future.

Notice also wishes about the future.

I'm not going on holiday.   *I wish I was going on holiday.*
I'm having lunch with Susan.   *I wish I wasn't having lunch with Susan.*

We can say **I wish . . . would** to refer to a *definite* time in the future, but only if we think the action may *not* happen.

I wish you would mend the gate tomorrow. (You probably won't do it.)

If our wish is *likely* to be realized, then we need a different structure such as *I hope* + Present Simple.

I hope it snows tomorrow.
I hope you feel better soon.

3 Third conditional

Third conditional sentences express *imaginary* situations about the *past*.

if + past perfect	would + perfect infinitive
Condition	Result
If you hadn't told me	*I would never have known.* (certainty)
	I might have made a mistake. (possibility)
	I could have got lost. (possibility)

The verb in the *condition* clause can be simple or continuous. Compare the following sentences.

If I had seen the man,	*I wouldn't have hit him.*
If I had been watching the road	

UNIT 12
Articles

The use of articles in English is complex, and there are a lot of exceptions that need to be remembered and learned.

Here are the basic rules.

1 A/an

Use **a/an** to refer to a *singular countable* noun which is *indefinite* – either we don't know which one, or it doesn't matter which one.

They live in a lovely house.
I'm reading a good book at the moment.
She's expecting a baby.

Use **a/an** to describe what something or someone is.

That's an instrument for measuring distance.
She's a lawyer.

2 The

Use **the** before a *singular* or *plural* noun, when both the speaker and the listener know which *specific* object is being referred to.

They live in the green house on top of the hill.
The book I'm reading is all about the emancipation of women.
Mind the baby! She's near the fire.
The sweater I bought is blue.

Use **the** before a noun if it is the *only* one (**the Queen, the Earth, the Atlantic**). Also use it with certain public places, especially when referring to them in a general way:

*I went to **the theatre** last night.*
*I have to go to **the bank**.*

It should also be used when referring to general groups of people (**the French, the rich and famous**)

3 **Zero article**

Use *no* article with *plural* and *uncountable* nouns when talking about things in general.

Compare the use of articles in the following sentences.

***Money** is the root of all evil.* (general)
*Put **the money** on the table.* (specific)

***Love** conquers all.* (general)
***The love** I have for you will last for ever.* (specific)

***Gas** is cheaper than electricity.* (general)
*I forgot to pay the bill, and now **the gas** has been cut off.* (specific)

4 **Final points**

Notice the difference between the use of articles in the following sentences:

*My daughter is **at school**.*
*The meeting will be held **at the school**.*

*I go **to church** on Sundays.*
*The firemen went **to the church** to put out the fire.*

*He was rushed **to hospital** immediately.*
*I'm going **to the hospital** to visit him.*

The use of **the** emphasizes the place simply as a *building*. The use *without* **the** suggests that the place is being used for its proper function as an *institution*, i.e. a place of learning, healing etc.

Pubs, hotels, theatres, and *cinemas* usually have **the**
the *Prince William*
the *London Hilton*
the *Albany Empire*
the *Odeon*

Some *geographical areas* have **the.**

seas   **the** *Mediterranean*
rivers   **the** *Seine*; **the** *Mississippi*
island groups   **the** *Seychelles*
mountain groups   **the** *Alps*
deserts   **the** *Sahara*

Streets, roads, and *squares* etc. in towns usually have *no* article.

Oxford Street
Portobello Road
Hyde Park
Leicester Square
Victoria Station

Other nouns which take *no* article are:

lakes   *Lake Superior, Lake Victoria*
countries   *Spain, Norway, China*
continents   *Asia, Europe*

The following types of noun take no article when referred to generally:

games   *squash, football, chess*
academic subjects   *medicine, literature, physics*
abstract nouns   *freedom, understanding*
meals   *dinner, tea, breakfast*

Compare these sentences:
*Do you prefer **hockey** or **football**?*
***The football** they play in America is different from the kind they play in England.*

***Dinner** is usually at eight o'clock.*
***The dinner** they served yesterday was the best I remember.*

Tapescript section

UNIT 1

Tapescript 1

A variety of accents

1 The capital city of my country was specially designed and built with wide tree-lined streets, radiating out in all directions, er . . . from the city centre. They join concentric ring roads, and are all pretty well identical. This is in federal territory, on the border of New South Wales and Victoria. The drawback is, that it's almost impossible to find your way around it, even after you've lived there for years! (Canberra)

2 Well, it's the capital city of the country. Now it's famous really for er . . . well, I think it's famous for two things. It's famous for the writers that have come from there. People like er . . . George Bernard Shaw, Oscar Wilde, James Joyce. And it's also famous for . . . er, for a drink. A drink called Guinness. A wonderful drink. It's known locally as Liffey water, after the river that flows through the centre of the town, the river Liffey. (Dublin)

3 This . . . er city is a very large city. It's the capital city of our country, and it's very busy with a lot of traffic. It has a big river running through it, which used to be used by quite big boats, although the docks aren't used very much now. A very good way to see the city is . . . er from a bus, because buses have er . . . two decks, and they're bright red. (London)

4 My capital is unusual because, although it's in a state, it's considered a separate district, with its own laws and regulations. In the middle of it there's a big house, where our country's leader lives. It has a west wing and an east wing, and parts of it are open to the public. There's also a house where senators work, and where representatives work, and there's a five-sided building where everybody that's in power works. (Washington)

5 I come from an ancient city, sometimes referred to as the Athens of the North. The main picturesque shopping street in the city centre is called Princes Street, and is overlooked by the castle, built on a hill of volcanic rock. (Edinburgh)

6 Well, it lies on the south coast of the country, on the banks of the River Taff. It's the capital city of course, and about fifty years ago, it used to be a very important port indeed, really, but since the . . . er, you know, the traditional industries of steel and coal have been in decline, well, the old docks have gone a bit downhill as well. But . . . er . . . it's got a lot of history, of course, it goes back to the days of Julius Caesar at least. It's got an old castle in the middle. And it's got a brand new concert hall, which is very appropriate for the Land of Song, I think. (Cardiff)

Tapescript 2

Esperanto, a world language

P = Presenter
N = Professor Nesbit

P Hello, and welcome to today's *Worldly Wise*, the programme that examines world issues and the way they affect each and every one of us.
Today we turn our attention to languages, or more specifically, to language. What would the world be like if everyone spoke the same language? Would we understand each other better and be more sympathetic to each other's causes? I'm not talking about everyone sharing the same first language, but sharing the same second language, and I'm not talking about English, but Esperanto.
What are the facts about this artificial language? Well, it was invented in 1887 by a Polish doctor, Ludwig Lazarus Zamenhof. The vocabulary comes mainly from Western European languages, and the grammar is similar to Slavic languages. It sounds like Italian.
From the learner's point of view, it has the advantage that there are no exceptions to rules. It is spoken all over the world by approximately eight million people, and there are many who would like Esperanto to be the official second language of the world.
I spoke to Professor Desmond Nesbit of the University of Edinburgh for more information and asked him, hasn't the world got enough natural languages, so why make an artificial one?

N I prefer the term planned to artificial. Esperanto means 'hopeful', and it was Zamenhof's hope that a common language would promote a friendship and an understanding amongst all people of the world. His er . . . inspiration is summed up by the Esperanto term *interna ideo* which means central idea, and it is an idea of human peace and justice.

P What are the advantages that you see of Esperanto as a world language?

N I see many. The advantages of the world being able to talk freely to each other about business, politics, culture, sport, hobbies, well – are obvious. The costs of translation at any international conference are staggering. Did you know that 55 per cent of the EEC's budget in Strasbourg is taken up by translation costs?

P My goodness!

N The main advantage, as I see it, is that Esperanto is a neutral language. It doesn't have the national, political, and cultural bias that all others of course have. If everybody has to learn a second language, then everybody is equal.

P But isn't it making a difficult situation even more difficult? I mean, there are already so many people who speak English throughout the world, why should they have to learn another language? Why not English as the world language?

N I think I've partly answered that question already. Why should people have to learn English? For many it's a waste of time, energy, and money. The other thing that must be said is that English is by no means an easy language to learn. There is the problem of spelling, of the large number of exceptions to any rule, it is very idiomatic and the prepositions are terrible! English is one of those languages which for many seems easy in the beginning, but then the bridge between basic knowledge and mastery takes a long time to cross, and many people give up.

P On the subject of ease of learning, how does Esperanto compare?

N Esperanto is a very easy language to learn. The tense system has none of the complications of English, and the grammar is based on just sixteen rules which have no exceptions. There are five vowel sounds, and . . .

P How many vowel sounds does English have?

N Twenty. The most remarkable thing is that after a very short time learners find that they can express quite sophisticated ideas, the same sort of things that they would want to say in their own language.

P That's remarkable. But Professor, do you really see Esperanto becoming the World language? There's quite a difference between the four hundred million speakers of English and the eight million speakers of Esperanto.

N I think it will happen, yes. I think it's happening now. Esperanto is taught in many schools in Yugoslavia and Hungary. China is very interested. It has such internal logic that it could become the international computer language, and that would really establish it.

P Professor Nesbit, thank you very much.

N Thank you.

Tapescript 3

A number dictation

Hello, and good evening.
It is feared that 182 people may have died in a plane crash this morning. The accident happened at 20 past 7. It was Bel Air flight 409, going from Singapore to New York. The plane had covered ¾ of the 12,000 mile trip, and had stopped to refuel. Eye witnesses said that the plane had reached its take-off speed of 150 mph when a fire broke out in the rear engine. 106 people managed to escape the blaze.
672 car workers walked out on strike today in Coventry. They had asked for a pay rise of 8·7%, but management said they could only offer 5½%. This would mean an extra £27.50 per week. A union spokesman said 'It's not enough'.
A man armed with a shotgun held up cashiers at the National Bank today and stole £5,500. Police have appealed for witnesses. The number to ring is 0106 744391.
Unemployment figures were released today. Last month there were 3,649,712 registered unemployed. That's 14.5% of the work force. Over the past year this number has increased by over 260,000.
And that's the end of tonight's news. Good night.

UNIT 2

Tapescript 4

All the world's a stage

See page 11.

Tapescript 5

The audition

P = Producer
D = Director

P Well, that was very interesting, wasn't it, Derek?

D Mmm, very interesting indeed, yes. But I think it's given us more problems than um ... than it's taken away. I mean, I don't think there's one obvious candidate – did you feel that?

P Oh, yes, I think so. I thought they all had strengths, and I don't think it's going to be an easy choice.

D No ... Well, let's go through them, shall we? Let's take Bill first. I thought he did rather well in the audition. The voice was right, and, well, he was very funny in places, he caught that comic side of Micawber when everything's gone wrong all around him. No?

P Um, yes, I agree. Yes, I think he caught the character very well, certainly, but er ...

D What?

P ... It's his past that worries me a little, I know he's had a lot of experience in character parts, but it's all been in the theatre, hasn't it, not on television, and as you've found yourself, it's not the same at all. The camera's so close on television, isn't it?

D Yeah. What's he been doing recently? Has he been in much?

P Well, no, in fact. He's been out of work for about nine months, and not helped by a bit of a drink problem. I don't know if you noticed ...

D Mmm, yes, he forgot one or two lines, didn't he?

P Mmm.

D Well, I don't know. I still think he did well. What about the next? Who was it? Harry, wasn't it?

P Yes. Now I thought Harry was *great*. He said his lines so confidently, and his timing was superb. I think he was really made for the part.

D You seem to have made up your mind, don't you?

P Yes. Well, no, it was just that when I closed my eyes, I could really picture him in the part.

D Yes, well, for me Polly that's just the point. I agree, he sounded very convincing. Hasn't he just written a book on Dickens, or something?

P Yes, it's called *The Spirit of Dickens*.

D Well, that's just what he did, he caught the spirit of this rather self-important old man, but to me he just doesn't look the part. I mean, how old is he?

P He's er ... let me look ... erm, he's ... thirty-eight.

D Yes, you see, too young, and I think too tall. Now Bill's the right age, at least.

P I know what you mean, but he's got so much experience of the stage and the television.

He's been with the Royal Shakespeare Company for years, and I think we could probably work on the appearance side, you know. Make-up would age him.

D Harry didn't look right, whereas Bill did. And I do wonder about make-up to make someone look older on television. It never looks quite right.

P Well, maybe another part for him? Not Micawber?

D Possibly. You might be right. Let's move on to Victor. Now there's a problem.

P How do you mean?

D He's the one with the greatest strengths and also the greatest weaknesses. I mean, he's a household name, everybody knows him, and well I think having him in the part would attract a lot of viewers, but ...

P ... but his experience is light comedy, situation comedy, not character parts like this.

D You took the words right out of my mouth – that's just what I was going to say. The problem is, he plays himself, and it's true, he's a very funny man.

P But could he adapt? I thought he auditioned quite well, actually. He's the right age, and the face fits.

D But the audience would identify with his other characters, and say 'Oh look! There's Victor O'Brian playing a Dickens character!' They wouldn't say 'Isn't Mr Micawber good! I wonder who he is?'

P The question is, how adaptable is he? I think with guidance he could be OK. And he's very keen. He's been trying to break away from those situation comedy roles for years, but producers won't let him.

D Well, you're the producer!

P (laughs) Oh well, what are we going to do?

D Let's just make a note of their good points and bad points again. Let's take Bill ...

Tapescript 6

A dictation of names and places

1 My name's Jameson. That's J-A-M-E-S-O-N. I'll spell it again for you. J-A-M-E-S-O-N.

2 Do you need my full name? My first name's Juliet. J-U-L-I-E-T. Yes, J-U-L-I-E-T. And my surname's Henderson. Hen-der-son – H-E-N-D-E-R-S-O-N.

3 **A** My Christian name is Stephen.
  B Now, there are different ways of spelling that, aren't there?
  A Yes. Mine's P-H.
  B Pardon?
  A You spell it S-T-E-P-H-E-N.
  B Thank you.

4 **A** Place of birth, please madam.
  B Loughborough. L-O-U-G-H-B-O-R-O-U-G-H. Would you like me to spell it again? L-O-U-G-H-B-O-R-O-U-G-H.

5 Hello, I'd like to order a book by Gerald Leary. Hello? It's not a very good line, is it? Gerald Leary. Gerald – G-E-R-A-L-D. Leary – L-E-A-R-Y. That's it. The title of the book is *The Secret Life of Plants*.

6 Hello, er – I have a reservation. The name's Mahoney – M-A-H-O-N-E-Y.

7 My surname's Bailey – B-A-I-L-E-Y.

8 **A** Where do you live?
  B A suburb of London called Greenwich.

A G-R-E-N-
B No, no. G-R-double E-N-W-I-C-H. Greenwich.

9 **A** Hello. I have an appointment with Miss Jenkins.
  B Your name please?
  A Seabourne. S-E-A-B-O-U-R-N-E.

10 **A** I'm living in a place called Gloucester.
  B How do you spell that?
  A G-L-O-U-C-E-S-T-E-R. Gloucester.

UNIT 3

Tapescript 7

My first job

I = Interviewer
L = Liz

I What was your first job, Liz?

L Erm. Oh, I can remember it very well. Erm, I'd just graduated and I'd just got married – er two important things – and my husband got a teaching job in Tanzania. And erm ... we went out there together and my idea was ... what I hoped to do was erm ... get a job shortly after getting there. And I didn't really know what kind of job it would be.

I So you were just taking pot luck, really?

L Well, what happened was I thought I'd take some time to settle us in to this small town on the coast of Tanzania, north of Dar es Salaam, a town called Tanga, and I thought I'd settle us in – wherever we were going to live, I – we didn't know. But on the very first day we were there, erm ... somebody came running up to me, literally in the street, and said 'We hear you're – you're a graduate, and the local junior school's going to close down. Please, do you think you could be the teacher?'

I The only teacher?

L No, one of two. I was to teach the six to thirteen year-olds, all nationalities, and there was also a class of five and six year-olds, all nationalities, in this small, erm ... local school. It was called Nuguvumali School. It was a very small school just outside, through the banana plantation on the hill outside of Tanga.

I But you had no experience of teaching at all?

L No. It was ... I look back now, now that I am a teacher – because I ultimately became a teacher – I look back with horror and think, 'The only way that I think that I coped was because of ... I was so ignorant, I didn't know any better'. Erm ... and ... erm ... every day ... I took the job ... I felt as if I was doing a really good deed. I don't think I did, looking back, but ... and every day we drove out, erm ... to this small school, just a little wooden school – it had a veranda all round – and the kind of thing that happened was ... because it was out in the bush, er ... there was a lot of snakes. And we had ... something that was very important with these children was snake drill. It was important to me too, I was terrified of snakes. Unfortunately, the children weren't frightened of snakes, so whenever the cry went up 'A snake!', instead of running in the opposite direction, the children would all run straight towards the snake. And I had the job of getting in between the children and the snake, and trying to say 'No, no!' you know, 'Back you go – Remember the snake drill!' and they'd cheer and cheer until . . . and they used to come along and chop the snake's head off, and the snake would go on wriggling. And then the children would cheer, and only after the final wriggle could we go back and start classes again.

I So the kids actually had a knife or something on them, did they?

L Well, the caretaker had a knife. It was . . . not a knife, something called a *panga*. It's a big African knife that they cut the grass with and the caretaker would run up with this *panga* and go 'Chop! – snake finished'.

I And did you have any discipline problems with these kids?

L Well, no. The thing was, when I took over the job, I was told by this very strict teacher that in Tanzania you had to punish the children very firmly. And the way you did that was you slapped them on the leg. And I was, I was twenty remember, yeah twenty years old, and I thought . . . 'You slap them on the leg', and she said . . . and she gave me a list of things where they were slapped on the leg. If they forgot a library book – they had a little library. And one day a little girl forgot a library book, and I thought 'Oh dear! I'm supposed to slap her on the leg!' And I thought 'I can't do that'. So I didn't, and in fact I never really had discipline problems.
It was quite funny. I was supposed to teach them everything, I mean it was a junior school, and one of the things I was supposed to teach them was geography, and I knew nothing about geography, but as part of my university course, I'd done something about Sweden, and Swedish – mainly about the language, but as part of the course for some reason we'd done something on Swedish geography. So here I was in Africa – and I thought 'I have to teach them geography, I don't know any geography' – there were no books. So I taught them about Sweden. And funnily enough of all the things I taught I think that was the most successful. They were fascinated in a country with snow, and a country where it didn't always get light at six o'clock, and it didn't always get dark at six o'clock, and I think that was erm . . . one of my main successes. Every day I went in, and they'd say 'Tell us some more about Sweden!' and I didn't have a lot to tell, really. But erm . . . I don't know if I did anything else very well, but I was very good in telling them about Sweden . . .

Tapescript 8

A dream come true

I = Interviewer
D = David

I For most of us, work is something we have to do to stay alive and pay the bills. It's not something we particularly enjoy, unless you're one of the lucky few who manage to make a living out of a hobby. David Crook used to work for a firm of accountants in the City of London. He gave up a six figure salary to come to live and work in the tiny village of Little Hampton. I went to visit him last week, and I asked him what made him do it.

D Well, living in London was becoming more and more depressing. My wife and I had always wanted to live in the country, but the problem was finding some sort of job to do – erm because we didn't have enough money to give up work entirely. Then one weekend, we were driving home after visiting friends, and we happened to see this beautiful windmill for sale. The building itself was in quite good condition, but the machinery for the mill was either – either broken or missing. I think both Lesley, my wife, and I had the same idea at the same time. You see, I've always enjoyed playing with engines and motors, taking them to pieces and mending them, and we thought we could buy the mill, renovate the machinery, and make enough from milling wheat to pay the bills.

I And that's what you did?

D That's right. The very next day I handed in my notice, and a few weeks later, we were here.

I Was it easy to repair the mill?

D No, not at all. It was terribly difficult to get hold of all the parts I needed. I had to travel all over the country, and I even had to make some of the parts myself. But we finally got it working just before Christmas last year.

I So you've been operating now for . . . eighteen months?

D That's right.

I And how is the business going?

D Well, I think it's going all right, actually. We even considered buying another mill, restoring it and selling it for a profit, but then we thought that it would be too much, and that wasn't the reason we came here, so we didn't. And we just keep this one mill going.

I Right. And do you have any regrets? Is there anything you miss, for example?

D No, not a thing. It's hard work, but it's for ourselves, and I think working together is something we've always wanted.

I And what about your boys? You have two teenage sons, don't you?

D Yes, well at first they missed all their friends, naturally, and living in a small village isn't at all like living in a London suburb. But it's fine now, they like it as much as we do.

I Well David, it sounds as though it's all worked out very well indeed.

D Well, touch wood it seems to have done.

UNIT 4

Tapescript 9

A ghost story

S = Stephanie
R = Rob

S This particular incident happened while my husband and I were living with friends in an old house in Highgate, in north London, and we had this large bedroom. And at one end of the room I also had a desk where I used to do my work. I could never really explain it but I often had this strange feeling that I was being watched . . . and . . . I started talking to myself . . . in my head, not out loud, saying 'Oh, don't be silly, there's nobody there, there's nothing at all'. And I carried on having this feeling, so I began to talk actually out loud,

saying 'Now, come on, I know you're there, don't worry, just don't bother me'. And the same would happen while I was working, I would suddenly feel that someone was there, and once I'd talked to it, it was OK.

R Did you tell Jeremy this? Did he know about it?

S Yes, I'd told him, but he didn't believe me. You see, I'd had one or two strange experiences before, when I was a child, but Jeremy just said that I was imagining things and that it was all nonsense. Anyway, we were lying in bed one night, and suddenly we both woke up, and there was somebody standing at the bottom of the bed, this figure, and we presumed it was John, one of the friends we were living with, who wanted something. So we said 'What's the matter, what do you want?', and there was no answer . . .

R (nervous laugh)

S So er . . . I said 'It's not John, it doesn't look like John'. It was this tall figure. I put the light on, and . . . there was nothing there . . .

R But you both saw it?

S Oh yes, we both saw it, not just me. We got up and checked. The door was closed, so goodness knows what it was. Then a few days later, Jeremy woke me up in the middle of the night. You see, in this room, we had lots of posters up on the walls, and also lots of postcards of art and pictures, and I had these postcards stuck on boards, about fifteen postcards to a board . . . He woke me up . . . it was freezing cold . . . each picture was falling off the wall . . . one by one . . . from left to right around the room. And when Jeremy woke me up, he was absolutely petrified . . . About half the pictures were on the floor, and each one dropped off one by one, all the postcards . . . off the board . . . and then the board and then the next board . . .

R What!

S And it went right round the room, until every single piece of paper was on the floor or the bed. We were sitting in bed covered in pieces of paper, absolutely terrified of what was going to happen next.

R And what *did* happen?

S No, that was it.

R That was enough!

S Yes. We got up, had a cup of tea, and tried to explain to the others the next day. They just thought we were crazy. Anyway, I still went on talking to this thing, and by this time Jeremy was convinced that there was something very strange going on . . .

R You're not kidding!

S Another night he woke up, felt there was something there, which was unusual, because he's so down to earth, it's not like him at all. And he wanted to know what this thing was. He didn't know much about contacting spirits, but knew people tried to ask them questions, so he said out loud 'When I ask a question, make a sign, any sign, to show me that you're there, once for yes and twice for no'. He didn't really expect anything to happen, so anyway he asked a question out loud, 'Is anybody there?'

R Just like in the films!

S Right. Suddenly I started breathing really deeply . . . and then . . . he told me later . . . my head . . . jerked . . . really strongly . . . once . . .

R (gasp)

S Well, he thought 'Well, it could be coincidence', and he ... er ... he asked another question, and said 'Are you a man?' and again my head jerked once ... in my sleep. And the next question after that was 'Do you live in this house?', and again the answer was 'Yes'. And by this time Jeremy couldn't stop, because he wanted ...

R Yes.

S ... to test it out ... and he was thinking ... 'Let's find out ...' and of course I was unconscious, this is what he told me later. I don't think he would have imagined it though, knowing him. Anyway, the next thing that happened was, he asked it various questions and the same thing would happen, my head jerked once if the answer was 'Yes' and twice if the answer was 'No'. And he ... er, well he found out that it was a man. It lived there when the house was built, it had been built for him in the early nineteenth century, and in fact that it ... had been his room, and that's why he came there ... he wasn't an unhappy spirit ... I mean, I never really felt frightened by him, just the experience of something happening ... And Jeremy established that he was really quite a happy spirit, and he was just around the house and had been all the time, and he was on his own in the house ...

Tapescript 10

English spelling

See page 34.

Tapescript 11

Phobias

P = Presenter
D = Doctor

P Did you know that about fifty per cent of the population of Britain say they couldn't touch a snake? And that another twenty per cent say they could, but not without feeling scared? Fear of snakes is one of the most common phobias of all. But there are many others. I spoke to Doctor Jones of the Institute of Psychiatry.

D Surprisingly enough, there is not a great range of things we are frightened of. Most are to do with open spaces, confined spaces, insects such as spiders, situations where there are a lot of people or too few people.

P And are many of us affected by these fears?

D Indeed yes, though of course, reactions vary from a minor feeling of discomfort which is easy to cope with, to an absolutely crippling fear which can destroy a person's life.

P And what are typical reactions when people begin to feel afraid?

D Well, patients break out in a cold sweat, they say they have shivers down their spine, they begin to breathe quickly and the heartbeat increases.

P And can these people be helped?

D Yes certainly, by what we call 'graded exposure'. Many fears are born of ignorance. People say they couldn't bear to touch a snake because its skin is slimy, which isn't true. So to a certain extent knowledge can help to break down a phobia. Then we gradually let a person become more familiar with the object of his or her fear, and try to

accustom them to the realities behind the phobia.

P And does it work?

D Oh yes.

P So there we are, You needn't let your phobia ruin your life. Help is at hand at the Institute of Psychiatry. Oh – what's that crawling along the floor?

Tapescript 12

Tag questions

M = Man
W = Woman

M I'm really looking forward to going away.

W Mmm, it'll be lovely to have a break. We haven't been away for ages, have we? We'd better take some warm clothing, because it's winter there now, isn't it?

M Yes, it is. You haven't seen my camera anywhere, have you? I've been looking for it for days.

W I thought you had it last Saturday. You took some pictures while we were out for a walk, didn't you?

M So I did. It might still be in the car. That reminds me. We'll have to order a taxi. The plane leaves at ten, doesn't it, so I suppose we should leave here about eight. What do you think?

W Yes, that should be all right. Now what about money? You've got the travellers cheques, haven't you?

M No. I thought you had them. You picked them up yesterday, didn't you?

W No. You said you were going to.

M Never mind. We can get them when we go shopping this afternoon, can't we? We'll have enough time.

W Yes, OK.

UNIT 5

Tapescript 13

What happened while the train was in the tunnel?

One day, a few years ago, a train was travelling through the English countryside. This was in the days when trains had small compartments, and in one particular compartment there were four people. There was a young girl, quite pretty, who looked like a student or someone who was starting her first job; there was an old lady, dressed in black with bags and magazines and knitting; there was an army officer in his mid-thirties, immaculately dressed in his uniform and very stiff and proper in his manner; and finally there was a young cockney, casually dressed with a sparkle in his eye and ever ready to have a joke. It was quite obvious that both the men were attracted to the young girl, though the officer certainly wouldn't show it and the cockney felt inhibited by the presence of the others.

Suddenly the train went into a tunnel; the lights had not been put on, so for half a minute the carriage was in complete darkness, and in the darkness came the sound of a large kiss followed almost immediately by a loud slap. What had taken place while the train was in the tunnel? When the train finally emerged and it was light again in the carriage, there for all to see was the

officer with a bleeding nose and a swollen eye. And the old lady, seeing this, thought to herself, 'What a brave young lady, who dared to hit the officer for stealing a kiss in such a cowardly way!'

And the young girl, seeing the suffering of the officer, was puzzled. 'How strange', she thought, 'that the officer should kiss the old lady, and not me!'

The poor officer, nursing two injuries that caused him more than a little pain and embarrassment, considered to himself 'That cockney's quite a clever chap! He kissed the girl, and the girl hit me!'

And the cockney laughed silently to himself at the trick he had played. 'I am a clever chap,' he thought to himself. 'I kissed the back of my hand, hit the officer in the face and nobody said a word!'

Tapescript 14

The lorry driver

B = Brian
A = Andy

B Have I ever told you the story of my career as a lorry driver?

A No. When was this?

B While I was a student at Bristol University. It was during the holidays, the Easter holidays, I think, and I needed some money. I'd just passed my driving test, and I was feeling very pleased with myself, so I went to the job agency. They phoned me up the next day and asked me if I had a driving licence, so I said 'Yes', and they said 'Right. We've got a job for you. Driving. Go down to Bristol fruit market at five thirty tomorrow morning.' And I thought 'Ha – this'll be great – I'll be driving a car or a small van. I'll really enjoy it.' So I went down there the next morning. It was quite a large place with fruit and vegetables everywhere, and lots of small lorries and vans ... and there was this huge three-ton lorry!

A And they expected you to –

B And I said to them that I wasn't really –

A Don't you need a special licence for that?

B Well, you see, they said 'There's your lorry. In you get and off you go!' And I said 'I can't drive that. I've only got an ordinary licence!' So they said 'That's all right. We've taken a few things off the back. It's just under the weight. Don't worry, you'll be all right!' I still said I couldn't drive it, so they sent someone round with me for the first few calls. He drove and I watched. It was OK at that time of the morning because there was very little traffic. We went round some shops and delivered the goods, and then I drove for about five minutes, and then he said 'Right. You can do it. You've got to go to Weston-super-Mare and then to Bridgwater.' And this was a hundred-mile trip! 'I'll leave you here,' he said. And he got out and just left me!

A Oh no!

B Yes. He left me on a busy roundabout just outside Bristol, and there I was, on my own. So I started off, let my foot off the clutch and immediately I heard this huge crash, within five seconds. So I looked round and saw that I had crashed into the side of a car parked at the side of the road, but I didn't stop. I was so scared that I just drove off.

A I don't blame you ...

B So anyway, I got to Weston-super-Mare, and

I was beginning to feel quite pleased with myself, and made the deliveries to the various shops there, and then I set off to Bridgwater. And on the way I decided I needed some petrol, or diesel because it was a lorry, you see. So I drove into a petrol station, and the man came running out shouting 'No, no, no, no, no!' And I thought 'What's wrong?' So I put the brakes on, and the man said 'Get out, you fool!' So I got out and I looked, and the roof of the garage . . .

A Oh . . . you'd forgotten what you were –

B I'd forgotten that I was driving a lorry, not a car, and of course the lorry was about fifteen feet high, and the lorry was literally about an inch away from the roof. I had nearly brought the whole roof crashing down.
So, then I said 'Fill it up with diesel', and he said 'Are you going anywhere today, then?' 'Yes.' 'Well, if I fill it up with diesel you won't get very far. This is a petrol driven lorry.' By this point I was really beginning to panic, so I rang back to the fruit market and said 'I can't do it. I can't do it at all!' And they said 'It's all right. Don't worry.' I told them I'd probably have an accident, but they said 'Nooo'. Anyway, I drove on, joined the motorway, and was driving along the motorway when a car came screaming past me. By this time my lips were bleeding because I had been biting them so hard . . .

A (laughs)

B . . . I was so scared. This car passed me and made me stop, and I braked and got out and the man said 'You're on fire!' You see, it was quite an old lorry and the brakes had stuck but I hadn't noticed. There were flames pouring out of the back. I managed to put them out and carried on. I got to Bridgwater, and by this time it was pretty busy. I mean, it was . . . oh . . . ten o'clock in the morning and I was tired. I'd been driving since six o'clock. I was driving round a corner, right in the middle of Bridgwater, and . . . you see, the thing with a lorry is that the front wheels are behind you, so when you're turning, it's not like in a car, you've got to go out into the road and then turn. But anyway, I turned this corner and I felt the back wheels go up on the pavement, and I thought 'Oh oh, that feels a bit odd', and the next thing there was one almighty crash. And I stopped . . .

A You hadn't hit someone?

B No, no. The entire back of the lorry was in a gentleman's clothes shop.

A (laughs)

B And there was glass everywhere, and fruit and vegetables all over the road, and I just stood there and thought 'Whoops!' And the best thing was, the man who owned the shop, this very respectable gentleman's clothes shop, the manager whoever he was, came out and said 'Can I help you, sir?'

Tapescript 15

Dictation

There has been a major bank robbery in central London. It happened at nine o'clock this morning, and fifty thousand pounds was stolen. Three men dressed as cleaners surprised bank clerks just as the bank was opening for business. The men had been waiting by a side entrance. They seized the cash and escaped in a stolen car. The police were called but the thieves had already disappeared. The police have appealed for witnesses to help them with their enquiries.

Tapescript 16

Exclamations

1 **A** Hey, Peter! Come and have a look at this.
  B What is it?

2 **A** Carefully with the box! Put it down slowly! That's it.
  B Ouch! That's my toe!

3 **A** So anyway, we went on to the cinema . . .
  B Shh! This is a library.

4 **A** What do you think of the soup?
  B Mmm! You haven't cooked this before.

5 **A** This government has done all it can to bring down unemployment . . .
  B Boo! Boo! Rubbish!

6 **A** I've just bought a new car. It's lovely. Come and see it.
  B Oh! I thought you didn't have any money.

7 **A** Are you ready? Shall we go?
  B Uh-huh. Coming.

8 **A** And then we had this lovely dish of raw meat and brains . . .
  B Ugh! I don't know how you can.

9 **A** How old are you?
  B Thirteen.
  A Tut-tut. Smoking at your age.

10 **A** Excuse me – could you open the door for me?
  B Of course.
  A Whoops! I knew that would happen.
  B I'll pick it up, don't worry.
  A Thank you.

UNIT 6

Tapescript 17

Changing rates of employment

West Germany had one of the lowest rates of unemployment back in 1980. It stood at just three per cent. But then over the next three years it rose quite sharply and steadily. In 1982 it was nearly six per cent, and in 1983 it was the same as France. 1984 saw a slight increase, and 1985 a slight fall. The 1985 figure was eight per cent, inbetween France and the United States. The United States have had ups and downs, or rather, it's the only country to show a significant drop in the number of unemployed. This is due to high interest rates, which haven't helped the rest of the world. In 1980 the rate was about the same as France and Great Britain, slightly higher than France, actually, at about seven per cent. This rose to 7.5 per cent in 1981, and then peaked the following year at over nine per cent. Since then things have looked up for the United States. 1983 brought a slight improvement, but then in 1984 we saw a drop of two per cent to return to the 1980 figure. In 1985 there was another small drop.
I'm afraid Great Britain heads this chart. As I said, they began in 1980 in pretty much the same situation as the United States. There followed a sharp rise in 1981, when the rate was ten point five per cent. This rose gradually over the next two years to thirteen per cent. In 1984 there was no great change, but 1985 saw another increase to about thirteen point five, and figures don't look as though they are on their way down yet.

Tapescript 18

Holistic medicine

P = **Presenter**
W = **Henry Wilson**
G = **Glenna Gillingham**
J = **John**

P Good morning, and welcome to our programme *Worldly Wise*. Today our attention turns to medicine and health care, and we examine a move which is becoming more and more popular, a move away from Western attitudes to medicine towards what is known as the holistic approach. But what is it? What does holistic mean? I spoke to Doctor Henry Wilson, of the National Homeopathic Centre.

W Well, holistic means 'whole', no more than that. But in terms of health care, what it means is looking at the whole body, the whole person when it comes to treating them.

P And how does that differ from a more Western approach?

W Modern medicine treats patients as a series of parts that are all isolated. It looks at the part which isn't working and tries to remove the symptoms until everything's working well again – a bit like a mechanic repairing a car. The opposite of holistic is symptomatic. Too often, modern medicine treats the symptoms and not the cause of an illness. Drugs and surgery can remove the symptoms –

P But what's wrong with that? Surely that's what a person who's ill wants, isn't it – to feel better, to not have the pain any more?

W Yes, but as I said, the cause remains. If you have backache, pain killers will take away the pain, but there's still something wrong somewhere that caused the backache in the first place.

P So what does the holistic approach think about illness?

W Well, it takes into account not only the symptoms, but also the age, habits, emotions and life-style of the individual, and tries to build an overall picture. You see, being healthy means there is a balance, or a harmony, between your mind and your body. When you're ill, it's because there's an imbalance somewhere, and this imbalance is shown by symptoms. The symptoms themselves aren't very important. For example, two people suffering from headaches might be given very different treatment, because the cause of the headache is not the same.

P You mentioned treatment. If holistic medicine doesn't prescribe drugs, how does it treat illness?

W It's important to understand that what holistic medicine tries to do above all is *prevent* illness, and we all know that prevention is better than cure. A good diet, with lots of fresh food, not processed food with its preservatives and chemicals, is essential; a healthy life-style, without too much pressure and worry, and lots of exercise and rest, not too much, not too little – these are the things that will prevent illness.

P Well, that's the theory, but what about the practice? Does it really work? I went along to the Park Clinic in Bath, run by Glenna Gillingham, who learned the arts of acupuncture in Hong Kong and China.

G Of course it works. I could quote you hundreds of success stories, of people who had been suffering for years, taking drugs that didn't work and having major operations that weren't necessary, and then coming to us and feeling better within weeks, sometimes days. It happens all the time.

P What sort of illnesses were these people suffering from?

G All sorts – migraine. Bob, a mechanic, had had blinding headaches for ten years. He couldn't work, he had to stay in bed with the curtains drawn, but after a few courses here he was better. Gill, a thirty year-old who had had arthritis for years and was going to have an operation to replace her hip – after six treatments, she recovered completely. Also insomnia, coughs, drug addiction, high blood pressure.

P Right . . . Now with us here is John. John, could you tell us your story?

J Well, for about a year I had a terrible back. It used to get me up at five in the morning, every morning, and I was in agony all the time. I couldn't move.

P And what happened when you saw your acupuncturist?

J We had a long chat, talked about my medical history, and my parents' medical history, my job, my life, my diet. She looked at my eyes, tongue and general colour, and took my pulse, and after an hour and a half told me to stop drinking coffee.

P Really? Why?

J Well, I had damaged kidneys, and the coffee was accumulating in my kidneys making them worse, and this came out as backache.

P So there wasn't in fact anything wrong with your back?

J No, nothing. And from that day I've never had a backache.

P Oh . . . So Miss Gillingham, do you reject Western medicine totally?

G Certainly not. It has a very important place, particularly in accidents and emergencies. What I would like to see is Western and holistic medicine working hand in hand. We both have things to offer. What I'm trying to start here is a system where in a medical practice there are four doctors and an acupuncturist, all working in their own specialist areas.

P And what do the doctors think of this?

G They're slowly beginning to accept us.

P Why do you think holistic medicine is becoming so popular?

G Because people are becoming disillusioned with their own doctor. They come to us complaining that the doctors don't listen, that the six minutes they're allowed isn't enough to explain all they have to say, and that the doctor is almost writing the prescription as they're walking in the room, before they've even begun to speak!

P I can hardly believe it!

G And I think the other thing is that we're becoming more health conscious generally, and aware that we are basically responsible for our own health.

P And that was Doctor Henry Wilson and Glenna Gillingham, telling us how to get the best health treatment by marrying Eastern and Western approaches. And I must admit, to me it sounds very sensible.

Tapescript 19

What sort of shop are they in?

1 A Good morning.
  B Good morning. I'd like to cash this, please.
  A How would you like it?
  B Erm . . . Could I have some fives and a few one pound coins, please?
  A Certainly.
  B Thanks.

2 A Can I help you?
  B Yes. I'd like some Cheddar.
  A Is it for cooking?
  B No, it's to have with biscuits.
  A Then I recommend this one. It's mature, and quite strong.
  B Could I try a little, please?
  A Yes, of course.
  B Mmm, very nice. I'll have half a pound, please.
  A Anything else, sir?
  B No, that'll be all, thank you.

3 A I'd like some nice lamb chops, please.
  B English or New Zealand?
  A Is there much difference in price?
  B The New Zealand is a little cheaper, but of course it's not quite the same quality.
  A Could I have a look at the New Zealand?
  B Of course.
  A They look fine. Six please.
  B Two pounds thirty, please.
  A Thank you.

4 A I like the style very much, and they're very comfortable.
  B Yes, they fit extremely well.
  A I'm afraid I don't like the colour. Have you got something a bit brighter? Brown is such a dull colour.
  B I'll have a look. What about a red?
  A Yes, I've got quite a few things that might go with red. Could I try them on?
  B Yes, I'll just fetch them. One moment.

5 A Good morning.
  B Hello. A large wholemeal loaf, please.
  A Thank you. 57p, please.
  B And a half-a-dozen soft white rolls.
  A Do you want the ones with sesame seeds?
  B They're for hamburgers, so yes, that'd be all right, wouldn't it?
  A Yes.
  B Yes, that's fine.
  A Anything else?
  B No, thanks. Not today.

6 A Hello, Tom. How are you today?
  B Not bad, thanks. You?
  A OK. What can I do for you?
  B I'd like some sprouts, Alf, please.
  A I couldn't get any today. Sorry.
  B Oh. Well, I'll have some beans, then.
  A How many?
  B A pound will do. Have you got any avocados?
  A Lovely ones. When are they for?
  B Tonight, please.
  A Here we are. Two beauties.
  B A lettuce and a cucumber, please.
  A Righto.
  B That's it, thanks.

7 A Hello. Have you got any of that stuff for getting stains out of furniture?
  B Yes. Do you mean that sort that comes in bottles? Do you want large, small or medium?

A Oh, just the small one please.
  B 75p, please.
  A And I need some nails, some six-inch nails.
  B They come in packs of twenty-five, sir.
  A But I don't want that many. Can I just have a few?
  B I'm sorry, I can't split them up.
  A All right, then, I'll have the packet.

8 A Twenty Benson and Hedges, please.
  B King size?
  A No, just the ordinary ones. Oh, and some matches please.
  B There you are.
  A Do you have any computer magazines?
  B Yes, they're over there on the middle shelf.
  A Ah, yes.

UNIT 7

Tapescript 20

Sentences for completion

1 In the month just finished, Britain's exports rose by ten per cent. In the same period, it's –

2 A Did you take those shoes back to the shop?
  B Oh, yes. The shop-assistant was very good, –

3 A It's my birthday today.
  B Is it? Many happy returns! Did you –

4 Yesterday in the High Court, Barry Thompson was sentenced to ten years in prison. He was –

5 A The things she said to me!
  B Yes, she has a very nasty temper.
  A But the names she called me! I've never been so –

6 He began taking drugs ten years ago. Now he's completely –

7 A How's my wife doing, Doctor?
  B I think we can say that she'll be home soon. We're very pleased –

8 UFO stands for –

9 There was a large demonstration in Paris today. Three thousand people marched through the streets –

10 And finally we come to the award for Best Actress. And the winner is . . . Bella Dickinson! Bella, it gives me great pleasure to –

11 I'm sorry, madam. You can't park here. You see, this is a restricted zone. You need a –

12 The teachers' strike looks like it's going to continue. The government's latest offer of a six per cent pay rise –

Tapescript 21

An interview with Jonathon Porritt

I = Interviewer
P = Jonathon Porritt

Part 1

I Could I ask you please, how did your interest in the environment, and the need to protect it, begin?

P It really all began because I was a teacher, and teaching in an inner London comprehensive school near Shepherd's Bush, and obviously a lot of the work we were doing were . . . was making assumptions about the shape of the future, and the world into which those children would have to go out, after they'd finished their five years' schooling. And I became more and more involved in trying to think what the shape of the planet would be like after the year two thousand, and one of the big projects that we did with some of our kids was to look more carefully at the relationship between humankind and the planet. And that got me interested in the whole subject, and I started reading much more about ecology. And then I began to realize that you can't really talk about ecology as a science, you have to consider ecology within a social and political context. And that's what drew me into Green politics. I became increasingly involved in several organizations, tried to wrap my . . . mind more and more around the economics of the issues, as that's really the key to it all, and eventually ended up with 'Friends of the Earth', as . . . as director.

Part 2

I I see. When you look into the future, the next thirty years, a reasonably long term, you perhaps see reasons to be both optimistic and pessimistic. What changes and developments do you think we might see over the next thirty years?

P It is very hard to predict – it has to be said – and I do feel a strange mixture of pessimism and optimism. I call myself a constructive pessimist, erm . . . because you can't help but be pessimistic, looking at some of the issues we face, and yet if we don't face them in a constructive way, then that pessimism merely feeds on itself, and becomes fatalism, and the world really will get into a very sorry state. But obviously, the crucial problems we face now are largely those of population, which is a problem . . . which is unfolding remorselessly, and will really hit us in the middle of the next century; the misuse or abuse of the world's resources, both the renewable resources, such as the clean air, clean water, and the non-renewable resources, the speed with which we're using up oil, gas, whatever else it may be; the appalling problems of poverty and famine and hunger, which er . . . what we saw last year in Ethiopia and the Sudan, I'm sorry to say, is merely a very small indication of the kind of things we're going to see before now and the turn of the century; the arms build-up, which has reached really staggeringly immoral levels er . . . one thousand million million dollars now being spent on arms every year, instead of being spent on the kinds of things that it ought to go on. And all of those problems, to us, which we, which we consider to be the problems of er . . . the misuse of the planet are very daunting. And they're not separate, they are all interconnected. And what I think is only just dawning on people, is that a lot of these problems do have the same roots, namely the unsustainable system that we insist upon at the moment, believing that the only way we can increase human wealth is by producing more and consuming more, even if we destroy the planet in the process.

Part 3

I They are –

P They're all pessimistic, they're all pessimistic. On the other side of the coin, it has to be said, that I would think there are three main things that are now beginning to . . . allow us to be a little more optimistic. First is awareness. I mean, in the last ten years there has been an astonishing array of books, and er . . . different ideas forthcoming about the state of the planet, and how we need to change our ways to cope with that. And that's wholly good, because many more people are now better informed than they used to be. Secondly, there is an increasing political awareness that these things have to be given political expression, people need to involve themselves in organizations, in groups; they need to put pressure on politicians so that they don't get away with the absurd things they're doing at the moment. And again, there is a sense – a growing strength of – within the Green Movement that we can actually do things. And thirdly, and I personally consider this to be as important as the first two, there is an increasing awareness of the spiritual values of the alternative that we're putting across, namely alternatives to materialism, as a better way of meeting people's needs, rather than this absolutely crude pursuit of material affluence, as the only way of satisfying people. And I think that spiritual aspect, combined with the political aspect, set within a context of greater awareness, is really the path that the 'Green Movement' is trying to carve out for itself at the moment.

Part 4

I Do you personally find your job depressing?
P (laughs)
I Do you find reasons for . . . for satisfaction?
P I personally love the work I do, although I am depressed by the er . . . sheer irrationality and selfishness of the way in which people treat the planet and treat each other, and I do find that a . . . a permanently depressing feature of human nature. But also, because of the nature of the work, and the people one is working with, there is the other side of human nature, that is . . . you know . . . very uplifting, and for every example of this short-sightedness and selfishness and so on, there are more and more examples building of people who are prepared to do things for others in an unstinting way, to take care for the planet, to think responsibly about the fate of other people in the Third World. And that means that however much the – the – kind of the dark bits of the job may erm . . . threaten to overwhelm one, there are always enough points of light to ensure that doesn't happen.
I Mr Porritt, thank you very much indeed.
P Thanks.

Tapescript 22

Arranging to meet

B = **Sally Beecham**
A = **Henry Adams**
T = **Telephonist**
S = **Secretary**

T Good morning. International Products Limited. Can I help you?
B Could I speak to Mr Adams, please?
T It's ringing for you.

B Thank you.
S Hello. Mr Adams' office.
B Hello. This is Sally Beecham from the Bristol office. Could I speak to Mr Adams, please?
S Certainly. One moment.
A Hello, Sally. How are you?
B Hello, Henry. Fine thanks. How's everything in Leicester?
A Not bad, not bad.
B I've just had Jeremy on the phone . . .
A . . . Oh, yes. Next week's meeting. Were the arrangements all right for you? Did you mind –
B No, no, no, that's fine. Wednesday morning suits me. **I'm going away** on Thursday, so I couldn't have made it after that. **I'll come** to you in Leicester. You're in the middle, after all, well, just about. I had a word with Jeremy about what time the meeting should start, because **he's coming** from Glasgow, so he's got the furthest to travel. **He's getting** a plane to the East Midlands airport, so how long **will it take** him to get to your office?
A What time **does his plane get in**? It depends on the traffic.
B At . . . oh, let me just check . . . ten twenty-five.
A Well, he should be here by . . . about eleven.
B That's fine. That's what we thought. So **I'll be** there at eleven. How's that?
A OK. What about you? How **are you getting** here?
B **I'll be coming** by car. It's motorway all the way, so **it won't take** me long.
A Right, then. **I'll see** you both here, next Wednesday at eleven.
B That's it.
A I look forward to it.
B Right. See you then. Bye Henry.
A Goodbye Sally.

Tapescript 23

A Victorian family

A = **Annie**
G = **Grandmother**

A Grannie?
G Yes, my dear?
A How many brothers and sisters did you have?
G I had . . . now let me see . . . there was . . . me, Alice, James, then Henry – that's four, isn't it? Then Robert and Emily, the twins – so that makes two sisters and three brothers.
A What were they all like? Did they look like you?
G Well, some did and some didn't. My sister Alice and I were very similar. People used to think *we* were the twins, but she was two years older than me. We both had fair hair, and when we were young, we used to have lovely ribbons in it. People said I was the pretty one – my sister Alice was so moody, she always looked miserable.
A Who were you closest to?
G Ah, my brother James. He was such a kind boy, always smiling, and so gentle. We were inseparable, we went everywhere together.
A Who did he look like?
G Well, people said James had my mother's features; same nose, same mouth, while Henry, who was older, was more like Father. Henry had thick, dark hair, but James had fair hair like me, and he used to have a parting down the middle. Henry was quite a plump boy, not fat, but he was always well-built, like Father.

A What about the twins?

G They were very plain, I seem to remember. When they were babies, no-one could tell them apart, they were so similar. They both had long faces with high foreheads. Robert was very severe and serious – I was quite afraid of him – but then he was so much older than me, we didn't have much to do with each other. Robert looked middle-aged before he was twenty.

A What about your Mummy and Daddy?

G Ah, Mother was a darling. She used to have her hair in a tight bun, and she looked quite fierce, but she wasn't really. She had smiling eyes and a heart of gold. Father was a very quiet man, he always looked distant as though he were lost in his own thoughts.

A What were their names?

G Daniel and Clare.

UNIT 8

Tapescript 24

Hitch-hiking in the snow

J = John

L = Linda

J Have I ever told you about the time I nearly froze to death?

L No. When was that?

J Well, it's a bit of an exaggeration to say I nearly froze to death, but it wasn't far off.

L Where were you, I mean when –

J It was while I was working in Corsica. Have you ever been to Corsica?

L No, no I haven't.

J Well, it's quite a remarkable place, actually. It's in the Mediterranean, so it's very hot in summer, and the winters are either mild or quite severe, you know . . . it depends . . .

L Mmm.

J And the interior is really wild and mountainous. Anyway, I was living in the north in a town called Bastia, and I had friends who lived down in the south in the capital, Ajaccio. It's not very far away, but the roads are so bad that the journey takes ages. And it was around Easter time, you know, March, April, something like that, and I'd gone down to see them for the weekend, and it had been warm – warm enough to go sunbathing, not enough for actual swimming. And then on the Sunday, we had lunch sitting outside, and it was time for me to get back to Bastia, so I started hitching.

L Had you done that before?

J Oh, yes, no problem. It usually took about three hours. So there I was, standing next to the road, in shirt-sleeves because it was a warm spring day, and I was rather puzzled . . .

L Why?

J Well, all these cars were going past with people in jackets and hats and scarves, and skis on the car roof.

L Why? Had it been snowing?

J Yes, you see. We hadn't heard the weather forecast, but apparently it had been snowing extremely heavily in the mountains, so all these people were setting off for a day's skiing.

L How odd . . .

J Mmm. Well I soon got a lift, that was easy, and they took me to the top of the mountain,

but, there had been loads of people going up to the top of the mountain, but there just wasn't anyone going down, not in a car, anyway.

L Oh, no, on skis!

J Right. So I had no choice, I had to start walking. Can you imagine? There I was, in sandals and just a jumper, trying to walk through snowdrifts that came up over my knees!

L Oh, so what did you do? I mean, how . . .?

J Well, I just carried on walking. At first it wasn't too bad. It was mid-afternoon, it wasn't very pleasant but it was very beautiful, and not too cold.

L And did you get a lift?

J Well, every now and again I'd get a lift that took me a few miles, just to the next village, and then I'd have to start walking again. By this time, it was getting dark, and awfully cold. And I started to panic. I was miles from anywhere, it was nearly night time, and I was supposed to be at work at nine o'clock the next day. But all I could do was walk. And the amazing thing was that the snow-ploughs had been round, and where the road was quite wide, they'd pushed huge piles of snow into the middle of the road, and the local kids had pushed holes like doorways into this snow, so it looked like a wall of snow with doors or archways in it. It was very strange. And then it was around seven-ish I think, and finally this chap stopped to give me a lift, and . . . I got in, you know, so pleased at last, and I was going to say 'Oh thank-you, thank-you, thank-you', but I couldn't talk!

L Why not?

J My jaw had frozen. Honestly. I couldn't move it.

L Because it was so cold?

J My jaw was absolutely frozen solid. And, would you believe, it didn't defreeze for ages because this chap's windscreen had smashed so we drove all the way back to Bastia with the wind and the snow pouring into the car. By this time, I didn't really care. All I cared about was the fact that he was going to Bastia, and that ultimately we'd get there.

L And you did?

J Yeah. It took a long time. And of course, when I did get back, people didn't believe that it had been snowing like that, and they certainly didn't believe my story, but it's quite true, I assure you.

L So what did you do then?

J Well, I had one or two brandies to help me thaw out. That did the trick. It was quite an experience, and really quite frightening.

L I'm sure it was.

UNIT 9

Tapescript 25

An arranged marriage

I = Interviewer

R = Raj

I How old were you when you met your husband, Raj?

R Mm . . . I was erm, sixteen.

I And what were you doing at the time?

R Oh I was at home. I had left school, and I was having private tuition actually, at home, to prepare me for my exams.

I And your father arranged your marriage, is that right?

R Yes, that's right.

I Could you tell me how he did that?

R Yes. He looked around for a suitable husband. He asked friends and relatives if they knew anybody, and found out about their education, their background, and most importantly, the family's background. He got all the information about them, you know.

I And did this take a long time?

R In my case, no, but it depends you see, erm . . . sometimes a father can see up to a hundred men before he chooses one. My elder sister . . . for my elder sister my father saw over a hundred men. You know, sometimes it can be difficult to decide. But for my brother he saw only one girl.

I And for you?

R He saw only two, one in the morning and one in the evening, and er . . . he chose the second one.

I My goodness! Tell me about that day.

R Yes . . . well, in the morning the first man came. He was very wealthy, but er . . . not very well educated, but he had a lot of money. And he was well-dressed, and he had very good manners.

I And the other one?

R He wasn't terribly wealthy, but he was well-educated, and he came from a good background. His family owned a village, and were like princes. And all his relatives were suitable. He was twenty-two, and studying law.

I And your father chose him?

R Yes.

I Why, do you know?

R I think he thought that money wasn't everything. He didn't want the . . . you know, he didn't want the family's money. Education was more important. If he's well-educated, he'll earn it later. Actually, Shyam, that's my husband's name, didn't want to get married. He wanted to wait, but you know his father persuaded him. You know when he came to my house to meet my father, he was very badly dressed because he wanted my father to refuse him, so he could say to his father 'Look, they didn't like me'. But luckily my father did like him and – erm – so he had to say 'yes'.

I And did you meet him that day?

R Yes. First my family spoke to him, and then they called me in, and we talked for four, four or five minutes. My father decided immediately.

I And did you agree?

R Of course. My father had decided.

I But did you prefer the second?

R Um – well I wasn't sure, actually. I left it to my father.

I And what happened next?

R Well, after a certain time, there was a special day when I went to see his family and he came to see my family. It was a sort of engagement party. But we – you know – we used to be on the phone every day, we'd see each other regularly, but never without a chaperon. We were married ten months later.

I And how long have you been married?

R Oh for twenty-two years now.

I And . . . it's been a successful marriage? Have you been pleased with your father's choice?

R Oh . . . yes, of course.

I Now you have two sons, don't you, one twenty-one and one fifteen. Are you going to arrange their marriages?

R Yes, we are planning them now. We've er . . . we've been asking families in India for some time, and we've found some suitable ones.

I Do you think that the system of arranged marriages is a good one? I can see that you've had a good marriage, but what about other people? How common is this system of arranged marriages?

R Well, most marriages in India are still arranged in this way, and generally it is a system that works. Erm of course it depends a lot on the – you know – family choosing the right person, but one reason it works is that the couple enter the marriage not expecting too much, if you see what I mean. Actually – actually, there are many more divorces between couples who thought that they were marrying for love and who then find that it isn't there. Arranged marriages seem to last, and that is a good thing.

I And is sixteen the age when girls get married?

R Well, my mother was married at thirteen, but that is considered too young now and er . . . at one time it used to be twenty, but it was found that the girls were then too old to be integrated into their new families, so now it is usually when the girls are sixteen or seventeen, yeah.

Tapescript 26

The Prime Minister's pay rise

I = Interviewer
PM = Prime Minister

I We are very pleased to have with us in the studio tonight the Prime Minister, who has very kindly found time to come to explain to us his point of view on the crisis that is facing his government. Prime Minister, good evening.

PM Good evening. May I say straight away that this is not a crisis. The situation is very much under control, and the vast majority of the population do in fact support this government and the action –

I Prime Minister, if I may, I'd like to put a question to you. Your government has announced that there can be no pay increases above four per cent for the next financial year, and although this has been difficult for many workers in a year where inflation has been six per cent, teachers, nurses, and miners have all settled for four per cent. Then suddenly we hear that Members of Parliament have voted for themselves a pay rise of thirty-five per cent. How can you justify this?

PM Let me say first of all that the pay rise would in fact be nearer twenty per cent. The rest of the money would be for a politician's many expenses, such as air fares, personal secretaries, and of course a large entertainment budget. You can't expect a Member of Parliament to travel second class, and eat in second-class restaurants, and do a first-class job.

I But Prime Minister, you're still expecting the public to accept that a politician's pay rise should be five times higher than anyone else's. Is that fair?

PM Two points will answer your question. Firstly, when the opposition party were in power, they allowed a Member of Parliament's salary to fall way behind the national average. This was a terrible thing to do, and yet again, my party is having to correct the mistakes of the previous administration. Secondly, I don't think people realize just how difficult it is to be a politician. All those late nights, receptions, and the decisions that have to be made, make life very difficult. If we were in industry, we would without doubt be earning figures vastly in excess of what we are prepared to accept.

I And would the Prime Minister also be getting an increase of twenty per cent?

PM No.

I Ah! Are you going to take less?

PM No. The responsibilities that a Prime Minister has to carry are enormous. You must understand the pressures of the position.

I Are you prepared to say what the increase might be?

PM I, of course, could not vote for my own salary increase, but my colleagues and members of the Cabinet suggested that, given the sacrifice of one's private life, the endless dedication to duty and public service, and the need to attract the very best person for the job, they suggested that the Prime Minister's salary should be reviewed separately.

I Are you prepared to tell us what the proposed salary would be?

PM I don't think this is the right moment to make such an announcement, do you? It will be announced to the House in the near future.

I Very well, Prime Minister. Thank you very much.

Tapescript 27

Two telephone conversations

1 Hello, 40974.

Oh, it's you.

We're all right. Why are you ringing?

Next Saturday? Is it the second Saturday of the month already? Yes, I suppose it is. All right. That's the eleventh, isn't it?

Oh, yes, so it is. The twelfth, then. Where are you thinking of taking them? The children always pester if they don't know, especially Paul.

The zoo? You took them there last month. I didn't think they enjoyed that visit. Lizzie didn't, anyway.

That's not what she told me. Anyway, it doesn't matter. What time are you going to pick them up?

OK. I'll have them ready. I haven't had my money for this month yet. It's always late. What's your excuse this time?

Oh, are you? Well, I hope you'll both be very happy.

I know your promises. All right. I'll tell them you rang. Bye.

2 Hello. Epsom 4778.

This *is* Jeremy Brook speaking.

Sorry – Janice who?

I'm, sorry. I don't think I know anyone by that name.

On holiday? Did we? When was that?

In Greece! Of course! You're the American girl who was in the next room. I remember. Good Lord! That was years ago! How are you?

I'm fine, thanks. What a surprise! What are you doing? Where are you?

In Epsom?

Erm . . . well . . . I'd love to, but erm . . . well, it's not very convenient, actually.

Yes, I know I said that, but . . . well, our house isn't all that big, and er –

Yes, I am. I got married last year.

Well, I'm glad you understand. I'm sorry to let you down. I'd have liked to help, but you see what I mean. Maybe we could meet for a drink?

No, I suppose you're right. Well, it was nice talking to you anyway. Have a good trip round Europe.

Thanks. Bye, Janice. Take care of yourself.

UNIT 10

Tapescript 28

Johnny Morris, the animal expert

'The crowd behaved like animals, just like animals.' I suppose we hear that about twice a week nowadays, 'The crowd behaved like animals'. Well it just isn't true. Animals do not behave like that. Animals are not hooligans, animals do not go out in gangs inflicting pain, damage and destruction and death on their own kind. Animals are concerned with the stability of their own species and the need for them to prosper and multiply. They do not destroy their own kind in large numbers as we do. In fact, I am amazed that animals have condescended to have anything to do with us at all. They should stay well away from us and most of them do but such is the nature of some of them that they have volunteered to share their lives with ours and we have accepted, for as we know animals are of enormous use to us. When we talk of people behaving like animals, I suggest that it is because animals must be kept in their places, that we are far, far better than they are, we simply must not let them appear to be superior. And yet of course in many cases they are. We could not use our noses with the sensitive skill of a dog, we couldn't possibly run with the speed and beauty of the horse, and no way could we fly like those wonderful birds. We grudgingly admire their splendid attributes, we wear their feathers and their skins because they are so beautiful. And we know in our heart of hearts that we are inferior. Oh yes we are in many respects inferior. So we are very lucky indeed that so many animals have come to help us, for on our own we are pretty helpless.

You know, scientists are quite incredible people. They're always telling us what we already know. They might express it differently, and come to their conclusions by experiments that we come to by instinct, but nevertheless it's true. I was reading not so long ago about these scientists who'd been doing experiments with dogs and cats and people. And they found out – you'll never believe this – they found out that animals are comforting to us, and that we can be reassuring to animals. Now what about that? Did you know that? Of course you did! What perhaps you didn't know is that the scientists came to their conclusion by measuring the blood pressures of the people and the animals. If you stroke a dog or a cat, and talk to it, the blood pressure of the animal and the person will go down. Here's something else. Did you know that people who have been ill, in hospital or having an operation, did you know that if they have a pet to care for, they'll get better more quickly? I can believe it. There are even hospitals that are experimenting with having animals for long-stay patients to look after.

I have known all my life, that I do not like to live in a house that does not shelter a cat. Oh, I have had some truly terrific dogs, but a cat has a different quality about it. Cats have got all the time in the world, and most of the time they're curled up asleep, and at peace. I know that after a heated telephone conversation or a difficult interview, I have to find the cat. He'll be sleeping in one of half a dozen different places, and I stroke him for a while. He'll open half of one eye and say 'You do get yourself worked up, don't you? Calm down, calm down, calm down.' Cats, the great comforters.

Animals have always been in our lives. Dogs have been around us for thousands of years, and they've served as hunters and of course guards. Dogs, it seems, have always been easy to train. Obedience, and a desire to please, has really let the dog in for a subservient role with us. In the ancient Roman town of Pompeii, there is a house that bears the warning *cave canem* – 'beware of the dog'. Apart from catching things, and guarding things, dogs are of course very good at guiding people. The Romans used to have guide dogs for the blind – well, not exactly blind, but blind drunk. For when a Roman went on a pub crawl, he would take his dog with him to lead him home. He had nothing to worry about, staggering home behind his dog, singing away, happy as Claudius.
Can you imagine guide cats for the blind? Never! For the philosophy of the cat is surely 'Look, mate. If you can't look after yourself, you've had it.' The only guiding I've known a cat to do is the upright tail in front of you leading to the feeding bowl. Cats seem to have come amongst us much later than dogs, but when they did, they made a great impact.

The ancient Egyptians used to worship their cats, and lots of them believed that they were descended from cats. Egyptian women used to try to walk like cats, slinking round the pyramids, minding their own business, but knowing everybody else's. You see, cats are like that. They're psychic. They have powers – don't know exactly what they are, but they've got them. And the Egyptians knew this – they made cats sacred. They worshipped them, and quite right too. If your cat died, the whole family would mourn for it. You would shave off your eyebrows. Eyebrows were things of great beauty, so you shaved them off. You closed the cat's eyes, put a delicate blue collar around its neck, and then you had it embalmed. And if you killed a cat in Ancient Egypt, you were put to death.
I have known a great many animals in my life, and not all of them were very nice. They had to get used to you, and you had to get used to them. Now gorillas take a bit of getting used to, and I knew a young female gorilla at Bristol Zoo, and when I first went in with her, she hit me, quite a bump – it's one of the things gorillas do. So I had in my hand a small sort of scrubbing brush with a handle, and I went over to her, and I bopped her one, not very hard but I just

bopped her one, and she sulked. Bit by bit, we got used to each other.

Tapescript 29

Relationships with parents

1 I don't remember very much about my childhood, actually. My wife's always asking me 'When you were a boy, did you use to . . .' and I reply 'I don't know, I can't remember.' We didn't . . . we didn't use to talk very much, we weren't very close, or if we were, we didn't show it. I remember I used to have my hair cut every Friday. My father and I would go together. I had the shortest hair in the school. When they'd finished cutting it, they'd burn the ends with a sort of candle. Oh I'll never forget that smell.

2 I got on very well with my mother. I used to tell her everything – or nearly everything – and she'd talk to me very openly too. Sometimes she'd say to me 'Don't go to school today. Stay with me.' And we'd go out shopping or something like that. It's a wonder I had any education at all, the number of days I missed from school.

3 I'm not a very tidy person, but my mother's very house-proud, so she's always telling me to pick things up and put them away, and do this and do that. She goes on for hours about 'Cleanliness is next to godliness'. My father isn't like that at all. He lets me do what I want. I think he's learned not to pay attention.

4 I have very fond memories of my childhood. To me it represented security. We used to do a lot together as a family. I remember walks, and picnics, and going for rides on a Sunday afternoon. Every Friday, when my father came home from work, he had a treat for each of us. My mother used to say he was spoiling us, but why not? It didn't do us any harm.

UNIT 11

Tapescript 30

The driving test

B = Bob
J = Jill

B Well? Did you?
J No.
B Oh no! That's the fourth time! What went wrong?
J Everything. I didn't do a thing right. Not in the test, anyway. In the lesson before, I did it all perfectly – three-point turn, emergency stop, moving off on a hill, great. The instructor said if I drove like that in the test, I'd pass.
B So what happened?
J Oh it's the usual thing. I just get so nervous. And the examiner was horrible. He really put me off, right from the start.
B How? What did he do?
J Well, he was so rude and sarcastic, so I was shaking like a leaf before we even started. If he'd been nicer and had tried to put me at ease a bit, I'm sure I'd have felt better.
B How was he sarcastic?
J Just to show you how nervous I was, right, I forgot to take the handbrake off when we started . . .

B . . . oh, no . . .
J Alright, I know. And we were going down the road, and he says 'Don't you think it's about time you took the handbrake off? We seem to be moving now, and I can smell it burning.'
B (laughs)
J Well I didn't think it was very funny.
B Sorry.
J I felt terrible after that. I'd made a mess of things even before we got into the car. He asked me . . . you know, you have to read a number plate about thirty yards away, and I don't know the names of any cars. He said 'What's the number of the Mercedes Two Thousand?', or something, and I got the wrong car, and he was really impatient, 'No, no, no!'
B That's not very fair, is it?
J Then we were going along, coming to a junction, and I slowed down too soon, so the people behind got held up. They started hooting, I stalled the car . . .
B . . . Oh Jill . . .
J and then when I got it going again, I didn't look right before pulling out into the main road . . .
B But there was nothing coming, was there?
J No, no. But I still should have looked, shouldn't I?
B Oh . . . did he say anything?
J He didn't have too. He just slammed the brakes on, you know, his dual controls, and put his hand to his forehead, like this, you know, as though he's thinking 'I wonder how long I'll stay in this job', and then signalled me to go on. Well, after that there was no point in going on, and I said so, but he just said 'Drive us back to the centre, please, Mrs Gibson'. Oh my knees were knocking, honestly.
B I bet. Poor old you. Never mind. You'll get it, of course you will.
J I know, but what annoys me is that I know I can do all these things, really well, but not in the actual test. That's when I mess them up. When I was reversing round a corner, and doing really well, a cyclist arrived wanting to turn into the same road. I didn't know who should wait for who, so I waited, but the cyclist waved me on, or at least, I thought he had, but when I started to move he was right in front of me, and I made him swerve. If that cyclist hadn't been there, it would have been fine. When I did the emergency stop, I skidded, and I never usually do that, I just lost control for a split second, and finally when we got back to the centre and I had to park, I got too close to another parked car – just ever so slightly touched it, you know, scraped it . . .
B Oh, boy. I bet you were glad when it was over, weren't you?
J The examiner certainly was, but he didn't show it, oh no, he just calmly filled in his form, and without looking at me at all, he was looking at the sky, he said 'I'm sorry to have to inform you, Mrs Gibson, that you have failed to reach the required standard'. And he got out and walked away.
B Oh, my love. Never mind. Next time.
J It makes me so mad. Why do people have to be so horrible?

Tapescript 31

Panic in a restaurant

A = Wife
B = Husband
C = Waiter

A Did you enjoy that, darling?

B Yes, not bad. The sauce tasted a bit strange, and I don't think the pastry was quite cooked enough.

A Well, you should have had what I had. The chicken was lovely. And that dessert, the Chef's surprise, was delicious. You really should be more adventurous, Gerald.

B Don't nag, please. My stomach hurts, it's so full. I wish I hadn't eaten that pudding. Talking of surprises, I'm dreading what the bill's going to come to. Did you look at the prices?

A Gerald, this is our wedding anniversary! Of course I didn't. You should have looked before we came in.

B Could we have the bill, please?

C Certainly, sir.

A There's no point in worrying about the bill now. It wouldn't have been so much if we'd ordered a house wine, but no, you had to have champagne.

C Your bill, sir.

B Thank you. Oh, no! I wish we hadn't come here.

Tapescript 32

Facts about Jack Higgins: right or wrong?

Jack Higgins is a best-selling author. He lives in New York with his wife and six children. He was born in London, and is now forty-three years old.
A lot of his friends left school at fifteen, but he didn't. When he was eighteen he did his National Service and went to Australia.
He is now rich and famous, and doesn't write any more. He has a very happy life. He enjoys meeting the Royal Family.

UNIT 12

Tapescript 33

An interview with Mrs Thatcher

This is an extract from an interview that Mrs Thatcher gave to the London Broadcasting Company (LBC). Mrs Thatcher had said that she was a great admirer of Victorian values. The interviewer asks her why this is so.

T Well, there's no – there's no great mystery about those. Erm, I was brought up by a Victorian grandmother. We were taught to work jolly hard: you were taught to improve yourself; you were taught self-reliance; you were taught to live within your income; you were taught that cleanliness was next to godliness; erm . . . you were taught self-respect; you were taught always to give a hand to your neighbour; er, you were . . . taught tremendous pride in your country; you were taught to be a good member of your community. All of these things are Victorian values.

I The Victorian values also seemed to encompass –

T – But they are also perennial values, as well.

I But they encompassed as well workhouses and – and shocking conditions in industry, all sorts of deplorable things that are also part of the Victorian scene.

T There's – there's some values which are eternal, and in fact you found a tremendous improvement in conditions during Victorian times, because people were brought up with a sense of duty. I was brought up with a very strong sense of duty, and part of the sense of duty was that if you were getting on better, so you turned yourself to help others, that as you did better yourself, so you had a duty to your community to turn to help others. And so, as you got an increasing prosperity during Victorian times, and as you got an immense national pride during Victorian times, so as you got greater prosperity, so you had a duty, voluntarily, to help others. And many of the very good things, improvements, that were made, er were made voluntarily in those times er – for example erm – people built hospitals, voluntary hospitals erm – many of the church schools were built during that time, many people say we simply must do better with the prisons, a better prison system, prison reform. But it came from this tremendous sense of reliance and duty. Erm . . . you don't hear so much about those things these days. But they were good values, and they led to tremendous improvements in the standard of living.

I So that's what you're trying to get back to, that's what you'd like to see happen, a society where we had those sorts of values, where perhaps the state steps back again then, and individuals get far more involved?

T What I am saying is that I think there are some values which are eternal, and I think the ones that I've indicated are.

I Yes, but what kind of society does that result in if people adopt those values, then we have –

T – Well, if I might say so, a very good society. If people are self-reliant, self-respecting, if they always lend a hand to others, if they wish always to improve themselves and work very hard to do it, if they reckon they've got to be very good members of the community, not because anyone tells them to, but because that's the way we live, and if they live within their income, and save, and that saving there is therefore for investment, if they're prepared to take responsibility for their own actions and responsibility for their own families, er . . . and to respect erm other people's rights, it seems to me that you have the basis of an excellent society.
You asked me how I see life quite apart from those things. I am very keen that every person should have the opportunity to be what I would call a man or woman of property . . .

I . . . own their own house . . .

T Therefore . . . you start by owning your own house. We're nearly up to sixty per cent, it is tremendous, because people – er, a man of property isn't someone else, it's oneself. And so therefore if you have a chance to own your own house then it gives you an interest in the future, it gives you respect for your own property, it gives you ability to improve your own standard of living and housing, and (*unclear*) to respect other people's property, and you'll have something to hand on to your children and grandchildren in years to come. This is the kind of independence, this is the kind of personal initiative and personal choice, which I believe is the kind of independence which used to belong to a few people, which I want to extend to the many.

I Right. You'd like everybody to have the freedom of choice to buy their own property, probably to – to choose the kind of education their children have, to choose the kind of medicine in which – er – their family partakes, whether private or National Health, but surely those kinds of advantages, to return to what we said earlier, are only offered to those with, offered to the 'haves', not to the 'have-nots', not to people without jobs. They're for people with money.

T But with all due respect, we unfortunately have just over three million unemployed in this country, and we have betw- twenty-two to twenty-three million people who are working. Nearly sixty per cent of the houses in this country are now owner-occupied, er . . . many, many more people are applying to buy their own homes. I'm trying to make certain that people who save – the value of their savings, is kept. Wouldn't life have been very much different for many of our old folk if the money they'd put aside out of very much lower wages in Victorian values, years ago, had in fact kept its value because we'd had governments which tried to keep inflation down? We'd have a very, very much better society, and we wouldn't have cheated those old people of the value of their savings.

Tapescript 34

The things that matter

See page 106.

Oxford University Press
Walton Street, Oxford OX2 6DP

Oxford New York Toronto
Delhi Bombay Calcutta Madras Karachi
Petaling Jaya Singapore Hong Kong Tokyo
Nairobi Dar es Salaam Cape Town
Melbourne Auckland

and associated companies in
Berlin Ibadan

OXFORD and OXFORD ENGLISH are trade
marks of Oxford University Press

ISBN 0 19 433559 3
© Oxford University Press 1987

First published 1987
Fourteenth impression 1992

Filmset in Linotron 202 Times by
Tradespools Ltd., Frome, Somerset
Printed in Hong Kong

Acknowledgements

The publishers and authors would like to
thank the following for their kind
permission to use articles, extracts, or
adaptations from copyright material:

Celia Brayfield: 'How's your timing?'
British Reader's Digest and *Newsweek
International*: 'Nightmare of the monster
cities' by Spencer Reiss (July 1984)
Business Magazines International: extract
from *Executive Travel Magazine* (October
1985)
William Heinemann Ltd. and the Executors
of the Estate of W. Somerset Maugham
for extracts from 'The Lotus Eater', from
The Complete Short Stories, Vol. 3 (1959
edition) by Somerset Maugham
Hodder & Stoughton Ltd.: *Audrey Rose* by
Frank de Felitta
London Standard: 'Life is not a rehearsal'
(May 1984) and 'Allen is a little disaster'
(March 1980)
Methuen London: extracts from *The Secret
Diary of Adrian Mole Aged 13¾* by Sue
Townsend
Nelson/Harrap: Poem on page 34 from
Take Five by Michael Carrier
Pan Books Ltd.: *The Story of Language* by
C. L. Barber
Associated Book Publishers (U.K.) Ltd:
extracts from *The Book of Heroic Failures* by
Stephen Pile
Saville & Holdsworth Ltd.: Job
Questionnaire (16 December 1984)
Sunday Express Magazine: 'Things I wish
I'd known at 18' by Jack Higgins (August
1982)
The Daily Telegraph: 'Litter wrecked untidy
handyman's marriage' (2 November 1984)
The Economist: 'The Western way to die'
(31 August 1985)
The Standard: 'Bride No. 26 — a record
for Mr Wolfe' (30 January 1984)

Every effort has been made to trace the
owners of copyright material used in this
book, but we should be pleased to hear
from any copyright holder whom we have
been unable to contact.

The authors would like to express their special
thanks to Stephanie Taylor and Brian Brownlee
for allowing us to use their copyright material;
authors of standard reference books, especially
Randolph Quirk, Sidney Greenbaum, Geoffrey
Leech and Jan Svartvik: *A Comprehensive
Grammar of the English Language*, Michael
Swan: *Practical English Usage*, Jake Allsop:
English Grammar, and W. Stannard Allen:
Living English Structure; and all at Oxford
University Press, particularly Suzanna Harsanyi
(Editor) and her staff, Pearl Bevan (Designer),
and Liz Hunter (Audio Director) for their
never-ending help and encouragement.

We thank the following for their permission
to use photographs, logos, and cartoons:

Air Canada
Alitalia
Andes Press Agency
Aviation Picture Library
Barnaby's Picture Library
BBC Enterprises
BBC Hulton Picture Library
Anthony Blake Photo Library
J. Allan Cash Photolibrary
Colorsport
Countryside Commission
Mary Evans Picture Library
Friends of the Éarth Trust
Sally and Richard Greenhill
The Green Party
Greenpeace
Susan Griggs Agency
Robert Harding Picture Library
Heath © Times Newspapers
Hodder & Stoughton
Japan Airlines
Kobal Collection
B. Langrish
Pan Am
Photographers Photo Library
Photo Library International
Photo Service Vivant Univers
The Pontifical Mission Aid Society
Ken Pyne © Private Eye
Quantas
Rex Features
S & G Press Agency
Transworld Features (UK)
Young Artists
Yoram Kahana
Welsh Tourist Board

Illustrations by:

Bill Belcher
Kevin Faerber
Martına Farrow
Sue Hillwood-Harris
Gray Joliffe
Conny Jude
David Murray
Liz Pyle
Jim Robins
Mark Rowney
Lee Stannard·
Paul Thomas
Anne Wilson

Studio and location photography by:

Rob Judges
Mark Mason
Philippa Foord-Kelcey

We thank the following for their time and
assistance:

B. H. Blackwell Ltd (Booksellers)
Designing Woman (Oxford)
The staff of The Duke of Cambridge (Oxford)